# HHhH

# HHhH

## Laurent Binet

# WINDSOR
# PARAGON

First published 2012
by Harvill Secker
This Large Print edition published 2012
by AudioGO Ltd
by arrangement with
The Random House Group Ltd

Hardcover      ISBN: 978 1 4713 1573 2
Softcover      ISBN: 978 1 4713 1574 9

British Library Cataloguing in Publication Data available

Printed and bound in Great Britain by
MPG Books Group Limited

# Part One

Once again, the writer stains the tree of History
with his thoughts, but it is not for us to find the
trick that would enable us to put the animal back in
its carrying cage.
OSIP MANDELSTAM, 'The End of the Novel'

# 1

Gabčík—that's his name—really did exist. Lying alone on a little iron bed, did he hear, from outside, beyond the shutters of a darkened apartment, the unmistakable creaking of the Prague tramways? I want to believe so. I know Prague well, so I can imagine the tram's number (but perhaps it's changed?), its route, and the place where Gabčík waits, thinking and listening. We are at the corner of Vyšehradská and Trojická. The number 18 tram (or the number 22) has stopped in front of the Botanical Gardens. We are, most important, in 1942. In *The Book of Laughter and Forgetting*, Milan Kundera implies that he feels a bit ashamed at having to name his characters. And although this shame is hardly perceptible in his novels, which are full of Tomášes, Tominas, and Terezas, we can intuit the obvious meaning: what could be more vulgar than to arbitrarily give—from a childish desire for verisimilitude or, at best, mere convenience—an invented name to an invented character? In my opinion, Kundera should have gone further: what could be more vulgar than an invented character?

So, Gabčík existed, and it was to this name that he answered (although not always). His story is as true as it is extraordinary. He and his comrades are, in my eyes, the authors of one of the greatest acts of resistance in human history, and without doubt the greatest of the Second World War. For a long time I have wanted to pay tribute to him. For a long time I have seen him, lying in his little

3

room—shutters closed, window open—listening to the creak of the tram (going which way? I don't know) that stops outside the Botanical Gardens. But if I put this image on paper, as I'm sneakily doing now, that won't necessarily pay tribute to him. I am reducing this man to the ranks of a vulgar character and his actions to literature: an ignominious transformation, but what else can I do? I don't want to drag this vision around with me all my life without having tried, at least, to give it some substance. I just hope that, however bright and blinding the veneer of fiction that covers this fabulous story, you will still be able to see through it to the historical reality that lies behind.

## 2

I don't remember exactly when my father first told me this story, but I can see him now, in my council-flat bedroom, pronouncing the words 'partisans', 'Czechoslovaks', perhaps 'operation', certainly 'assassinate', and then this date: '1942'. I'd found *History of the Gestapo* by Jacques Delarue on his bookshelves, and started to read it. Seeing me with this book in my hands, my father had made some passing remarks: he'd mentioned Himmler, the leader of the SS, and then his right-hand man, Heydrich, the Protector of Bohemia and Moravia. And he'd told me of a Czechoslovak commando sent by London, and an assassination attempt. He didn't know the details—and I had no reason to ask for them at the time, as this historic event hadn't yet taken hold of my imagination. But I had sensed

4

in him that slight excitement he always gets when recounting something he finds striking. I don't think he was really aware of the importance he gave this anecdote. When I told him recently of my intention to write a book on the subject, all I sensed was polite curiosity without a trace of any particular emotion. But I know that this story has always fascinated him, even if it never made as strong an impression on him as it did on me. So one of the reasons I am embarking on this book is to reciprocate his gift—those few words spoken to an adolescent boy by a father who, at the time, was not yet a history teacher. But who, in a few awkward phrases, knew how to tell it.

The story, I mean. History.

## 3

When I was still a child, well before the separation of the two countries, I already knew the difference between the Czechs and Slovaks. How? Because of tennis. For example, I knew that Ivan Lendl was Czech while Miroslav Mečř was Slovak. And if Mečř the Slovak was a flashier player, more talented and likable than the cold, workmanlike Czech Lendl (who was, all the same, the world number one for 270 weeks—a record he held until Pete Sampras topped him, holding the number one spot for 286 weeks), I had also learned from my father that, during the war, the Slovaks had collaborated while the Czechs had resisted. In my child's mind, this meant that all Czechs had been resistance fighters and all Slovaks collaborators,

5

as if by nature. Not for a second did I consider the case of France, which called into question such an oversimplification: hadn't we, the French, both resisted *and* collaborated? Truth be told, it was only when I learned that Tito was a Croat—so not all Croats had been collaborators, and perhaps not all Serbs had been resistance fighters—that I began to have a clearer understanding of Czechoslovakia's situation during the war. On one side, there was Bohemia and Moravia (in other words, the current Czech Republic), occupied by the Germans and annexed to the Reich—that is, having the unenviable status of protectorate, and considered part of Greater Germany. On the other side there was the Slovak state, theoretically independent but turned into a satellite by the Nazis. Obviously, this does not presuppose anything about any individual person's behaviour.

4

On arriving in Bratislava in 1996, before going to work as a French teacher in a Slovakian military academy, one of the first things I asked the secretary to the military attaché at the embassy (after asking for news of my luggage, which had gone missing near Istanbul) concerned the story of the assassination. I learned the first details of the affair from this man: a warrant officer who had specialized in phone-tapping in Czechoslovakia and, since the end of the Cold War, had been redeployed as a diplomat. First of all, there were two men involved in the attack: a Czech and a Slovak. I was pleased to find out that a representative of my host country had taken part in the operation—and that there really had been Slovak resistance fighters. I didn't learn much about the operation itself, except that one of the guns had jammed when they shot at Heydrich's car (and I discovered simultaneously that Heydrich was in a car at that moment). But it was above all what happened afterward that piqued my curiosity: how the two partisans had taken refuge with their friends in a church, and how the Germans had tried to drown them . . . A strange story. I wanted details. But the warrant officer didn't know much more.


5


A little while after arriving in Slovakia, I met a very beautiful young Slovak woman with whom I fell madly in love and went on to have a passionate affair that lasted nearly five years. It was through her that I managed to obtain further information. Firstly, the protagonists' names: Jozef Gabčík and Jan Kubiš. Gabčík was the Slovak, and Kubiš the Czech—apparently you can tell their nationality from their surnames. These two men have become part of the historical landscape: Aurélia, the young woman in question, had learned their names at school, like all the little Czechs and Slovaks of her generation. She knew the broad outline of the story, but not much more than my warrant officer. I had to wait two or three years before I knew for sure what I had always suspected—that this story was more fantastic and intense than the most improbable fiction. And I discovered that almost by chance.

I had rented an apartment for Aurélia in the centre of Prague, between the castle of Vyšehrad and Karlovo náměstí (Charles Square). From this square runs a street, Resslova ulice, that goes down to the river, where you will find that strange glass building which seems to undulate in the air and which the Czechs call Tančící dům: the dancing house. On Resslova Street—on the right-hand side as you go down—there is a church. And in the church's wall is a basement window bordered by stone where you can see numerous bullet marks and a plaque mentioning Gabčík and Kubiš—and Heydrich, whose name is now forever linked with theirs. I had passed this basement window dozens of times without noticing either the bullet marks or the plaque. But one day I stopped and read the words—and realized I had found the church where the parachutists took refuge after the assassination attempt.

I came back with Aurélia at a time when the church was open, and we were able to visit the crypt.

In the crypt, there was everything.

6

There were still fresh traces of the drama that had occurred in this room more than sixty years before: a tunnel dug several yards deep; bullet marks in the walls and the vaulted ceiling. There were also photographs of the parachutists' faces, with a text written in Czech and in English. There was a

8

traitor's name and a raincoat. There was a poster of a bag and a bicycle. There was a Sten submachine gun (which jammed at the worst possible moment). All of this was actually in the room. But there was something else here, conjured by the story I read, that existed only in spirit. There were women, there were careless acts, there was London, there was France, there were legionnaires, there was a government in exile, there was a village by the name of Lidice, there was a young lookout called Valčík, there was a tram which went by (also at the worst possible moment), there was a death mask, there was a reward of ten million crowns for whoever denounced the gunmen, there were cyanide pills, there were grenades and people to throw them, there were radio transmitters and coded messages, there was a sprained ankle, there was penicillin that could be procured only in England, there was an entire city under the thumb of the man they nicknamed 'the Hangman', there were swastika flags and death's-head insignias, there were German spies who worked for Britain, there was a black Mercedes with a blown tyre, there was a chauffeur and a butcher, there were dignitaries gathered around a coffin, there were policemen bent over corpses, there were terrible reprisals, there was greatness and madness, weakness and betrayal, courage and fear, hope and grief, there were all the human passions brought together in a few square yards, there was war and there was death, there were Jews deported, families massacred, soldiers sacrificed, there was vengeance and political calculation, there was a man who was (among other things) an accomplished fencer and violinist, there was a locksmith who never managed to do his job, there was the spirit of the Resistance engraved forever in these walls, there were traces of the struggle between the forces of life and the forces of death, there was Bohemia, Moravia, Slovakia, there was all the history of the world contained in a few stones.

There were seven hundred SS guards outside.

## 7

On the Internet, I discovered the existence of a telefilm, *Conspiracy*, with Kenneth Branagh as Heydrich. I eagerly ordered the DVD—only five euros, postage and handling included—and it arrived three days later.

*Conspiracy* is a historical reconstruction of the Wannsee Conference, where, on January 20, 1942, in only a few hours, Heydrich and his assistant Eichmann set down the methods of enforcing the Final Solution. By this time, mass executions had already begun in Poland and the USSR but they had been entrusted to the SS extermination commandos, the Einsatzgruppen, who simply rounded up their victims by the hundreds, sometimes by the thousands, often in a field or a forest, before killing them with submachine guns. The problem with this method was that it tested the executioners' nerves and harmed the troops' morale, even those as hardened as the SD or the Gestapo. Himmler himself fainted while attending one of these mass executions. Subsequently, the SS had taken to asphyxiating their victims by cramming them inside trucks and hooking up

10

the exhaust pipe to a length of hose, but the technique remained relatively unsophisticated. After Wannsee, the extermination of the Jews—which Heydrich entrusted to the tender care of his faithful Eichmann—was administered as a logistical, social, and economic project on a very large scale.

Kenneth Branagh's portrayal of Heydrich is quite clever: he manages to combine great affability with brusque authoritarianism, which makes his character highly disturbing. I don't know how accurate it is—I have not read anywhere that the real Heydrich knew how to show kindness, whether real or faked. But one short scene does a good job of showing his true psychological and historical nature. Two men at the conference are having a private discussion. One confides to the other that he's heard Heydrich has Jewish origins and asks if he thinks there might be any truth to this. The second man replies venomously: 'Why not go and ask him yourself ?' His questioner goes pale at the thought. Now, it turns out that a persistent rumour claiming his father was Jewish did in fact pursue Heydrich for many years and that his youth was poisoned by this. Apparently the rumour was unfounded. But let's be honest, even if that wasn't the case, Heydrich—as head of the secret services of the Nazi Party and the SS—would have been able to erase all suspect traces in his genealogy without the slightest effort.

This is not the first time that Heydrich has made it to the big screen: in 1943, less than a year after the assassination, Fritz Lang shot a propaganda film entitled *Hangmen Also Die!* with a screenplay by Bertolt Brecht. This film recounts the events in

11

a way that is utterly fanciful—Lang didn't know what had really happened, and even if he had he naturally wouldn't have wished to risk revealing the truth—but quite ingenious: Heydrich is assassinated by a Czech doctor, a member of the Resistance who takes refuge in the house of a young girl. Then the girl's father, an academic, is rounded up by the Germans along with other local worthies and threatened with execution if the assassin doesn't give himself up. The crisis, treated in an extremely dramatic way (thanks to Brecht, presumably), is resolved when the Resistance manages to pin the blame on a traitorous collaborator, whose death ends both the affair and the film. In reality, neither the partisans nor the Czech people got off so lightly.

Fritz Lang chose to represent Heydrich rather crudely as an effeminate pervert, a complete degenerate who carries a riding crop to underline both his ferocity and his depraved morals. It's true that the real Heydrich was supposed to be a sexual pervert and that he spoke in a falsetto voice at odds with the rest of his persona, but his stiffness, his haughtiness, his absolutely Aryan profile, were worlds away from the mincing creature in the film. If you wanted to find a more lifelike screen representation, you should watch Charlie Chaplin's *Great Dictator* again: there you see Hinkel, the dictator, flanked by two henchmen, one of them a smug, bloated fat man clearly modelled on Göring, and the other a tall, thin man who looks much colder, stiffer, and more cunning. That isn't Himmler, a coarse little moustached fox, but rather Heydrich, his very dangerous right-hand man.

12

For the hundredth time, I returned to Prague. Accompanied by another young woman, the gorgeous Natacha, I went back to the crypt. (She's French, this one, in spite of her name, and the daughter of Communists, like all of us.) The first day we went, it was closed for a national holiday, but across the road I spotted a bar—I'd never noticed this place before—called the Parachutists. Inside, the walls were covered with photos, documents, paintings, and posters relating to the assassination. At the back, a large painted mural depicted Great Britain, with points indicating the various military bases where the exiled Czech army commandos prepared for their missions. I drank a beer there with Natacha.

The next day, we returned during opening hours and I showed Natacha the crypt. She took several photos at my request. A short film reconstructing the assassination was playing in the foyer. I tried to pinpoint the places where the drama took place in order to go there myself, but it was quite far from the centre of town, out in the suburbs. The street names have changed: even now I have trouble situating the exact location of the attack. On my way out of the crypt, I picked up a flyer, written in Czech and English, advertising an exhibition entitled 'Assassination'. Beside the title was a photo of Heydrich surrounded by German officers and flanked by his local right-hand man, the Sudeten German Karl Hermann Frank—all of them wearing full uniform and climbing a wood-panelled staircase. A red target had been printed on Heydrich's face. The exhibition was taking place at the Army Museum, not far from the Florenc metro station, but there was no mention of dates, only the museum's opening hours. We went there the same day.

At the museum entrance, a little old lady welcomed us with great solicitude: she seemed happy to see some visitors and invited us to take a tour of the building's various galleries. But I was interested in only one of them. The entrance was decorated by an enormous pasteboard announcing, in the style of a Hollywood horror film, the exhibition on Heydrich. I wondered if it was permanent. It was free, in any case, like the rest of the museum. The little lady, having asked us where we were from, gave us a guidebook in English (she was sorry to be able to offer a choice of only English or German).

The exhibition surpassed all my expectations. Here, there really was everything: as well as photos, letters, posters, and various documents, I saw the parachutists' guns and personal effects, their dossiers filled out by the British commanders, with notes, appraisals, and reports. I saw Heydrich's Mercedes, with its blown tyre and the hole in the right rear door, and the fatal letter from the lover to his mistress that led to the massacre at Lidice. I saw their passports and their photos, and a great number of other authentic, deeply moving traces of what happened. I took notes feverishly, knowing full well that there were way too many names, dates, details. As I was leaving, I asked the lady if it was possible to buy the guidebook that she'd lent me, in which all the captions and commentaries had been transcribed. Sounding very sorry, she said no. The book was handbound and clearly not intended for general sale. Seeing that I was at a loss, and probably touched by my jabbering attempts to speak Czech, she ended up taking the book from my hands and stuffing it determinedly into Natacha's handbag. She signalled us not to say a word, and to leave. We parted effusively. It's true that given the number of visitors to the museum, the guidebook was unlikely to be missed by anyone. But even so, it was really kind. Two days later, an hour before our bus left for Paris, I went back to the museum to give the little lady some chocolates. She was embarrassed and didn't want to accept them. The guidebook she gave me is so important that without it—and therefore without her—this book probably wouldn't exist in the form it's going to take. I regret not having dared ask her name, so that I could have thanked her a bit more ceremoniously.

9

When she was sixteen or seventeen, Natacha took part two years running in a national essay-writing contest about the Resistance, and both times she finished first—a feat that as far as I know has never been matched, before or since. This double victory gave her the opportunity to be a standard-bearer in a commemorative parade and to visit a concentration camp in Alsace. During the bus journey she sat next to an old Resistance fighter who took a liking to her. He lent her some books and documents, but afterward they lost touch. Ten years later, when she told me this story—somewhat guiltily as you'd imagine, seeing that she still had his documents and that she didn't even know if he was alive—I encouraged her to contact him again. And even though he'd moved to the other end of France, I managed to track him down.

That's how we came to visit him in his beautiful white house near Perpignan, where he lived with his wife.

Sipping sweet muscat wine, we listened as he told us how he had joined the Resistance, how he'd gone underground, all the things he'd done. In 1943, aged nineteen, he was working at his uncle's dairy farm. Being of Swiss origin, this uncle spoke such good German that the soldiers who came to get fresh supplies had taken to hanging around in order to chat with someone who spoke their language. First of all, our young Resistance fighter was asked if he could glean any interesting information from the talks between the soldiers and his uncle, about troop movements, for example. Then they put him on parachute duty, where he helped to pick up the boxes of materials parachuted down at night from Allied airplanes. When he became old enough to be drafted by the STO—which meant he was under threat of being sent to work in Germany—he went underground, serving in combat units and taking part in the liberation of Burgundy. Actively, it would seem, judging by the number of Germans he claims to have killed.

I was genuinely interested in his story, but I also hoped to learn something that could be useful for my book on Heydrich. What exactly, I had no idea.

I asked him if he'd received any military

16

instruction after going underground. None, he told me. Later, they taught him how to handle a heavy machine gun, and he had a few training sessions: dismantling and reassembling the gun blindfolded, and shooting practice. But when he first arrived, they stuck a machine gun in his hands and that was it. It was a British machine gun, a Sten. A completely unreliable weapon, so he told me: all you had to do was hit the ground with the butt and it went off. A piece of junk. 'The Sten was shit, there's no other way of saying it.'

You might wish to remember this. It turns out to be important.

## 10

I said before that one of the characters in Chaplin's *Great Dictator* was based on Heydrich, but it's not true. Let's ignore the fact that in 1940 Heydrich was a shadowy figure, largely unknown to the majority of people—Americans most of all. That is obviously not the problem: Chaplin could have *guessed* at his existence, and somehow got it exactly right. But while it's true that the dictator's henchman in the film is depicted as a snake—whose intelligence contrasts with the ridiculousness of the actor parodying big fat Göring—he is equally a caricature of buffoonery and spinelessness. And in those characteristics we cannot recognize the future Hangman of Prague at all.

On the subject of screen portrayals of Heydrich, I've just seen an old film on TV entitled *Hitler's Madman*. It's directed by Douglas Sirk, who was of Czech origin, and it's an American propaganda film, shot in a single week and released in 1943, just before Fritz Lang's *Hangmen Also Die!* The story, which is (like Lang's) utterly fanciful, places the heart of the Resistance in Lidice, the village of martyrs that would end up like Oradour. [Oradour-sur-Glane was a village in France whose 642 inhabitants were all massacred by SS troops in 1944.] The film is about a parachutist flown in from London and the dilemma of the villagers who find him. Are they going to help him or keep away from him—or even betray him? The problem with the film is that it reduces the organization of the attack to a local scheme, based on a series of coincidences (Heydrich happens to be passing through Lidice, which happens to be sheltering a parachutist, who in turn happens to find out what time the Protector's car will go past). The plot is therefore much weaker than that of Lang's film, where, with Brecht writing the screenplay, the dramatic power of this one event is used to create a genuine national epic.

On the other hand, the actor who plays Heydrich in the Douglas Sirk film is excellent. For a start, there is a physical resemblance. But he also manages to convey the character's brutality without overdoing the facial tics—whereas Lang sacrificed subtlety in order to emphasize Heydrich's degenerate soul. Now, it's true that Heydrich was an evil, pitiless swine, but he wasn't Richard III. The actor in Sirk's film is John Carradine, the father of David Carradine, alias Bill in the Tarantino films. The most successful scene is that of Heydrich on his deathbed: eaten away by fever, he delivers a cynical speech to Himmler that is not without a kind of Shakespearean resonance, but which seems at the same time quite plausible. Neither cowardly nor heroic, the Hangman of Prague passes away without repentance, without fanaticism, regretting only that he must leave a life to which he felt attached—his own.

I did say *plausible*.


# 11

Months flow past, they become years, and all that time this story keeps growing inside me. And while my life passes—made up, like everyone's, of private joys, dramas, hopes, and disappointments— the shelves of my apartment fill up with books on the Second World War. I devour everything I can find, in every possible language. I go to see all the films that come out—*The Pianist, Downfall, The Counterfeiters, Black Book*—and my TV remains stuck on the History Channel. I learn loads of things, some with only a distant connection to Heydrich, but I tell myself that everything can be useful, that I must immerse myself in a period to understand its spirit—and the thread of knowledge, once you pull at it, continues unravelling on its own. The vastness of the information I amass ends up frightening me. I write two pages for every thousand I read. At this rate, I will die without even having mentioned the preparations for the attack. I get the feeling that my thirst for documentation, healthy to begin with, is becoming a little bit dangerous—a pretext, basically, for putting off the moment when I have to start writing.

At the same time, I have the impression that everything in my daily life is bringing me back to this story. Natacha rents a studio apartment in Montmartre: the entry code for the door is 4206; I think straightaway of June 42. Natacha tells me the date of her sister's wedding: I yell cheerfully, 'May twenty-seventh? Unbelievable! The day of the assassination!' Natacha shakes her head. Going through Munich last summer on our way back from Budapest, we witness something staggering in the main square of the old town: a neo-Nazi rally. The shamefaced locals tell me they've never seen such a thing. I don't know if I believe them. I watch, for the first time, an Eric Rohmer film on DVD: the main character, a double agent in the 1930s, meets Heydrich in person. In a Rohmer film! It's funny how, as soon as you take a close interest in a subject, everything seems to bring you back to it.

I also read lots of historical novels, to see how others deal with the genre's constraints. Some are keen to demonstrate their extreme accuracy, others don't bother, and a few manage skilfully to skirt around the historical truth without inventing too much. I am struck all the same by the fact that, in every case, fiction wins out over history. It's logical, I suppose, but I have trouble getting my head around it.

One successful model, in my opinion, is *The Bloody Baron*, by Vladimir Pozner, which tells the story of Baron Ungern—the one encountered by Corto Maltese in *Corto Maltese in Siberia*. Pozner's novel is divided into two parts: the first takes place in Paris and recounts the author's research as he collects various accounts of his character. The second plunges us into the heart of Mongolia, and we find ourselves all at once in the novel itself. I reread this passage from time to time. In fact, the two parts are separated by a short transitional chapter entitled 'Three Pages of History', which ends with the line '1920 had just begun'.

I think that's brilliant.


## 12

Maria has been clumsily trying to play the piano for perhaps an hour when she hears her parents return. Bruno, the father, opens the door for his wife, Elizabeth, who is carrying a baby in her arms. They call the little girl: 'Come and see, Maria! Look, it's your little brother. He's very small and you have to be really nice to him. His name is Reinhardt.' Maria nods distractedly. Bruno leans gently over the newborn: 'How handsome he is!' he says. 'How blond he is!' says Elizabeth. 'He will be a musician.'


## 13

Of course I could, perhaps I should—to be like Victor Hugo, for example—describe at length, by way of introduction, over ten pages or so, the town of Halle, where Heydrich was born in 1904. I would talk of the streets, the shops, the statues, of all the local curiosities, of the municipal government, the town's infrastructure, of the culinary specialities, of the inhabitants and the way they think, their political tendencies, their tastes, of what they do in their spare time. Then I would zoom in on the Heydrichs' house: the colour of its shutters and its curtains, the layout of the rooms, the wood from which the living-room table is made. Following this would be a minutely detailed description of the piano, accompanied by a long disquisition on German music at the beginning of the century, its role in society, its composers and how their works were received, the importance of Wagner . . . and there, only at that point, would my actual story begin. I remember one interminable digression in *The Hunchback of Notre Dame* on the workings of judicial institutions in the Middle Ages. I thought that was very clever. But I skipped the passage.

So I've decided not to overstylize my story. That suits me fine because, even if for later episodes I'll have to resist the temptation to flaunt my knowledge by writing too many details for this or that scene that I've researched too much, I must admit that in this case—regarding Heydrich's birthplace—my knowledge is a bit sketchy. There are two towns in Germany called Halle, and I don't even know which one I'm talking about. For the time being, I think it's not important. We'll see.

## 14

The teacher calls the pupils one by one: 'Reinhardt Heydrich!' Reinhardt steps forward, but another child raises a hand: 'Sir! Why don't you call him by his real name?' A shiver of pleasure spreads through the class. 'His name is Süss, everyone knows that!' The class explodes, the pupils roar. Reinhardt says nothing: he clenches his fists. He never says anything. He has the best marks in the class. Later that day, he will be the best at P.E. And he's not a Jew. At least he hopes not. His grandmother remarried a Jew, apparently, but that's got nothing to do with his family. This, at least, is what he's understood from the public rumours and his father's indignant denials. But in all honesty he's not really sure. In the meantime, he's going to shut them all up in P.E. And this evening, when he gets home, before his father gives him his violin lesson, he'll be able to boast that he was top of the class again. And his father will be proud, and congratulate him.

But this evening the violin lesson won't happen and Reinhardt won't even be able to tell his father about school. When he gets home, he will learn that the country is at war.

'Why is there a war, Father?'

'Because France and England are jealous of Germany, my son.'

'Why are they jealous?'

'Because the Germans are stronger than they are.'

## 15

There is nothing more artificial in a historical narrative than this kind of dialogue—reconstructed from more or less firsthand accounts with the idea of breathing life into the dead pages of history. In stylistic terms, this process has certain similarities with hypotyposis, which means making a scene so lifelike that it gives the reader the impression he can see it with his own eyes. When a writer tries to bring a conversation back to life in this way, the result is often contrived and the effect the opposite of that desired: you see too clearly the strings controlling the puppets, you hear too distinctly the author's voice in the mouths of these historical figures.

There are only three ways you can faithfully reconstruct a dialogue: from an audio recording, from a video recording, or from shorthand notes. And even with this last method, there is no absolute guarantee that the contents of the conversation will be recorded exactly, down to the last comma. Indeed, the stenographer will often condense, summarize, reformulate, synthesize. But let's assume that the spirit and tone are reconstructed in a generally satisfactory manner.

If my dialogues can't be based on precise, faithful, word-perfect sources, they will be invented. However, if that's the case, they will function not as a hypotyposis but as a parable. They will be either extremely accurate or extremely illustrative. And just so there's no confusion, all the dialogues I invent (there won't be many) will be written like scenes from a play. A stylistic drop in an ocean of reality.

16

Little Heydrich—cute, blond, studious, hard-working, loved by his parents. Violinist, pianist, junior chemist. A boy with a shrill voice which earns him a nickname, the first in a long list: at school, they call him 'the Goat'.

24

At this point in his life, it is still possible to mock him without risking death. But it is during this delicate period of childhood that one learns resentment.

## 17

In *Death Is My Trade*, Robert Merle creates a novelized biography of Rudolph Höss, the commandant of Auschwitz, based on firsthand accounts and on notes that Höss himself wrote in prison before being hanged in 1947. The whole of the first part is given over to his childhood and his unbelievably deadening upbringing at the hands of an ultraconservative and emotionally crippled father. It's obvious what the author is trying to do: find the causes, if not the explanations, for the path this man would later take. Robert Merle attempts to guess—I say guess, not understand—how someone becomes commandant of Auschwitz.

This is not my intention—I say intention, not ambition—with regard to Heydrich. I do not claim that Heydrich ended up in charge of the Final Solution because his schoolmates called him 'the Goat' when he was ten years old. Nor do I think that the ragging he took because they thought he was a Jew should necessarily explain anything. I mention these facts only for the ironic colouring they give to his destiny: 'the Goat' will grow up to be the man called, at the height of his power, 'the most dangerous man in the Third Reich'. And the Jew, Süss, will become the Great Architect of the Holocaust. Who could have guessed such a thing?

I picture the scene:

Reinhardt and his father, bent over a map of Europe spread out on the large living-room table, moving little flags around. They are concentrating hard because this is a critical time—the situation has become very serious. Mutinies have weakened the glorious army of Wilhelm II. But they have also devastated the French army. And Russia has been swept away by the Bolshevik revolution. Thankfully, Germany is not such a backward country. German civilization rests upon pillars so solid that Communists could never destroy it. Not them, and not the French either. Nor the Jews, obviously. In Kiel, Munich, Hamburg, Bremen, and Berlin, German discipline will take back the reins of reason, of power, and of the war.

But the door opens. Elizabeth, the mother, bursts in. She's in a mad panic. The Kaiser has abdicated. They've proclaimed the Republic. A Socialist has been named chancellor. They want to sign the peace agreement.

Reinhardt, dumbstruck and goggle-eyed, turns towards his father. And he, after an awful pause, can mumble only one phrase:

'It's not possible.' It is November 9, 1918.

# 19

I don't know why Bruno Heydrich, the father, was anti-Semitic. What I do know, however, is that he was considered to be a very funny man. He was a barrel of laughs, apparently, the life and soul of the party. His jokes were so funny that everyone thought he must have been a Jew. At least this argument couldn't be used against his son, who was never renowned for his great sense of humour.

# 20

Having lost the war, Germany is now a prey to chaos and, according to a growing proportion of the population, the Jews and the Communists are leading it into ruin. The young Heydrich, like everyone else, makes a vague show of defiance. He enrols in the Freikorps, a militia that wishes to take over from the army by fighting everything to the left of the extreme right.

These Freikorps, paramilitary organizations dedicated to the struggle against Bolshevism, have their existence rubber-stamped by a Social Democrat government. My father would say there was nothing surprising about that. According to him, the Socialists have always been traitors. Joining forces with the enemy would be second nature to them. He has tons of examples. In this case, it was indeed a Socialist who crushed the Spartacist uprising and had Rosa Luxemburg executed. By the Freikorps.

I could give details of Heydrich's involvement in the Freikorps, but that seems unnecessary. It's enough to know that, as a member, he was part of the 'technical relief troops', whose duty was to prevent factory occupations and to ensure the smooth running of public services in the event of a general strike. Already this acute sense of duty towards the State!

The good thing about writing a true story is that you don't have to worry about giving an impression of realism. I have no need for a scene featuring the young Heydrich during this part of his life. Between 1919 and 1922, he is still living in Halle (Halle-ander-Saale, I've checked) with his parents. During this time, the Freikorps spread all over the place. One of them came from the 'white' navy brigade led by the famous Captain Erhardt. His insignia was a swastika and his battle song was entitled 'Hakenkreuz am Stahlhelm' ('Swastika on a Steel Helmet'). For me, that sets the scene better than the longest description in the world.

21

So it's the Depression: unemployment devastates Germany, times are hard. The young Heydrich had wanted to be a chemist, while his parents had dreamed of making him a musician. But in times of crisis, the tried and tested option is the army. Fascinated by the exploits of the legendary Admiral von Luckner—a family friend who nicknamed himself 'the Sea Devil' in an eponymous, bestselling, self-glorifying autobiography—Heydrich enlists in the navy. One morning in 1922, the tall young blond man appears at the officers' school in Kiel carrying a black violin case, a gift from his father.

## 22

The *Berlin* is a German navy war cruiser whose second-in-command is Lieutenant Wilhelm Canaris—First World War hero, ex-secret agent, and future Wehrmacht head of counterintelligence. His wife, a violinist, organizes musical evenings on Sundays in their quarters. A place becomes free in her string quartet, and the young Heydrich, serving on the *Berlin*, is invited to join. He plays well and his hosts, unlike his comrades, appreciate his company. He becomes a regular at Frau Canaris's musical evenings, where he listens, deeply impressed, to his boss's stories. 'Espionage!' he says to himself. And no doubt he begins to daydream.

## 23

Heydrich is a dashing officer of the Kriegsmarine and a fearsome swordsman. His swashbuckling reputation wins his comrades' respect, if not their friendship.

That year, there is a fencing tournament in Dresden for German officers. Heydrich competes with the sabre, the most brutal of weapons. It's his speciality. Unlike the foil, which touches only with the point, the sabre cuts and thrusts with its sharp edge, and its blows, like lashes from a whip, are infinitely more violent. The physical engagement between two men using sabres is also more spectacular. All of this suits the young Heydrich perfectly. But that particular day he takes a beating in the first round. Who is his opponent? I haven't been able to find out. I imagine a left-hander: quick, clever, dark-haired. Perhaps not Jewish— that would be a bit much—but maybe a quarter Jewish. A fencer who's not easily impressed, who shies away from direct combat, who provokes his opponent with feints and parries. Heydrich remains the favourite, however, and although he gets more and more worked up—his blows missing his man and hitting only thin air—he still manages to catch up his opponent's score. But at the end of the bout, he loses his temper. Striking too vigorously, he is parried, and allows a riposte that touches him on the head. He feels the other's blade strike his helmet. He is out in the first round. In a rage, he smashes his sabre on the ground. The judges reprimand him.

## 24

The first of May, in Germany as in France, is Labour Day, the origins of which go back to a decision of the Second International, made in tribute to a great workers' strike that took place on 1 May in Chicago in 1886. But it's also the anniversary of an event whose importance was not realized at the time, whose consequences would be incalculable, and that is for obvious reasons not celebrated anywhere: on May 1, 1925, Hitler founded an elite body of troops, originally intended to protect his safety. A bodyguard made up of overtrained fanatics corresponding to strict racial criteria. This was the 'protection squadron', the Schutzstaffel, better known as the SS.

In 1929 this special guard is transformed into a genuine militia, a paramilitary organization led by Himmler. After the Nazis take power in '33, Himmler gives a speech in Munich in which he declares:

'Every state needs an elite. The elite of the National Socialist state is the SS. It is here that we maintain, on the basis of racial selection, allied to the requirements of the present time, German military tradition, German dignity and nobility, and German industrial efficiency.'

25

I still don't have the book that Heydrich's wife wrote after the war, *Leben mit einem Kriegsverbrecher* ('Living with a War Criminal' in English, although the book has never been translated). I imagine it would be a mine of information, but I haven't been able to get my hands on it. It is an extremely rare work, and the price on the Internet is generally between 350 and 700 euros. I suppose German neo-Nazis, fascinated by Heydrich—a Nazi such as they would hardly dare to dream of—are responsible for these exorbitant prices. I did find it once for 250 euros and wanted to commit the folly of ordering it. Happily for my budget, the German bookshop that had put it up for sale didn't accept payment by card. I would have had to go to my bank's local branch. The mere prospect of this, a profoundly depressing one for any normal person, persuaded me not to take the transaction any further. Anyway, given that my German is no better than the average French twelve-year-old's (although I did do it for eight years in school), it would have been a risky investment.

So I should do without this book. But I've reached the point in the story where I have to recount Heydrich's first meeting with his wife. Here more than for any other section, that extremely rare and costly tome would undoubtedly have been a great help.

When I say 'I have to,' I do not mean, of course, that it's absolutely necessary. I could easily tell the whole story of Operation Anthropoid without even once mentioning Lina Heydrich's name. Then again, if I am to portray Heydrich's character, which I would very much like to do, it's difficult to ignore the role played by his wife in his ascent within Nazi Germany.

At the same time, I'm quite happy not to write the romantic version of their *affaire de coeur*, which Mrs Heydrich would not have failed to give in her memoirs. I prefer to avoid the temptations of a soppy love scene. Not that I refuse to consider the human aspects of a being such as Heydrich. I'm not one of those people who's offended by the film *Downfall* because it shows us (among other things) Hitler being nice to his secretaries and affectionate with his dog. I naturally suppose that Hitler could, from time to time, be nice. Nor do I doubt, judging by the letters he sent to her, that Heydrich fell genuinely in love with his wife from the moment he met her. At the time, she was a young girl with a pleasant smile, who could even have passed for pretty—far from the hard-faced evil shrew she would become.

But their first meeting, as told in a biography clearly based on Lina's memoirs, is really too kitsch: at a ball where she dreads being bored the whole evening because there aren't enough boys, she and her friend are approached by a black-haired officer, accompanied by a shy blond young man. She falls in love instantly with the shy one. Two days later, there's a rendezvous at the Hohenzollern Park in Kiel (very pretty, I've seen photos) and a romantic lakeside walk. A date at the theatre the next evening—then to a rented room, where, I imagine, they sleep together, even if the biography remains discreet on this point. The official version is that Heydrich arrives in his best uniform, they have a drink after the play, share a silence, and then suddenly, without warning, Heydrich proposes marriage. '*Mein Gott*, Herr Heydrich, you don't know anything about me or my family! You don't even know who my father is! The navy doesn't allow its officers to marry just anyone.' But as it's also made clear that Lina had got hold of the keys to the room, I suppose that either before or after the proposal, that very evening, they consummated their relationship. It turns out that Lina von Osten, from an aristocratic family fallen on slightly hard times, is a very suitable match. So they get married.

It's not a bad story. I just don't feel like doing the ballroom scene, and even less the romantic walk in the park. So it's better for me not to know

33

more of the details; that way, I won't be tempted to share them. When I happen upon the materials that allow me to reconstruct in great detail an entire scene from Heydrich's life, I often find it difficult not to do it, even if the scene itself isn't particularly interesting. Lina's memoirs must be full of such stories.

So, in the end, maybe I can do without this overpriced book.

All the same, there is one thing about the meeting of the two lovebirds that intrigued me: the name of the dark-haired officer who accompanied Heydrich was Manstein. First of all, I wondered if it was the same Manstein who would later direct the Ardennes offensive during the French campaign, who we would find afterward as an army general on the Russian front—in Leningrad, Stalingrad, and Kursk—and who would lead Operation Citadel in 1943, when the Wehrmacht's task was to deal with, as best they could, the Red Army counterattack. The same Manstein too who, to justify the work of Heydrich's Einsatzgruppen on the Russian front, would declare in 1941: 'The soldier must appreciate the necessity for the harsh punishment of Jews, who are the spiritual bearers of the Bolshevik terror. This is also necessary in order to nip in the bud all uprisings, which are mostly plotted by Jews.' The same, finally, who would die in 1973—meaning that, for one year, I lived on the same planet as him. In truth, it's unlikely: the dark-haired officer is portrayed as a young man, whereas Manstein, in 1930, was already forty-three. Perhaps someone from the same family, a nephew or a distant cousin.

At eighteen Lina was, as far as we know, already a firm believer in Nazism. According to her, she was the one who converted Heydrich. Yet certain clues lead us to believe that even before 1930 Heydrich was politically well to the right of most soldiers, and strongly attracted by National Socialism. But obviously the 'woman behind the famous man' version is always more appealing . . .


26


It's risky to try to determine the moments when a person's life is changed forever. I don't even know if such moments exist. Éric-Emmanuel Schmitt wrote a book, *La Part de l'autre*, in which he imagines that Hitler passes his art diploma. From that instant, his destiny and the world's are completely altered: he has a string of affairs, becomes a promiscuous playboy, marries a Jewish woman with whom he has two or three children, joins the Surrealists in Paris, and ends up a famous painter. At the same time, Germany fights a small war with Poland and that's all. No Second World War, no genocide, and a Hitler who is nothing like the real one.

Fictional gimmicks aside, I doubt whether one man's destiny can determine a nation's, never mind the whole world's. Then again, you'd be hard-pressed to find anyone else as utterly evil as Hitler. And the art exam probably was a decisive factor in his personal destiny, since after this failure Hitler ended up a tramp in Munich—a period during which he would develop a fatal resentment towards society.

If you wanted to find a key moment of this kind in Heydrich's life, it would undoubtedly occur the day in 1931 when he took home what he believed was just another girl. Without her, everything would have been very different—for Heydrich, for Gabčík, Kubiš, and Valčík, as well as for thousands of Czechs and, perhaps, hundreds of thousands of Jews. I won't go so far as to suggest that without Heydrich the Jews would have been spared. But the incredible efficiency he demonstrated throughout his Nazi career allows us to think that Hitler and Himmler would have had trouble coping without him.

In 1931 Heydrich is a navy lieutenant with the promise of a brilliant military career. He is engaged to a young aristocrat and his future is bright. But he is also an inveterate pussy hound, making endless sexual conquests and visits to brothels. One evening he brings home a young girl he'd met at a ball in Potsdam and who'd come to Kiel to pay him a visit. I don't know for sure if she became pregnant, but in any case her parents demanded that he do his duty by her. Heydrich didn't deign to respond, given that he was already engaged to Lina von Osten—whose pedigree was more suitable, and with whom, unlike the other one, he seemed genuinely in love. Unfortunately for him, the father of this young girl was Admiral Raeder himself, commander in chief of the navy. Raeder kicked up a huge fuss. Heydrich got bogged down in murky explanations that allowed him to exonerate himself in the eyes of his fiancée, but not of the military. He was court-martialled, disgraced, and finally booted out of the armed services.

So in 1931, at the height of the economic crisis devastating Germany, the young officer with the brilliant future finds himself unemployed—one man among five million without work.

Luckily for him, his fiancée hasn't dropped him. A rabid anti-Semite, she pushes him to get in touch with a Nazi who is quite highly placed in a new elite organization with a growing reputation: the SS.

April 30, 1931, the day Heydrich is ignominiously dumped from the navy—is this the day that seals the fate of Heydrich and his future victims? We can't really be sure, not least since at the 1930 elections Heydrich declared: 'Now old Hindenburg will have no choice but to name Hitler the chancellor. And then our time will come.' Leaving aside the fact that he was wrong by three years on Hitler's nomination, we see here Heydrich's political opinions in 1930, and can therefore suppose that even if he'd remained a navy officer, he would have ended up making a good career with the Nazis. Only perhaps not quite so monstrous.

## 27

Meanwhile, he goes back to his parents' house and, we're told, cries like a child for several days.

Then he enrolls in the SS. But in 1931 being a foot soldier in the SS does not pay much. It's practically voluntary work, in fact. Unless you climb the ladder.

There would be something comic in this face-to-face meeting were it not that it led to the deaths of millions. On one side, the tall blond in black uniform: horsey face, high-pitched voice, well-polished boots. On the other, a little hamster in glasses: dark brown hair, moustache, not very Aryan at all. It's in this pathetic willingness to ape his master Adolf Hitler by growing a moustache that we see the physical link between Heinrich Himmler and Nazism, otherwise not immediately apparent—unless you count the various uniforms already put at his disposal.

Against all racial logic, it's the hamster who's in charge. He is already a big wheel in a party poised to win the elections. Sitting across from this rodent-faced but increasingly influential little man, Heydrich tries to appear simultaneously respectful and self-assured.

It's the first time he's met Himmler, the supreme leader of the organization to which he belongs. Heydrich has been recommended by a friend of his mother's. He is applying to be chief of the intelligence service that Himmler wishes to create within the organization. Himmler hesitates. He prefers another candidate. He is unaware that this other candidate is an agent of the Republic sent to infiltrate the Nazi machine. So convinced is he by this man's suitability for the job that he wanted to cancel his meeting with Heydrich. But when she discovered this, Lina put her husband on the first train to Munich. Thus it is that he turns up at the house of the ex-chicken farmer and future Reichsführer Himmler—the man who Hitler will soon refer to only as 'my faithful Heinrich'.

So Heydrich forces his presence on Himmler, who is consequently in rather a bad mood. And if Heydrich does not want to continue teaching rich sailors in Kiel's yacht club, it's in his interests to make a good impression very quickly.

On the other hand, he does hold a trump card: Himmler's remarkable incompetence in the domain of intelligence.

In German, *Nachrichtenoffizier* means 'transmission officer', while *Nachrichtendienstoffizier* means 'intelligence officer'. It's because Himmler, notoriously ignorant about all things military, makes no distinction between these two terms that Heydrich—who used to be a transmission officer in the navy—is sitting opposite him today. In fact, Heydrich has practically no experience of intelligence. And what Himmler is asking him to do is nothing less than to create within the SS an espionage service that can compete with the Abwehr of Admiral Canaris, Heydrich's old navy boss. Now that he's here, Himmler expects him to outline his vision for the project. 'You have twenty minutes.'

Heydrich does not want to be a sailing instructor all his life. So he concentrates hard and gathers together everything he knows about the subject. This is limited mainly to what he's remembered from the English spy novels he's been reading for years. What the hell! Heydrich has figured out that Himmler knows even less about intelligence than he does, so he decides to bluff. He sketches out a few diagrams, taking care to use lots of military terms.

And it works. Himmler is impressed. Forgetting his other candidate, the Weimar double agent, he hires the young man for a salary of 1,800 marks per month, six times more than he's been earning since being kicked out of the navy. Heydrich is going to move to Munich. The foundations of the sinister SD are laid.

## 29

SD: Sicherheitsdienst, the security service. The least-known and the most sinister of all Nazi organizations. Including the Gestapo.

To begin with, though, it's just a small, underfunded agency: Heydrich keeps his first files in shoe boxes, and has only half a dozen agents. But already he's got into the spirit of intelligence work: *know everything about everyone*. Without exception. As the SD extends its web, Heydrich will discover that he has an unusual gift for bureaucracy, the most important quality for the management of a good spy network. His motto could be: Files! Files! Always more files! In every colour. On every subject. Heydrich gets a taste for it very quickly. Information, manipulation, blackmail, and spying become his drugs.

Add to this a rather childish megalomania. Having got wind that the head of the British intelligence service calls himself M (yes, like in James Bond), he decides in all seriousness to call himself H. It is in some ways his first proper alias, before the great era of nicknames: 'the Hangman', 'the Butcher', 'the Blond Beast', and—this one given by Adolf Hitler himself—'the Man with the Iron Heart'.

I don't believe that 'H' ever became a popular nickname among his men (they preferred the more graphic 'Blond Beast'). There were too many eminent Hs above him, creating the risk of some regrettable mix-ups: Heydrich, Himmler, Hitler . . . he must have dropped this childish affectation himself, out of prudence. But *H for Holocaust* . . . that might very well have worked as the title of a bad biography.


30


Natacha flicks through the latest issue of *Magazine littéraire*, which she kindly bought for me. She stops at the review of a book about the life of Bach, the composer. The article begins with a quote from the author: 'Has there ever been a biographer who did not dream of writing, "Jesus of Nazareth used to lift his left eyebrow when he was thinking"?' She smiles as she reads this to me.

I don't immediately grasp the full meaning of the phrase and, faithful to my long-held disgust for realistic novels, I say to myself: *Yuk!* Then I ask her to pass me the magazine and I reread the sentence. I am forced to admit that I would quite like to possess this kind of detail about Heydrich. Natacha laughs openly: 'Oh yes, I can just see it: Heydrich used to lift his left eyebrow when he was thinking!'

In the imagination of the Third Reich's sycophants, Heydrich has always exemplified the Aryan ideal—because he was tall and blond and he had fairly delicate features. In the more gushing biographies he is generally described as a handsome man, a charming seducer. If they were honest—or less blinded by the dark fascination they feel for everything to do with Nazism—they would see, by looking more closely at the photos, not only that Heydrich was no oil painting but that he also had certain physical traits that are hardly compatible with the demands of Aryan classification: thick lips, admittedly not without a certain sensuality, but of a type that might almost be described as negroid, and a long prominent nose that could easily pass as hooked if it belonged to a Jew. Add to this a pair of large and fairly stuck-out ears and a long face generally agreed to look a bit horsey, and you obtain a result that, while not necessarily ugly, falls way short of Gobineau's ideal. [Arthur Gobineau (1816–82) was a French aristocrat and man of letters who became famous for developing the racialist theory of the Aryan master race in his book *An Essay on the Inequality of the Human Races*.]

32

The Heydrichs, newly installed in a nice apartment in Munich that Lina loves (I admit it, I ended up buying her book, and I've had it indexed by a young Russian student who grew up in Germany—I could have found a German, but it's fine this way), have prepared a meal fit for a king. This evening, Himmler is coming to dinner, along with another eminent guest: Ernst Röhm, head of the SA. He looks like a pig, with his round belly, his big head, his little deep-set eyes, his thick neck ringed with a roll of fat, and his mutilated nose turned up like a snout—a souvenir of the First World War. Proud of his soldier's manners, Röhm is also in the habit of behaving like a pig. But he's the head of an irregular army of more than 400,000 Brownshirts and it's said that he's on first-name terms with Hitler. In the eyes of the Heydrichs, therefore, he is perfectly commendable. And in fact, it's a very merry evening. They laugh a lot. After a delicious meal cooked by the lady of the house, the men feel like having a smoke and a nightcap. Lina brings them matches and goes down to the cellar to find some brandy. Suddenly, she hears an explosion. She rushes upstairs and realizes what's happened: in her excitability at serving these eminent guests, she mixed up the ordinary matches with the exploding New Year's matches. Hilarity ensues. All that's missing is the canned laughter.

## 33

Gregor Strasser is an old friend of Hitler's. A member of the NSDAP since its inception, he runs the *Arbeiter Zeitung*, the Berlin newspaper he set up when he got out of prison in 1925. Because of his prestige and position, certain matters are deferred to him. There is a dispute that cannot be settled by the local Party section. In 1932, accusing an SS officer is not without risks, even for a high-ranking Nazi, and the Schutzstaffel's growing reputation invites caution. This is why the Gauleiter of Halle-Merseburg prefers to hand over this delicate matter to Strasser: in an old edition of a musical encyclopedia, there is an entry on 'Heydrich, Bruno, real name Süss.'

So Himmler's new protégé might be the son of a Jew! Gregor Strasser, probably wishing to prove that he is still a man to be reckoned with, orders an inquiry. Does he want to take the scalp of this rising star? Does he feel the need to polish his own reputation, now going dull within the party he helped to found? Is it a genuine fear of seeing the Jewish virus infect the heart of the Nazi machine? In any case, a report is sent to Munich and it lands on Himmler's desk.

Himmler is dismayed, of course. He has already sung the praises of his young recruit to the Führer, and he fears for his own credibility if the accusation is proven. He follows the Party's inquiry with great attention. The suspicions concerning the paternal branch of Heydrich's family must have been abandoned fairly quickly: the name Süss belonged to Heydrich's grandmother's second husband, so there is no direct genetic link—and anyway the man wasn't Jewish, despite his surname. Then again, the inquiry may have led to doubts over the purity of the maternal branch. Due to a lack of evidence, Heydrich ends up being officially exonerated. But Himmler wonders if it wouldn't be better to get rid of him anyway, because he knows that from now on

44

Heydrich will remain at the mercy of rumours. On the other hand, Heydrich's activities in the SS have already made him, if not indispensable, at least very promising. Unsure of what to do, Himmler decides to seek the advice of the Führer himself.

Hitler summons Heydrich, with whom he converses privately for a long time. I don't know what Heydrich says to him, but after this meeting, the Führer's mind is made up. He tells Himmler: 'This man is extraordinarily gifted and extraordinarily dangerous. We would be stupid not to use him. The Party needs men like him, and his talents will be particularly useful in the future. What's more, he will be eternally grateful to us for having kept him and he will obey us blindly.' Himmler is vaguely disturbed to have at his command a man who can inspire such admiration in the Führer, but he agrees all the same: he is not in the habit of disputing his master's opinion.

So Heydrich has saved himself. But he has lived through the nightmare of his childhood once again. What strange fate allows *him* to be accused of being Jewish, he who is clearly such a perfect incarnation of the Aryan race in all its purity? His hatred for that cursed people grows ever stronger. In the meantime, he writes down the name of Gregor Strasser.


34


I don't know when exactly it happens, but I tend to think it's during these years that Heydrich decides upon a slight modification in the spelling of his

first name. He drops the *t* from the end: Reinhardt
becomes Reinhard. It sounds tougher.

## 35

I've been talking rubbish, the victim of both a faulty
memory and an overactive imagination. In fact, the
head of the British secret service at this time was
called 'C'—not 'M' as in James Bond. Heydrich too
called himself 'C', and not 'H'. But it's not certain
that, in doing so, he wished to copy the British: the
initial more probably referred to *der Chef*.

While I was checking my sources, however, I
came upon this statement, disclosed to I don't
know whom, but which shows that Heydrich had a
very clear idea of his job: 'In a modern totalitarian
system of government, the principle of state
security has no limits. Therefore whoever is in
charge must aim to gather a degree of power almost
without restraints.'

You can accuse Heydrich of many things, but
you can't say he didn't keep his promises.

## 36

April 20, 1934, is a significant date in the history of
the Schutzstaffel: Göring surrenders the leadership
of the Gestapo, which he created, to the two
heads of the SS. Himmler and Heydrich take
possession of the magnificent headquarters on
Prinz Albrecht Strasse in Berlin. Heydrich chooses

his office. He moves in. Sits down at his desk. Gets to work straightaway. He places some paper in front of him. Takes his pen. And starts making lists.

Obviously, Göring isn't happy to give up the leadership of his secret police, already one of the jewels in the crown of the Nazi regime. But it's the price he must pay to win the support of Himmler against Röhm: the petit bourgeois of the SS worries him less than the left-leaning agitator of the SA. Röhm likes to brag that the National Socialist revolution is not finished. But Göring doesn't see things that way: they've got the power, their only task now is to keep it. Heydrich undoubtedly subscribes to this point of view too, even if Röhm is godfather to his son.


# 37

Berlin hums with conspiracy as a document circulates the city. It's a typewritten list. Neutral observers are stunned by the carelessness with which this sheet of paper is passed around in the cafés, going from hand to hand under the eyes of waiters whom everybody knows to be informers in the pay of Heydrich.

It is nothing less than the blueprint of a hypothetical ministerial cabinet. In this future government, Hitler remains chancellor but the names of Papen and Göring vanish. In their place appear those of Röhm and his friends—Schleicher, Strasser, Brüning.

Heydrich shows the list to Hitler. The Führer, who likes nothing more than having his paranoid tendencies confirmed, chokes with rage. However, the heterogeneity of the coalition leaves him puzzled: Schleicher, for example, has never been counted among the friends of Röhm, whom he despises. Heydrich retorts that General von Schleicher has been seen deep in conversation with the French ambassador—proof that he is part of the plot.

In fact, the disparate couplings of this strange coalition show above all that Heydrich still needs to refine his knowledge of internal politics. Because he's the one who has drawn up and distributed this list. The prevailing principle behind it is very simple: he has, naturally enough, written down the names of his enemies, along with the enemies of his two masters, Himmler and Göring.

## 38

From outside, the imposing grey stone building reveals nothing. At most you might guess at an unusual activity in the movements of the silhouettes that enter and exit. But inside this SS hive there is frenzied agitation: men run in all directions, shouts echo in the great white hall, doors slam on every floor, telephones ring endlessly in offices. At the heart of the building and of the unfolding drama, Heydrich plays what will become his greatest role— that of the killer bureaucrat. Around him are tables, telephones, and men in black who dial and hang up. He takes all the calls.

'Hello! He's dead? . . . Leave the corpse where it is. Officially, it's suicide. Put your gun in his hand . . . You shot him in the back of the neck? Well, never mind, that doesn't matter. Suicide.'

'Hello! It's done? . . . Very good . . . The woman too? . . . All right, you'll say that he was resisting arrest . . . Yes, the woman too! . . . That's right, she tried to intervene, that will work fine! . . . The servants? . . . How many? . . . Take their names, we'll deal with them later.'

'Hello! Finished? . . . Good, now throw it all in the Oder.'

'Hello! . . . What? . . . At his tennis club? He was playing tennis? . . . He jumped over the hedge and disappeared in the woods? Are you fucking with me? . . . You comb the woods and you find him!'

'Hello! . . . What do you mean, "another"? What do you mean, "the same name"? . . . The first name too? . . . All right, bring him here, we'll send him to Dachau while we find the right one.'

'Hello! . . . Where was he last seen? . . . The Adlon Hotel? But everyone knows the waiters work for us, that's idiotic! He said he wanted to give himself up? . . . Very well, go back and wait at his house, then send him to us.'

'Hello! Let me speak to the Reichsführer! . . . Hello? Yes, it's done . . . Yes, that too . . . It's happening now . . . It's done . . . And where are you with number one? . . . The Führer refuses? But why? . . . You must convince the Führer! . . . Talk about his morals! And all the scandals that we've had to suppress! Remind him of the trunk left behind at the brothel! . . . Understood, I'll call Göring now.'

'Hello? Heydrich speaking. The Reichsführer tells me that the Führer wants to spare the SA Führer! . . . Naturally, under no circumstances!

49

'. . . You must tell him that the army will never accept it! We have executed Reichswehr officers: if Röhm doesn't die, Blomberg will refuse to back the operation! . . . Yes, there you go, a question of justice, absolutely! . . . Understood, I'll wait for your call.'

An SS guard enters. He looks worried. He approaches Heydrich and bends down to speak in his ear. They both leave the room. Five minutes later, Heydrich returns, alone. His face reveals nothing. He goes back to answering calls.

'Hello! . . . Burn the body! Send the ashes to his widow!'

'Hello! . . . No, Göring won't let us touch him . . . Leave six men at his house . . . Nobody enters and nobody leaves!'

'Hello! . . .' et cetera.

At the same time, he methodically fills out little white sheets of paper.

This goes on all weekend.

Finally, he gets the news he's been waiting for: the Führer has given in. He will give the order to execute Röhm—his oldest accomplice, and the head of the Sturmabteilung. Röhm may be godfather to Heydrich's eldest son but he is above all Himmler's direct superior. By decapitating the SA leadership, Himmler and Heydrich liberate the SS, which becomes an autonomous organization answerable only to Hitler. Heydrich is named Gruppenführer, a rank equivalent to major general. He is thirty years old.

Gregor Strasser is eating lunch with his family on Saturday, June 30, 1934, when the doorbell rings. Eight armed men are here to arrest him. Without even giving him time to say goodbye to his wife, they take him to Gestapo headquarters. He is not interrogated but finds himself locked in a cell with several SA men who crowd around him excitedly. They are reassured by his prestige as an old companion of the Führer, even if he hasn't exercised any political power in months. He does not understand why he is here with them, but he knows the mysteries of the Party well enough to fear its arbitrary, irrational side.

At 1700, an SS guard comes to take him to an individual cell with a large window in the roof. Alone in his cell, Strasser does not know that the Night of the Long Knives has begun, but he can guess what's going on. Should he fear for his life? True, he's a historical figure in the Party, linked to Hitler by the memory of past struggles: they were, after all, in prison together after the Munich putsch. But he knows too that Hitler is not a sentimental man. And even if he can't grasp how he could be considered a threat comparable to Röhm or Schleicher, one must take the Führer's boundless paranoia into account. Strasser realizes he will have to play his cards cleverly if he wants to save his neck.

He is thinking this when he feels a shadow pass behind his back. With an old fighter's instinct, he understands he is in danger and ducks at the very moment that a gun is fired. Someone has reached through the window and shot at him from point-blank range. He ducks, but not fast enough. He collapses.

Facedown on the cell floor, Strasser hears the bolt of the door slide open, then the sound of boots around him, the breath of a man bending over his neck, and voices:

'He's still alive.'

'What shall we do? Finish him off ?'

He hears the click of a pistol being loaded.

'Wait, I'll go and ask.'

A pair of boots moves away. A moment passes. The boots return, accompanied. Heels snap to attention at the entry of the new arrival. Silence. And then this falsetto voice that he would recognize anywhere, and which sends a final chill down his spine.

'He's not dead yet? Let him bleed like a pig.'

Heydrich's is the last human voice he will hear before dying. Well, when I say 'human' . . .

## 40

Fabrice comes to visit, and talks to me about the book I'm writing. He's an old university friend who, like me, is passionate about history. This summer evening we eat on the terrace and he talks about my book's opening with an enthusiasm that is encouraging. He fixes on the construction of the chapter about the Night of the Long Knives: this series of telephone calls, according to him, evokes both the bureaucratic nature and the mass production of what will be the hallmark of Nazism—murder. I'm flattered but also suspicious, and I decide to make him clarify what he means: 'But you know that each telephone call corresponds to an actual case? I could get almost all the names for you, if I wanted to.' He is surprised, and responds ingenuously that he'd thought I'd invented this. Vaguely disturbed, I ask him: 'What about Strasser?' Heydrich going there in person, giving the order to let him suffer a slow death in his cell: that, too, he thought I'd invented. I am mortified, and I shout: 'But no, it's all true!' And I think: 'Damn, I'm not there yet . . .'

That same evening, I watch a TV documentary on an old Hollywood film about General Patton. The film is soberly entitled *Patton*. The documentary consists essentially of showing extracts from the film, then interviewing witnesses who explain, 'In fact, it wasn't really like that . . .' He didn't take on two Messerschmitts that were machine-gunning the base, armed only with his Colt (but no doubt he would have done, according to the witness, if the Messerschmitts had given him time). He didn't make such-and-such a speech before the whole army but in private, and besides, he didn't actually say that. He didn't learn at the last moment that he was going to be sent to France, but had in fact been informed several weeks in advance. He didn't disobey orders in taking Palermo, but did so with the backing of the Allied High Command and his own direct superior. He certainly didn't tell a Russian general to go fuck himself, even if he didn't much like the Russians. And so on. So, basically, the film is about a fictional character whose life is strongly inspired by Patton's, but who

53

clearly isn't him. And yet the film is called *Patton*.
And that doesn't shock anybody. Everyone finds it
normal, fudging reality to make a screenplay more
dramatic, or adding coherence to the narrative
of a character whose real path probably included
too many random ups and downs, insufficiently
loaded with significance. It's because of people
like that, forever messing with historical truth just
to sell their stories, that an old friend, familiar
with all these fictional genres and therefore fatally
accustomed to these processes of glib falsification,
can say to me in innocent surprise: 'Oh, really, it's
not invented?'

No, it's not invented! What would be the point of
'inventing' Nazism?

## 41

You'll have gathered by now that I am fascinated by
this story. But at the same time I think it's getting to
me.

One night, I had a dream. I was a German
soldier, dressed in the grey-green uniform of
the Wehrmacht, and I was on guard duty in an
unidentified landscape, covered with snow and
bordered by barbed wire. This background was
clearly inspired by the numerous Second World
War video games to which I've occasionally been
weak enough to become addicted: Call of Duty,
Medal of Honour, Red Orchestra . . .

Suddenly, during my patrol, Heydrich himself
arrived to perform an inspection. I stood to
attention and held my breath while he circled me

with an inquisitorial air. I was terrorized by the idea that he might find fault with me. But I woke up before anything else happened.

To tease me, Natacha often pretends to worry about the impressive number of books on Nazism that line the shelves of my apartment, and the risk of ideological conversion she thinks I'm running. To join in the joke, I never fail to mention the innumerable tendentious—if not openly neo-Nazi—websites that I come across while researching on the Internet. It is obviously impossible that I—son of a Jewish mother and a Communist father, brought up on the republican values of the most progressive French petite bourgeoisie and immersed through my literary studies in the humanism of Montaigne and the philosophy of the Enlightenment, the Surrealist revolution and the Existentialist worldview—could ever be tempted to 'sympathize' with anything to do with Nazism, in any shape or form.

But I must, once more, bow down before the limitless and nefarious power of literature. Because this dream proves beyond doubt that, with his larger-than-life, storybook aura, Heydrich *impresses* me.

## 42

Anthony Eden, the British foreign minister, listens in stunned silence. The new Czech president, Edvard Beneš, is displaying a staggering confidence in his ability to resolve the question of the Sudeten Germans. Not only does he claim to be able to contain Germany's expansionist desires, but, what's more, to do so alone—in other words, without the help of France and Great Britain. Eden doesn't know what to make of this speech. 'I suppose that to be Czech in days like these, one must be an optimist,' he says to himself. It is still only 1935.

## 43

In 1936, Major Moravec, head of the Czechoslovak secret services, takes his colonel's exam. One of the hypothetical questions reads:

'Czechoslovakia is attacked by Germany. Hungary and Austria are also hostile. France has not mobilized her army and the Petite Entente is probably unworkable. What are the military solutions for Czechoslovakia?'

Analysis of the subject: with the Austro-Hungarian Empire having been carved up in 1918, Vienna and Budapest are now naturally eyeing up their former provinces—that is, Bohemia-Moravia, which had been an Austrian dependency, and Slovakia, which had been under Hungarian control. Moreover, Hungary is led by a fascist ally of Germany, Admiral Horthy. A badly weakened Austria, meanwhile, is having trouble resisting the calls from both sides of the German border for the country to be united with its Germanic big brother. The agreement signed by Hitler, which promises that he won't intervene in Austrian affairs, is not worth the paper it's written on. If there was ever a conflict with Germany, therefore, Czechoslovakia would also find itself pitted against the two heads of the fallen empire. The Petite Entente, agreed to in 1922 by Czechoslovakia, Romania, and Yugoslavia to protect one another from their old Austro-Hungarian masters, is not the most convincing of strategic alliances. And France's reluctance to keep its commitments to its Czech ally if a conflict arises has already been made clear. So the hypothetical situation proposed in the exam is completely realistic. Moravec's response is only five words long: 'Problem unsolvable by military means.' He passes with flying colours and becomes a colonel.

## 44

If I were to mention all the plots in which Heydrich had a hand, this book would never be finished. Sometimes in the course of my research I come upon a story that I decide not to relate, whether because it seems too anecdotal, or because there are details missing and I'm unable to fit the pieces of the puzzle together, or because I find the story questionable. Sometimes, too, there are several contradictory versions of the same story. In certain cases, I allow myself to decide which version is true. If not, I drop the story.

I had decided not to mention Heydrich's role in the fall of Tukhachevsky. First of all, because his role struck me as secondary, even illusory. Next, because Soviet politics in the 1930s doesn't really have much to do with the main flow of my story. Finally, I suppose, because I was afraid of getting involved on another historical front: the Stalinist purges, Marshal Tukhachevsky's career, the origins of his dispute with Stalin . . . all of this called for both learning and meticulousness. The danger was that it would drag me too far from my subject.

All the same, I have imagined a scene, just for the pleasure of it: we see the young General Tukhachevsky contemplating the rout of the Bolshevik army at the gates of Warsaw. It's 1920. Poland and the USSR are at war. 'The Revolution will step over the corpse of Poland!' declared Trotsky. It has to be said that in allying itself with Ukraine, in dreaming of a confederation that would also include Lithuania and Byelorussia, Poland was threatening the fragile unity of the nascent Soviet Russian state. On the other hand, if the Bolsheviks wanted to take the revolution to Germany, they were bound to go through the region.

In August 1920, the Soviet counterattack led the Red Army to the gates of Warsaw, and Poland's fate looked sealed. But the young nation's independence would last another nineteen years. What Poland was unable to do in 1939 against the Germans, it did that day against the Russians: it pushed them back. This is the 'miracle at the Vistula.' Tukhachevsky is defeated by an unparalleled strategist—Józef Piłsudski, the hero of Polish independence, and nearly thirty years Tukhachevsky's senior.

The two armies are more or less equal in numbers: 113,000 Poles against 114,000 Russians. Tukhachevsky, however, is certain of victory. He sends the main body of his forces north, where Piłsudski has fooled him into believing that there is a concentration of troops. In fact, Piłsudski attacks in the south, from behind. It is here that this tributary episode joins the main flow of my story.

Tukhachevsky calls for reinforcements from the 1st Cavalry—led by the no-less-legendary General Budyonny—who are fighting on the southwest front to take L'viv. Budyonny's cavalry is formidable, and Piłsudski knows that this intervention might turn the battle against him. But then something unbelievable happens: General Budyonny refuses to obey orders, and his army remains at L'viv. For the Poles, this is without doubt the real miracle at the Vistula. For Tukhachevsky, however, defeat is bitter, and he wants to understand why it happened. He doesn't have to search far: the political commissar of the southwestern front, under whose authority Budyonny is operating, has decided that the capture of L'viv is a matter of prestige. There is no question of him sending away his best troops, even if it is necessary to avoid a military disaster, because he knows that the disaster is not his responsibility. Never mind that the fate of the war depends upon it. The personal ambitions of this commissar have often taken precedence over all other considerations. His name is Joseph Dzhugashvili, though he is better known by his nom de guerre: Stalin.

Fifteen years later, Tukhachevsky succeeds Trotsky as head of the Red Army, while Stalin succeeds Lenin as head of state. The two men hate each other, they are at the pinnacle of their power, and they disagree over political strategy: Stalin seeks to delay a conflict with Nazi Germany, while Tukhachevsky advocates going to war now.

I wasn't aware of all this when I saw the Eric Rohmer film *Triple Agent*. But I decided to study the question seriously when I heard the main character, General Skoblin, an eminent White

Russian exiled in Paris, say to his wife: 'Do you remember? I told you that in Berlin I went to see the head of German intelligence, a certain Heydrich. And you know what I didn't want to tell him? Things about Comrade Tukhachevsky, whom I met secretly in Paris during his trip to the West for the funeral of the king of England. Oh, of course, he didn't open his heart to me, but from what he said I was able to make certain deductions. The Gestapo must have got wind of this meeting; Heydrich questioned me, I answered evasively, he gave me an icy look, and that's how we left it.'

Heydrich in a Rohmer film! I still can't get over it.

After this bit of dialogue, Skoblin's wife asks:

'And this Mr Heydrich, why does he want this information?'

'Well, it's in the Germans' interests to compromise the head of the Red Army, especially as they already know he's out of favour with Stalin ... at least, that's what I assume.'

Skoblin goes on to deny any links with the Nazis, and this, too, seems to be Rohmer's view, even if the director takes great care to stress the ambiguity of his character and politics. But I struggle to believe that Skoblin went to the trouble of meeting Heydrich in Berlin just to tell him nothing.

It seems to me more likely that Skoblin went to see Heydrich to inform him that a plot against Stalin had been hatched by Tukhachevsky, but that in doing so, Skoblin was acting on behalf of the NKVD—in other words, for Stalin himself. Why? To spread the rumour of the plot in order to make people believe an (apparently unfounded) accusation of high treason.

60

Did Heydrich believe Skoblin? I don't know, but either way he saw the opportunity of eliminating a dangerous enemy of the Reich: to remove Tukhachevsky in 1937 is to decapitate the Red Army. He decides to feed the rumour. He knows that such an affair is a matter for Canaris's Abwehr, as it's a military question. But, intoxicated by the sheer scale of his project, he manages to convince Himmler and Hitler to give him control of the operation. To carry it out, he calls on his best hired man, Alfred Naujocks, who specializes in dirty work. For three months, Naujocks will create a whole series of forgeries aimed at compromising the Russian marshal. He has no difficulty finding his signature: all he has to do is look through the archives of the Weimar Republic. Back then, when diplomatic relations between the two countries were more friendly, many official documents had been signed by Tukhachevsky.

When the dossier is ready, Heydrich assigns one of his men to sell it to the NKVD. This meeting gives rise to a wonderful spying double cross: the Russian buys the fake dossier from the German, whom he pays with fake rubles. Each thinks he's fooling the other, each is fooled in turn.

Eventually, Stalin gets what he wants: evidence that his most serious rival is planning a coup d'état. Historians disagree over how much importance should be given to Heydrich in this affair, but it should be noted that the dossier was sent in May 1937, and that Tukhachevsky was executed in June. For me, the closeness of the dates strongly suggests a link between cause and effect.

So, in the end, who fooled whom? I think Heydrich served Stalin's interests, in allowing him to get rid of the only man capable of eclipsing him. But this man was also the most able to lead a war against Germany. The total disorganization of the Red Army, caught off guard by the German invasion of June '41, would be the final aftermath of this murky story. But you can't really say it was Heydrich's masterstroke. Rather, Stalin shot himself in the foot. All the same, when Stalin begins a series of unprecedented purges, Heydrich is exultant. He is perfectly happy to take all the credit for this state of affairs.

## 45

I am thirty-three, considerably older than Tukhachevsky was in 1920. Today is the anniversary of the assassination attempt on Heydrich—May 27, 2006. Natacha's sister is getting married, but I'm not invited to the wedding. Natacha called me a 'little shit'. I don't think she can bear me anymore. My life is in ruins. I wonder if Tukhachevsky felt this bad when he realized that he'd lost the battle, when he saw his army routed and understood that he had failed miserably. Did he believe he was finished, done for, washed up? Did he curse fortune, or adversity, or those who'd betrayed him? Or did he curse himself? Anyway, I know he bounced back. That's encouraging, even if it was only to be crushed fifteen years later by his worst enemy. The wheel turns: that's what I tell myself. Natacha doesn't return my calls. I am in 1920, standing before the trembling walls of Warsaw, and at my feet, indifferent, flows the Vistula.

## 46

That night, I dreamed that I wrote the chapter about the assassination, and it began: 'A black Mercedes slid along the road like a snake.' That's when I understood that I had to start writing the rest of the story, because the rest of the story had to converge at this crucial episode. By pursuing the chain of causality back into infinity, I allowed myself to keep delaying the moment when I must face the novel's bravura moment, its scene of scenes.

## 47

Imagine a map of the world, with concentric circles closing in around Germany. This afternoon, November 5, 1937, Hitler reveals his plans to the army high command—Blomberg, Fritsch, Raeder, Göring—and to his foreign minister, Neurath. The objective of German politics, he reminds them (although I think everyone's understood by now), is to ensure the safety of Germany's racial identity, to guarantee its existence, and to aid its development. It is therefore a question of living space (the famous *Lebensraum*) and it is here that we can begin to trace the circles of the map. Not from the narrowest to the widest, to take in at a single glance the Reich's expansionist aims, but from the widest to the narrowest, focusing ruthlessly on the ogre's first targets. For reasons he never bothers to explain, Hitler decrees that the Germans have the right to a bigger living space than other races. Germany's future depends entirely on the solution to this problem. Where can this space be found? Not in some distant colony in Africa or Asia, but in the heart of Europe (he traces a circle around the Old Continent), in the immediate neighbourhood of the Reich. So the circle encompasses only France, Belgium, Holland, Poland, Czechoslovakia, Austria, Italy, and Switzerland—plus Lithuania, if we remember that the top of Germany at the time extended from Danzig to Memel and bordered the Baltic countries. So Hitler's question was this: Where can Germany obtain the greatest profit for the lowest price? France was ruled out because of its presumed military power and its links to Great Britain—and Holland and Belgium, too, due to their strategic importance for the French. Mussolini's Italy was naturally excluded straightaway. An eastward expansion towards Poland and the Baltic countries would create a premature conflict with the Soviet Union. Switzerland was saved as usual, less by its neutrality than by its role as the world's piggy bank. The circle is therefore retraced and moved above a zone reduced to two countries: 'Our first objective must be to overthrow Czechoslovakia and Austria simultaneously in order to remove the threat to our flank in any possible operation against the West.' As we see, no sooner has he targeted his 'first objective' than Hitler is thinking of widening the circle.

Apart from Göring and Raeder, both of whom were genuine Nazis, Hitler's audience is shocked by his plans—literally so in the case of Neurath, who suffers several heart attacks in the days that follow the unveiling of this brilliant scheme. Blomberg

64

and Fritsch—respectively, the war minister and commander in chief of the armed services, and commander in chief of the army—protested with a vehemence wholly inappropriate in the Third Reich. In 1937, the old army still believed that it could sway the opinions of the dictator it had, imprudently, helped to seize power.

They didn't understand Hitler at all. But they soon would. And Blomberg and Fritsch would pay dearly for their education.

Not long after this stormy conference, Blomberg married his (much younger) secretary. To his displeasure, and perhaps to his surprise, it was revealed that his wife was a former prostitute. And to make the scandal as great as possible, nude photos of her were passed around government circles. Though Blomberg bravely refused to divorce, he was forced to resign his post. Relieved of all military responsibility, he remained faithful to his wife till the end—that's to say, until 1946 in Nuremberg, where he died in detention.

As for Fritsch, he was the victim of an even more indecent plot, skilfully conducted by Heydrich.

## 48

Like Sherlock Holmes, Heydrich plays the violin. (He plays it better than does the fictional detective, however.) Also like Sherlock Holmes, he conducts criminal inquiries. Except that where Holmes seeks the truth, Heydrich just makes it up.

His mission is to compromise General von Fritsch, the commander in chief of the army.

Heydrich doesn't need to be head of the SD to know that Fritsch has anti-Nazi feelings: he has never made any secret of them. At a military parade in Saarbrücken, in 1935, he was heard openly and sarcastically abusing the SS, the Party, and many of its most eminent members. It would probably be quite easy to implicate him in a plot.

But Heydrich has something more humiliating in mind for the old baron. Knowing how proud and touchy the Prussian aristocracy are when it comes to their moral rectitude, he decides to compromise Fritsch, as he did Blomberg, in a sex scandal.

Unlike Blomberg, Fritsch is a confirmed bachelor. This is Heydrich's starting point. In cases of this kind, the angle of attack is obvious. In order to put together the dossier, Heydrich calls on the Gestapo's 'department for the suppression of homosexuality'.

And guess what he discovers? A shady individual, known to the police as a blackmailer of homosexuals, claims to have *seen* Fritsch, in a dark alley near Potsdam Station, having sex with a certain 'Jo the Bavarian'. Unbelievably, this story appears to be true, except for one minor detail: the Fritsch in question is not the general, but someone else with the same surname. To Heydrich, this is of little importance. He finds out that this second Fritsch is a retired cavalry officer—a soldier, then—which will help add to the confusion, even more so as the blackmailer, encouraged by the Gestapo, is ready to identify whoever Heydrich wants him to.

Heydrich has imagination, and it's a useful quality in his job. But in order to work properly, this type of plot also requires an attention to detail that Heydrich doesn't really demonstrate here. Still,

66

he almost gets away with it.

In the chancellery offices, before Göring and Hitler himself, Fritsch finds himself face-to-face with the blackmailer. This latter is, by all accounts, utterly degenerate, and the haughty baron does not even deign to respond to the accusations against him. Unfortunately, covering oneself in one's dignity is not the kind of attitude that goes down well in the higher echelons of the Third Reich. Hitler demands Fritsch's immediate resignation. Up to this point, everything is going to plan.

But Fritsch refuses. He asks to be court-martialled. And suddenly Heydrich is in a very delicate position. A court-martial entails a preliminary inquiry led not by the Gestapo but by the army itself. Hitler hesitates. He has no more desire than Heydrich for a full and proper trial, but he is also a little fearful of the reactions of the old military class.

Within a few days, the situation has been turned on its head: not only has the army discovered the truth, but it has managed to pull the two key witnesses—the blackmailer and the retired cavalry officer—from the claws of the Gestapo. Heydrich's plan fizzles out completely. His fate is now hanging by a thread: if Hitler agrees to the trial, his trickery will be exposed in broad daylight, which will lead at the very least to Heydrich's dismissal—and the end of all his ambitions. He will find himself more or less where he was in 1931, after his discharge from the navy.

Heydrich is not very happy at this prospect. The icy killer is now the terror-stricken prey. His right-hand man Schellenberg recalls how one day in the office, during this crisis, Heydrich asks for a gun. The head of the SD has his back to the wall.

But he is wrong to doubt Hitler. In the end, Fritsch is put on sick leave: no resignation, no trial. It's simpler this way, and his problems are solved. All the same, Heydrich did have a trump card up his sleeve: his interests were the same as Hitler's, because the latter had decided to take control of the army himself. In other words, Fritsch would have had to be eliminated, come what may—it was the Führer's unshakable will.

February 5, 1938—a prominent headline in the *Völkischer Beobachter*:

'All power concentrated in the hands of the Führer.'

Heydrich needn't have worried.

The trial does finally take place, but, in the meantime, the balance of power has shifted irrevocably: after the incredible euphoria provoked by the Anschluss, the army bows down before the genius of the Führer, and stops making trouble. Fritsch is acquitted, the blackmailer is executed, and the whole affair is forgotten.

<br>

### 49

Hitler never joked about morals. Since the Nuremberg Laws of 1935, it is officially forbidden for a Jew to have sexual relations with an Aryan. The crime is punishable by a prison sentence.

But, amazingly, only the man can be prosecuted. It was evidently Hitler's wish that the woman, whether Jewish or Aryan, should not be at the mercy of the law.

Heydrich, more Catholic than the pope, doesn't see it that way. This discrimination between men and women offends his sense of equity (although only when the woman is a Jew, of course). So in 1937 he gives secret instructions to the Kripo (criminal police) and the Gestapo that, in the event of any German man being found guilty of sleeping with a Jew, the woman would automatically be arrested and sent discreetly to a concentration camp.

In other words, when the Nazi leaders are—for once—ordered to show a degree of moderation, they are unafraid to thwart the Führer's will. This is interesting when you consider that obedience to orders, in the name of military honour and sworn oaths, was the only argument put forward after the war to justify these men's crimes.

## 50

A bombshell rocks Europe: it's the Anschluss. Austria has finally 'decided' to be 'reunited' with Germany. It's the first step in the birth of the Third Reich. It is also Hitler's first conjuring trick, soon to be repeated: conquering a country without meeting any resistance.

The news spreads like wildfire across the continent. In London, Colonel Moravec wishes to return urgently to Prague, but it's impossible to find a flight. He manages to take off for France but ends up in The Hague, from where he decides to complete his journey by train. The train is a fine way to travel, of course, but there is a slight problem. To reach Prague, he must cross Germany.

Unbelievably, Moravec decides to risk it.

So for several hours on March 13, 1938, the head of the Czechoslovak secret services is travelling through Nazi Germany by train.

I try to imagine the journey. Naturally, Moravec attempts to be as discreet as possible. He speaks German, admittedly, but I'm not sure that his accent is beyond suspicion. Then again, Germany is not yet at war, and the German people—though heated up by the Führer's speeches about the Jewish international conspiracy and the enemy within—are not yet as alert as they will later become. But, taking no chances, when Moravec buys his ticket he doubtless chooses the friendliest-looking clerk. Or better still, the most half-witted.

Once he was on the train, I suppose he sought out an empty compartment, and that he sat down either:

next to the window, so he could discourage anyone who attempted to begin a conversation by turning his back and pretending to admire the countryside, all the while watching the compartment's reflection in the glass

*or*

next to the door, so that he could watch all the comings and goings in the corridor.

Let's put him next to the door.

What I do know is that he believed—aware, and perhaps quite proud, of his own importance—that the Gestapo would pay a great deal of money to know who the German railway was transporting that day.

Each movement in the carriage must have been a test of nerves.

Each time the train halted in a station.

Eventually, a man boarded the train and sat down in his compartment. Soon, it was full of suspicious-looking people. Poor men, families—those wouldn't have worried him too much. But also some better-dressed men.

A man without a hat, perhaps, passes in the corridor, and this detail intrigues Moravec. He remembers from his journeys as a student in the USSR that they had told him how, in that country, any man in a hat must be either a member of the NKVD or a foreigner. In which case, what does it mean in Germany to be hatless?

I suppose there were changes of train, connections to be made, hours of waiting, and all the added stress they bring. Moravec hears newspaper vendors yelling out their headlines in hysterical, triumphant voices. He must surely buy several more tickets, if only to conceal for as long as possible his final destination.

And then . . . the customs barrier. I presume that Moravec had a fake passport, but I don't know what nationality it was. And, in fact, he might not have had a fake passport, because he'd been in London on a mission conducted with the agreement of the British authorities. Before London, he'd spent a few days in the Baltic countries, where I believe he went to see his local counterparts. So he didn't need a false identity, and perhaps hadn't prepared one.

Perhaps, after all, his passport being in order, the customs officer—having conscientiously examined it, during those special seconds in a life when time seems to stop—had simply given it back to him.

Anyway, he made it through.

71

When, at last, he got off the train and stood upon his native soil, free from danger, he surrendered himself to an immense wave of relief.

Much later, he would say that this was the last pleasant feeling he would experience for a long time.

## 51

Austria is the Reich's first acquisition. The next day, the country becomes a German province and 150,000 Austrian Jews suddenly find themselves at Hitler's mercy.

In 1938, no one is really thinking about exterminating them. The idea is to encourage them to emigrate.

In order to organize this emigration of Austrian Jews, a young SS sublieutenant, appointed by the SD, is sent to Vienna. He quickly gets to grips with the situation and he's full of ideas. The one he's most proud of—if we trust what he would later say at his trial, twenty-two years later—is the idea of the conveyor belt: in order to be allowed to emigrate, the Jews must put together a thick dossier made up of many different documents. Once the dossier is complete, they report to the Jewish Emigration Office, where they place their documents on a conveyor belt. The real aim of this process is to strip them of all their possessions as quickly as possible, so that they do not leave the country before having legally transferred everything they own. At the end of the conveyor belt, they retrieve their passport from a basket.

Fifty thousand Austrian Jews will thus escape Hitler's trap before it closes on them. In a way, this solution suits everyone at the time: the Jews can think themselves lucky to get out in one piece, while the Nazis get their hands on a great deal of loot. Heydrich, in Berlin, considers the operation a success. And for some time yet, the emigration of all the Reich's Jews is seen as a realistic solution, the best response to the 'Jewish question'.

As for the young lieutenant who does such a good job with the Jews, Heydrich will make a note of his name: Adolf Eichmann.


## 52

It's while he's in Vienna that Eichmann invents the method that will form the basis of all the Nazis' politics of extermination and deportation. This involves seeking the victims' active cooperation. The Jews are always invited to make themselves known to the authorities, and in the vast majority of cases—whether for emigrating in 1938 or for being sent to Treblinka or Auschwitz in 1943—this is exactly what they do. Without this, the Nazis would have had to deal with insurmountable demographic problems, and no policy of mass extermination would really have been possible. There would still undoubtedly have been countless crimes, but everything suggests that we would not be talking about genocide.

Neither Heydrich nor Eichmann can suspect that 1938 is paving the way for 1943, even if—with characteristic intuition—the former immediately

73

sees in the latter a talented bureaucrat, whom he can turn into a valuable assistant. And although the eyes of Nazi Germany begin now to turn towards Prague, Heydrich and Eichmann have no idea what roles they will play in that city.

## 53

There are signs, though. For years, Heydrich has been ordering numerous studies of the Jewish question from his heads of department. And this is the kind of response he's been getting:

> It would be advisable to deprive the Jews of their means of survival—and not only in the economic sphere. There should be no future for them in Germany. Only the old generation should be allowed to die here in peace— not the young ones. Hence the incitement to emigrate. As for the means, street-fighting anti-Semitism should be rejected. You don't kill rats with a revolver, but with poison and gas.

Metaphor? Fantasy? The subconscious rising to the surface? In any case, you feel that this department head already has an idea in the back of his mind. The report dates from May 1934. The man is a visionary!

In the heart of old Bohemia, east of Prague, on the Olomouc road, is a little town: Kutná Hora is on Unesco's World Heritage List, and has picturesque alleys, a beautiful Gothic cathedral, and above all a magnificent ossuary—a genuine local curiosity where the white vaults and ribs of the sepulchral architecture are constructed out of human skulls.

In 1237, unsuspected by the town's inhabitants, Kutná Hora carries within it the virus of history, which is about to begin one of its long, cruel, and ironic chapters. This chapter will last seven hundred years.

Wenceslaus I, the son of Premysl Ottokar I, part of the glorious founding dynasty of the Premyslids, rules over the lands of Bohemia and Moravia. The sovereign has married a German princess, Kunigunde, the daughter of Philip of Swabia, king of Germany and a Ghibelline—in other words, part of the fearsome house of Hohenstaufen. So, in the quarrel between the Guelphs (allies of the pope) and the Ghibellines (allies of the emperor), Wenceslaus chose the side of the Germanic Holy Roman Empire. From this point on, the split-tailed lion decorates the royal armouries, replacing the old eagle in flames. Dungeons proliferate, and the spirit of chivalry reigns.

Soon, Prague will have its Old New Synagogue.

Kutná Hora is still nothing but a village—not one of the biggest towns in Europe.

This could be like a scene from a medieval Western. As night falls, a Falstaffian tavern welcomes the inhabitants of Kutná Hora as well as a few rare travellers. The regulars drink and joke with the waitresses, pinching their asses, while the travellers eat in silence, exhausted, and the thieves watch and get ready for their night's work, hardly touching their drinks. Outside it's raining, and you can hear a few whinnies from the stable next door. An old white-bearded man appears at the door. His clothes are soaked, his leggings mud-stained, water streams from his cloth hat. Everyone in Kutná Hora knows him—he's an old madman from the mountains—and no one pays much attention to him. He orders drink, then food, then more drink. He demands a pig be killed for him. Laughter explodes from the nearby tables. The landlord, mistrustful, asks if he has enough money to pay. At this a look of triumph flashes in the old man's eyes: he puts a small, cheap leather purse on the table, and undoes the laces. He takes out a little greyish stone and, pretending to be casual, gives it to the landlord to inspect. The landlord frowns, takes the stone between his fingers, and holds it up to the light coming from the torches on the wall. Stunned, suddenly impressed, he takes a step backwards. He has recognized the metal. It's a silver nugget.

## 55

Premysl Ottokar II, son of Wenceslaus I, carries (like his grandfather) the name of his ancestor Premysl the Ploughman—who, in times immemorial, was taken for a husband by Queen Libuse, the legendary foundress of Prague. More than anyone else, except perhaps his grandfather, Premysl Ottokar II felt himself to be the guardian of his kingdom's greatness. And no one could say he wasn't worthy in this respect. From the beginning of his reign, Bohemia produced—thanks to its silver deposits—an average annual revenue of 100,000 silver marks, making it one of the richest regions of thirteenth-century Europe: five times richer than Bavaria, for example.

But the man nicknamed 'the King of Iron and Gold' (which hardly does justice to the metal that made his fortune) is, like all kings, not content to make do with what he's got. He knows that the kingdom's prosperity depends on its silver mines, and wishes to speed up their exploitation. All these sleeping deposits, still untouched, keep him awake at night. He needs more manpower. And the Czechs are peasants, not miners.

Ottokar contemplates Prague, his town. From the heights of his castle, he sees all the markets around the immense Judith Bridge. (This is one of the first bridges built from stone rather than wood, located on the site of the future Charles Bridge.) Little coloured dots bustle around goods of all kinds: fabrics, meat, fruit and vegetables, jewels and finely worked metals. All these merchants, Ottokar knows, are German. The Czechs are a people of the land, not of the city, and as he thinks this the king feels perhaps a tinge of regret, if not contempt. Ottokar also knows that it is towns that are responsible for a kingdom's prestige, and that a nobility worthy of its name does not remain on its lands but forms a court—as the French call it—around the king. But when Ottokar thinks of this great concept of chivalry, he thinks not of

France but of the Teutonic Knights, at whose side he fought in Prussia during the Crusade of 1255. Hadn't he himself founded Königsberg at the point of his sword? Ottokar turns to Germany because the German courts are, in his eyes, incarnations of nobility and modernity. To bring these qualities to his kingdom, he has decided to begin a vast policy of German immigration to Bohemia, justified by the need for mineworkers. Hundreds of thousands of German colonists will be encouraged to come and settle in his beautiful country. By favouring them, by giving them lands and financial privileges, Ottokar hopes at the same time to find allies who will weaken the position of the greedy and threatening local nobility—the Ryzmburks, the Viteks, the Falkenstejns—for whom he feels only distrust and disdain. History will show, with the rise in power of the German aristocracy in Prague, Jihlava, Kutná Hora, and eventually throughout Bohemia and Moravia, that the strategy worked perfectly, even if Ottokar won't live long enough to benefit from it.

But in the long term, you'd have to say it was a very bad idea.

56

The day after the Anschluss, Germany, showing uncharacteristic prudence, sends messages of appeasement to Czechoslovakia. The Czechs shouldn't have the slightest fear of being the next victim, they are told, even if the annexation of Austria and the consequent feeling of being encircled might seem a legitimate source of anxiety.

To avoid any needless tension, orders are given that no German troops in Austria should approach within ten to fifteen miles of the Czech border.

But in the Sudetenland, news of the Anschluss provokes an extraordinary enthusiasm. Suddenly people talk only of their ultimate fantasy: being reunited with the Reich. There are protests and marches everywhere, political tracts and propaganda pamphlets. The pervading atmosphere is of conspiracy. The Czech government gives orders aimed at suppressing this agitation, but they are systematically sabotaged by public workers and German employees. The boycott of the Czech minority in German-language zones is enforced on an unprecedented scale. Beneš will write in his memoirs that he was stunned by this mystical romanticism that seemed to suddenly seize all the Germans of Bohemia.

## 57

The Council of Constance is guilty of having called on our natural enemies—all the Germans who surround us—to fight an unjust war against us, when they have no reason to rise up against us except their unquenchable hatred of our language.

(HUSSITE MANIFESTO, c. 1420)

Once, and once only, France and Britain said no to Hitler during the Czechoslovak crisis. And even then, the British 'no' was rather half-hearted.

May 19, 1938: reports of German troop movements at the Czech border. On May 20, Czechoslovakia orders a partial mobilization of its own forces, sending out a very clear message: if the country is attacked, it will defend itself.

The French, reacting with a firmness we hardly expect of them anymore, immediately declare that they will honour their commitments to Czechoslovakia. In other words, that they will come to the military aid of their allies in the event of a German attack.

The British, unpleasantly surprised by the French attitude, nevertheless fall into line with their ally's position. With this small qualification: that they will under no circumstances guarantee a military intervention. Chamberlain makes sure that his diplomats do not promise more than is contained in this muddled phrase: 'In the event of a European conflict, it is impossible to know if Great Britain will take part.' Not the most decisive of statements.

Hitler will remember these weasel words, but at the time he takes fright and retreats. On May 23, he makes it known that Germany has no aggressive intentions towards Czechoslovakia, and withdraws the troops massed at the border as if nothing had happened. The official line is that these were simply routine manoeuvres.

But Hitler is mad with rage. He feels that Beneš

has humiliated him, and the urge to make war is rising within him. On May 28, he summons the Wehrmacht's field officers and barks at them:

'It is my staunch desire to wipe Czechoslovakia off the map.'

## 59

Beneš, worried by Great Britain's reluctance to honour its commitments, calls his ambassador in London for the latest news. The conversation, recorded by the German secret service, leaves no doubt about the Czechs' disillusionment with their British counterparts—beginning with Chamberlain, who gets it with both barrels:

'The dirty bastard just wants us to lick Hitler's ass!'

'You have to talk him around! Make him get his wits back!'

'The old bugger hasn't got any wits left. All he does is sniff the Nazis' shit.'

'So talk to Horace Wilson. Tell him to warn the prime minister that England, too, will be in danger if we don't show ourselves resolute. Could you make him understand that?'

'How do you want me to talk to Wilson? He's just a jackal!'

The Germans rush to get the tape recordings to the British.

Apparently, Chamberlain was dreadfully upset and never forgave the Czechs.

This same Wilson, Chamberlain's special adviser, made a bid for conciliation between the Germans and Czechs, with Britain acting as referee. Not long afterward, Hitler would talk about it in these terms:

'Why should I care about the British being involved? The filthy old dog is mad if he thinks he can con me like this!'

Wilson is surprised:

'If Herr Hitler is referring to the prime minister, I can assure him that the prime minister is not mad. He is simply interested in the outcome of the peace talks.'

Hitler then really lets loose:

'I'm not interested in what these ass-lickers say. The only thing that interests me is my people in the Sudetenland; my people who are tortured and assassinated by that vile queer Beneš! I won't take it any longer. It's more than a good German can bear! Do you hear me, you stupid swine?'

So there is at least one point on which the Czechs and Germans were in agreement: Chamberlain and his clique were a bunch of ass-lickers.

Curiously, however, Chamberlain was far less offended by the German insults than by those of the Czechs. With hindsight, you'd have to say that's a shame.

## 60

On August 21, 1938, Edouard Daladier, the French council president, gives an edifying speech on the radio:

Faced with authoritarian states who are arming and equipping themselves with no

82

regard to the length of the working week, alongside democratic states who are striving to regain their prosperity and ensure their safety with a forty-eight-hour week, why should France—both more impoverished and more threatened—delay making the decisions on which our future depends? As long as the international situation remains so delicate, we must work more than forty hours per week, and as much as forty-eight hours in businesses linked to national defence.

Reading this transcription, I was reminded that putting the French back to work was the French right's eternal fantasy. I was deeply shocked that these elitist reactionaries, understanding so little the true nature of the situation, would use the Sudeten crisis to settle their scores with the Popular Front. Bear in mind that in 1938, the editorials of the bourgeois newspapers shamelessly stigmatized those workers whose only concern was enjoying their paid holidays.

Just in time, however, my father reminded me that Daladier was a radical Socialist, and thus part of the Popular Front. I've just checked this, and staggeringly, it's true: Daladier was the defence minister in Leon Blum's government! I feel like I've been punched in the stomach. I can hardly bear to tell the story: Daladier, former defence minister of the Popular Front, invokes questions of national defence not to prevent Hitler carving up Czechoslovakia but to backtrack on the forty-hour week—one of the principal gains of the Popular Front. At this level of political stupidity, betrayal becomes almost a work of art.

## 61

On September 26, 1938, Hitler must deliver a speech to the crowds gathered at the Sportpalast in Berlin. He practises his speech on a British delegation who come to tell him that the Czechs have refused to evacuate the Sudetenland. 'They treat the Germans like blacks! On October 1, I will do what I please with Czechoslovakia. If France and England decide to attack, let them go ahead! I couldn't care less! It's pointless to continue negotiations—they're going nowhere!' And he leaves.

Then, on the podium, in front of his fanatical supporters:

For twenty years, the Germans of Czechoslovakia have been persecuted by the Czechs. For twenty years, the Germans of the Reich have watched this happen. They were forced to watch it: not because they accepted the situation, but because, being unarmed, they couldn't help their brothers fight these torturers. Today, things are different. And the democracies of the world are up in arms! We have learned, during these years, not to trust the world's democracies. In our time, only one state has shown itself to be a great European power, and at the head of this state, one man has understood the distress of our people: my great friend Benito Mussolini. [The crowd shouts *Heil Duce!* ] Mr Beneš is in Prague, and he thinks nothing can happen to him because he has the support of France and England.

[Prolonged laughter.] My fellow countrymen, I believe the moment has come to speak clearly. Mr Beneš has seven million people behind him, and here we have seventy-five million. [Enthusiastic applause.] I assured the British prime minister that once this problem has been resolved, there will be no more territorial problems in Europe. We don't want any Czechs in the Reich, but I tell the German people this: on the Sudeten question, my patience is at an end. Now it's up to Mr Beneš whether he wants peace or war. Either he accepts our offer and gives the Sudeten Germans their freedom, or we will go and free them ourselves. Let the world be warned.

## 62

It's during the Sudeten crisis that we have the first positive indications of the Führer's madness. At this time, the merest mention of Beneš and the Czechs would send him into such a rage that he could lose all self-control. He was reportedly seen throwing himself to the floor and chewing the edge of the carpet. Among people still hostile to Nazism, these demented fits quickly earned him the nickname Teppichfresser ('Carpet Eater'). I don't know if he kept up this habit of crazed munching, or if the symptom disappeared after Munich. [Some people claim that 'eating the carpet' is a German expression similar to 'eating one's hat' in English or French, and that the foreign reporters at the time were wrong to take the phrase literally. However, I've made inquiries and can find no evidence whatsoever that such an expression exists.—L.B.]

## 63

September 28, 1938: three days before the Munich Agreement. The world holds its breath. Hitler is more menacing than ever. The Czechs know that if they give up the natural barrier they call the Sudetenland, they are dead. Chamberlain declares: 'How horrible, fantastic, incredible it is that we should be digging trenches and trying on gas masks here because of a quarrel in a far-away country between people of whom we know nothing.'

## 64

Saint-John Perse belongs to that lineage of writer-diplomats, such as Claudel or Giraudoux, who fill me with disgust. In his case, this instinctive repugnance seems to me particularly justified. Consider his behaviour during September 1938:

Alexis Leger (his real name, fittingly, as *leger* means 'lightweight') accompanies Daladier to Munich in his position as general secretary of the Foreign Office. A hard-line pacifist, he has worked tirelessly to convince Daladier to give in to all the Germans' demands. He is there when the Czech representatives are shown in to be informed of their fate, twelve hours after the Munich Agreement, drafted without them, has been signed.

Hitler and Mussolini have already left. Chamberlain yawns ostentatiously, while Daladier tries and fails to hide his agitation behind a façade of embarrassed haughtiness. When the Czechs, crushed, ask if their government is expected to make some kind of declaration in response to this news, it is perhaps shame that removes his ability to speak. (If only it had choked him—him and all the others!) It is therefore left to his colleague to speak, and he does so with such casual arrogance that the Czech foreign minister says afterward, in a laconic remark that all my countrymen should ponder: 'Well, he's French.'

The Agreement being concluded, no response is expected. On the other hand, the Czech government must send its representative to Berlin this very day, by 3:00 p.m. at the latest (it is now 3:00 a.m.), to attend a meeting of the commission responsible for enforcing the Agreement. On Saturday, a Czechoslovak official must also appear in Berlin to settle the details of the evacuation. The diplomat's tone hardens with each command that he utters. In front of him, one of the two Czech representatives bursts into tears. Saint-John Perse, irritated by this, and as if to justify his own brutality, adds that the situation is beginning to get dangerous for the whole world. He's not joking!

Thus it is a French poet who pronounces, almost performatively, the death sentence of Czechoslovakia, the country I love most in the world.

## 65

At his hotel in Munich, a journalist asks him:

'But, Mr Ambassador, in the end this agreement must be a great relief, no?'

Silence. Then the Foreign Office secretary sighs:

'Oh yes, a relief . . . like when you do it in your pants!'

This belated truthfulness, coupled with a clever joke, is not enough to salvage his reputation. Saint-John Perse acted like a big shit. Or, as he would have said—with the ridiculous affectation of a stuffy diplomat—an 'excrement'.

## 66

*The Times* wrote of Chamberlain: 'No conqueror fresh from victory on the field of battle has come back adorned with more noble laurels.'

## 67

Chamberlain, on a balcony in London: 'My good friends, this is the second time in our history that there has come back from Germany to Downing Street peace with honour. I believe it is peace for our time.'

## 68

Krofta, the Czech foreign minister: 'They have put us in this situation. Now it's our turn; tomorrow it will be their turn.'

## 69

Out of some kind of childish pedantry, I have scrupulously avoided using the most famous French quotation to come out of this whole sad affair. But I can't not cite Daladier, who after getting off his airplane, cheered by the crowd, said: 'Oh, the fools! Those fools, if they knew what was coming . . .'

Some people doubt whether he actually spoke these words, whether he had enough clarity of mind, or enough wit. In fact, this apocryphal quotation became widely known because of Sartre, who used it in his novel *The Reprieve*.

## 70

Churchill's words, spoken in the House of Commons, are distinguished by their greater perceptiveness and, as always, their grandeur:

'We have sustained a total and unmitigated defeat.'

(Churchill has to stop speaking for some time while he waits for the whistles and shouts of protest to die down.)

'We are in the presence of a disaster of the first magnitude. The road down the Danube Valley to the Black Sea has been opened. All those Danubian countries will, one after another, be drawn into this vast system of power politics radiating from Berlin. And do not suppose that this is the end. This is only the beginning . . .'

Not long afterward, Churchill sums it all up with his immortal phrase:

'You had to choose between war and dishonour. You chose dishonour. You will have war.'

## 71

*It rings, it rings, the bell of betrayal.*
*Whose hands set it swinging?*
*Gentle France, faithful Albion,*
*And we loved them.*
                    (FRANTIŠEK HALAS)

## 72

On the half-corpse of a nation betrayed, France went back to belote and Tino Rossi. [Belote is a popular French card game. Tino Rossi (1907–83) was a famous French singer and movie idol.]
                    (MONTHERLANT)

Faced with Germany's arrogant pretensions, the two great Western democracies keep their mouths shut—and Hitler can gloat. Instead of which, he goes back to Berlin in a really bad mood, cursing Chamberlain: 'This person deprived me of my triumphant entry into Prague!' By forcing the Czech government to make all their concessions, France and Britain—these two cowardly countries—briefly prevented the German dictator from realizing his true goal: not only taking a slice of Czechoslovakia, but 'wiping it off the map.' In other words: turning it into a province of the Reich. Seven million Czechs, seventy-five million Germans . . . to be continued . . .

In 1946, at Nuremberg, the representative for Czechoslovakia will ask Keitel, the German chief of staff: 'Would the Reich have attacked Czechoslovakia in 1938 if the Western powers had supported Prague?' To which Keitel will reply: 'Definitely not. Militarily, we weren't strong enough.'

Hitler can curse all he likes. The truth is that France and Britain opened a door to which he did not have the key. And, obviously, by displaying such servility, encouraged him to start again.

This is where it all began, exactly fifteen years before, at the Bürgerbräukeller in Munich. But tonight, for once, the three thousand people gathered here have not come to celebrate the past. The speakers have taken their turn onstage and all of them have screamed for vengeance. The day before yesterday, in Paris, a seventeen-year-old Jew killed a German ambassadorial secretary because the Germans had deported his father. This is no great loss, as Heydrich is well placed to know: as a staunch anti-Nazi, the ambassadorial secretary was under Gestapo surveillance. But there is an opportunity here and it must be seized. Goebbels has entrusted him with a great mission. While the evening is in full swing, Heydrich gives his orders: there will be spontaneous demonstrations during the night. All police stations must immediately contact the commanding officers of the Party and the SS. The demonstrations will not be suppressed by the police. All the police need do is ensure that there is no danger to German lives or goods (for example, synagogues will be set on fire only if there is no risk to the neighbouring buildings). Jewish shops and private apartments may be destroyed, but not pillaged. The police must arrest as many Jews, especially rich ones, as the prisons can hold. As soon as they are under arrest, officers are advised to make immediate contact with the appropriate concentration camps so that they can be sent away at the earliest possible moment. This order is transmitted at 1:20 a.m.

The SA is already on its way, with the SS following. In the streets of Berlin, and all the other cities of Germany, the windows of Jewish shops are turned to flying shards of glass. Furniture is thrown from the windows of Jewish apartments, and the Jews themselves are arrested, beaten up, or even shot. Typewriters, sewing machines, even pianos, are seen smashed to pieces on the ground. The honest folk stay in their houses; the more curious go out to watch, careful not to get involved, like silent ghosts. Not that we can ever know the true nature of their silence: complicit? Disapproving? Incredulous? Satisfied? Somewhere in Germany, an eighty-one-year-old lady hears a banging at the door. When she opens to the SA, she sniggers: 'Oh, what important visitors I have this morning!' But when the SA tell her to get dressed and follow them, she sits on the sofa and declares: 'I won't get dressed and I won't go any where. Do with me what you will.' And when she repeats, 'Do with me what you will,' the squad leader draws his pistol and shoots her in the chest. She collapses on the sofa. He puts a second bullet in her head. She falls off the sofa and rolls over on the carpet. But she is not yet dead. Her head turned towards the window, she emits a quiet groan. So he shoots her again—in the middle of her forehead this time, from four inches away.

Elsewhere, an SA guard climbs onto the roof of a sacked synagogue, brandishing scrolls of the Torah and yelling: 'Burn yourselves with these, Jews!' And he throws them like carnival streamers. Already, we see the inimitable Nazi style.

In a report written by the mayor of a small town, we read: 'The acts against the Jews occurred promptly and without any particular tension. Following the measures taken against them, a Jewish couple threw themselves in the Danube.'

All the synagogues are burning, but Heydrich, ever the professional, has ordered that any official records to be found in them must be sent to SD headquarters. Boxes of documents arrive at Wilhelmstrasse. The Nazis love burning books, but not files. German efficiency? Who knows if the SA didn't wipe their asses with some of those precious archives . . .

The next day, Heydrich sends the first confidential report to Göring: the scale of destruction is not yet measurable in terms of numbers. According to the report, 815 shops have been destroyed, 171 houses burned or destroyed, but this is only a fraction of the actual damage. One hundred and nineteen synagogues have been set on fire, another 76 completely destroyed. Twenty thousand Jews have been arrested. The number of deaths is reported as 36. The number of serious injuries is also 36. All the dead and injured are Jewish.

Heydrich has also been informed about all rapes: in these cases, the Nuremberg racial laws apply. Anyone guilty of having sex with a Jew will be arrested, kicked out of the Party, and handed over to the courts. Those who have committed murder, on the other hand, have nothing to worry about.

Two days later, Göring chairs a meeting at the Air Ministry to find a way of making the Jews bear the costs of all the damage. As the spokesman for the insurance companies points out, the price of broken windows alone comes to five million marks (this is why it's called 'Crystal Night'). It turns out

94

that many of the Jewish boutiques are owned by Aryans, which means they must be compensated. Göring is furious. Nobody had thought about the economic implications, least of all the finance minister. He shouts at Heydrich that it would have been better to kill two hundred Jews than to destroy so much valuable property. Heydrich is upset. He replies that they did kill thirty-six Jews.

As solutions are found to make the Jews themselves pay for the damages, Göring calms down and the atmosphere lightens. Heydrich listens as Göring jokes with Goebbels about the creation of Jewish reservations in the forest. According to Goebbels, they ought to introduce certain Jewish-looking animals—like the moose, with its hooked nose. Everyone present laughs heartily, except for the representative of the insurance companies, who's unconvinced by the field marshal's finance plan. And Heydrich.

At the end of the meeting, when it has been decided to confiscate all Jews' goods and to forbid them from having businesses, Heydrich decides it would be useful to refocus the debate:

'Even if the Jews are eliminated from economic life, the main problem remains. We must kick the Jews out of Germany. In the meantime,' he suggests, 'we should make them wear some kind of sign so they can be easily recognized.'

'A uniform!' shouts Göring, always fond of anything to do with clothing.

'I was thinking of a badge, actually,' Heydrich replies.

The meeting, however, doesn't end on this prophetic note. Henceforth, the Jews are excluded from public schools and hospitals, from beaches and swimming pools. They must do their shopping during restricted hours. On the other hand, following objections from Goebbels, it is decided not to make them use a separate carriage or compartment on public transport: What would happen during rush hour? The Germans might be packed like sardines in one carriage while the Jews had another carriage all to themselves! And so on—you get the idea. Let's just say that the debate scales new heights of technical precision.

Heydrich suggests yet more restrictions on the Jews' movements. Then Göring—completely recovered from his brief loss of temper—raises, out of the blue, a fundamental question. 'But, my dear Heydrich, you will have to create ghettos in all our cities, on an enormous scale. It's unavoidable.'

Heydrich replies brusquely:

'As far as ghettos are concerned, I would like to define my position straightaway. From a policing point of view, I believe it's impossible to establish a ghetto in the sense of a completely isolated district where only Jews may live. We cannot control a ghetto where a Jew can melt into the rest of the Jewish population. That would provide shelter for criminals, and also a breeding ground for diseases. We don't want to let the Jews live in the same buildings as Germans, but at the moment—whether in whole districts or in individual buildings—

it is the Germans who force the Jews to behave correctly. Surely it would be better to keep them under the watchful eyes of the whole population than to cram them in their thousands into areas where I cannot adequately control their daily lives with uniformed agents.'

Raoul Hilberg sees in this 'policing point of view' the prism through which Heydrich views both his job and German society: the entire population is considered a sort of auxiliary police force, responsible for surveying and reporting any suspect behaviour among the Jews. The Warsaw Ghetto uprising in 1943, which will take the German army three weeks to crush, proves Heydrich right: you can't trust those Jews. He also knows, of course, that germs do not racially discriminate.

## 77

Physically, Monsignor Jozef Tiso is small and fat. Historically, he belongs with the biggest collaborators—his role as the Slovak version of Pétain being determined by the hatred he feels for centralized Czech power. The archbishop of Bratislava has worked his whole life for his country's independence and today, thanks to Hitler, he achieves his goal. On March 13, 1939, as the Wehrmacht's regiments prepare to invade Bohemia and Moravia, the chancellor of the Reich invites the future Slovak president into his office.

As always, Hitler talks and the other person in the room listens. Tiso isn't sure if he should be happy or fearful. His long-held wish is finally coming to pass—but why must it come in the form of blackmail and an ultimatum?

Hitler explains: were it not for Germany, Czechoslovakia would have been much more badly damaged. By contenting itself with the annexation of the Sudetenland, the Reich has made a great show of leniency. But are the Czechs grateful? Not in the slightest! In recent weeks the situation has become impossible. Too many provocations. The Germans who live there are oppressed and persecuted. It's the spirit of the Beneš government come back to haunt them. At the mention of his name, Hitler becomes heated.

The Slovaks have disappointed him. After Munich, Hitler fell out with his Hungarian friends because he wouldn't let them take over Slovakia. He was under the impression that the Slovaks wanted their independence.

So, yes or no, does Slovakia want its independence? It is a question not of days but of hours. If Slovakia wants its independence, Hitler will help: he will take the country under his protection. But if the Slovaks refuse to be separated from Prague, or if they even hesitate, he will abandon Slovakia to its fate: the country will be at the mercy of events for which he will no longer be responsible.

At this precise moment, Ribbentrop enters and hands Hitler a report, claiming it has just arrived. The report reveals the movements of Hungarian troops at the Slovak border. This little scene allows Tiso to comprehend the urgency of the situation— if he hadn't already. It also makes his choice quite clear: either Slovakia declares its independence and its allegiance to Germany, or it is swallowed up by

Hungary.

Tiso replies: the Slovaks will show themselves worthy of the Führer's kindness.

## 78

In return for the transfer of the Sudetenland to Germany, the integrity of Czechoslovakia's new borders was guaranteed at Munich by France and Britain. But Slovakia's independence alters the deal. Is it possible to protect a country that no longer exists? The commitment was made to Czechoslovakia, not to the Czechs alone. This, at least, is how the British diplomats reply when their counterparts from Prague come to ask for their help. We are now on the eve of the German invasion, and it turns out it is perfectly legal for France and Britain to act like cowards.

## 79

On March 14, 1939, at 10:40 p.m., a train coming from Prague arrives at Anhalter Bahnhof in Berlin. An old man dressed in black gets off the train: balding, dull-eyed, droopy-lipped. President Hácha, who replaced Beneš after Munich, has come to beg Hitler to spare his country. He didn't take the plane, because he has a heart condition. He is accompanied by his daughter and by his foreign minister.

Hácha is fearful of what awaits him here. He

knows that German troops have already crossed the border and that they are massing around Bohemia. The invasion is imminent, and he has come all this way only to negotiate an honourable surrender. I imagine he would be willing to accept similar conditions to those imposed on Slovakia: independent nationhood but under German protection. What he fears is nothing less than the total disappearance of his country.

So how surprised he must be, as soon as he sets foot on the platform, to be welcomed by a guard of honour. The foreign minister, Ribbentrop, has come in person. He gives Hácha's daughter a beautiful spray of flowers. The procession that accompanies the Czech delegation is worthy of a head of state—which he still is, of course. Hácha breathes more easily. The Germans have put him in the best suite of the luxurious Hotel Adlon. On her bed his daughter finds a box of chocolates: a personal gift from the Führer.

The Czech president is taken to the chancellery, where the SS forms a guard of honour. By this point, Hácha is feeling much better.

His impression changes slightly when he enters the chancellor's office. Hitler is flanked by Göring and Keitel, the heads of the German army, and their presence is not a good sign. Hitler's expression, too, is not what Hácha might have hoped for after his lavish welcome. The little serenity that he had managed to recover quickly vanishes, and Emil Hácha finds himself sinking into the quicksand of history.

'I can assure the Führer,' he says to the interpreter, 'that I have never got mixed up in politics. I have never had any involvement, so to

100

speak, with Beneš and Masaryk, and whenever I've been in their company I've found them disagreeable. I have never supported the Beneš government, indeed I have always opposed it, so much so that after Munich I wondered if it was even a good idea to remain as an independent state. I am convinced that Czechoslovakia's destiny is in the Führer's hands, and that it is in good hands. The Führer, I am certain, is precisely the right man to understand my point of view when I tell him that Czechoslovakia has the right to exist as a nation. We have been blamed because there are still too many Beneš partisans, but my government is doing all it can to silence them.'

Now Hitler begins to speak, and his words—according to the interpreter's version of events—turn Hácha to stone.

'The long journey undertaken by the president, despite his age, can be of great help to his country. Germany is indeed ready to invade in the next few hours. I do not harbour a grudge against any nation. If this stump of a state, Czechoslovakia, has continued to exist, it is only because I wished it to, and because I have loyally honoured my commitments. But even after Beneš's departure, your country's attitude has not changed! I did warn you! I said that if you kept provoking me, I would utterly destroy the Czechoslovak state. And still you provoke me! Well, the dice have been rolled now . . . I have given orders to German troops to invade your country and I have decided to incorporate Czechoslovakia into the German Reich.'

The interpreter said of Hácha and his minister: 'Only their eyes showed they were still alive.'

Hitler continues:

101

'Tomorrow at six a.m., the German army will enter Czechoslovakia from all sides and the German air force will occupy all the airfields. Two outcomes are possible.

'Either the invasion gives rise to fighting: in this case we will use brutal force to smash all resistance.

'Or the invasion will be allowed to occur peacefully, in which case I will grant the Czechs a regime that is to a large extent their own . . . giving them autonomy and a certain amount of national liberty.

'I am not moved by hatred. My only goal is the protection of Germany. But if Czechoslovakia had not given in to my demands at Munich, I would have exterminated the Czech people without hesitation, and nobody would have been able to stop me! Today, if the Czechs want to fight, the Czech army will cease to exist within two days. There will naturally be victims among the German army too: this will feed a hatred of the Czech people that will prevent me, out of self-preservation, from granting the country any autonomy.

'The world makes fun of people like you. When I read the foreign press, I feel sorry for Czechoslovakia. It makes me think of the famous quotation from Schiller: "The Moor has done his duty, the Moor can go . . ."'

Apparently this quotation is proverbial in Germany, but I don't really understand why Hitler used it here, nor what he meant . . . Who is the Moor? Czechoslovakia? But in what sense has it done its duty? And where could it go?

First hypothesis: from Germany's perspective, Czechoslovakia was useful to the Western democracies merely by existing, as it weakened Germany after 1918. Now that it's fulfilled its mission, it can cease to exist. But this is, at the very least, inaccurate: the creation of Czechoslovakia confirmed the dismantling of the Austro–Hungarian Empire, not of Germany. What's more, if Czechoslovakia's duty was to weaken Germany, 1939 seems an odd moment to abandon it, with Austria annexed and Germany restored to power and becoming ever more threatening.

So, second hypothesis: the Moor represents the Western democracies, who did what they could at Munich to limit the damage (the Moor has done his duty) but who are from then on careful not to get involved (the Moor can go) . . . Except we can tell that, in Hitler's mind, the Moor must be the victim—the foreigner that's been used—and that means it's Czechoslovakia.

Third hypothesis: Hitler doesn't really know what he means; he simply couldn't resist quoting something, and his meagre literary knowledge did not provide him with anything better. He might perhaps have contented himself with a *'Vae victis!'* more appropriate to the situation, simple but always effective. Or he might simply have kept his mouth shut.


80


Faced with the Führer, Hácha caved in. He declared that the situation was very clear and that all resistance was madness. But it's already 2:00 a.m., and he has only four hours to prevent the Czech

103

people from defending themselves. According to Hitler, the German military machine is already on the march (true) and nothing can stop it (at least, no one seems very keen to try). Hácha must sign the surrender immediately and inform Prague. The choice Hitler is offering could not be simpler: either peace now, followed by a long collaboration between the two nations, or the total annihilation of Czechoslovakia.

President Hácha, terrified, is left in a room with Göring and Ribbentrop. He sits at a table, the document before him. All he has to do now is sign it. The pen is in his hand, but his hand is trembling. The pen keeps stopping before it can touch the paper. In the absence of the Führer, who rarely stays to oversee such formalities, Hácha gets jumpy. 'I can't sign this,' he says. 'If I sign the surrender, my people will curse me forever.' This is perfectly true.

So Göring and Ribbentrop have to convince Hácha that it's too late to turn back. This leads to a farcical scene where, according to witnesses, the two Nazi ministers literally chase Hácha around the table, repeatedly putting the pen back in his hand and ordering him to sign the bloody thing. At the same time, Göring yells continuously: if Hácha continues to refuse, half of Prague will be destroyed within two hours by the German air force . . . and that's just for starters! Hundreds of bombers are waiting for the order to take off, and they will receive that order at 6:00 a.m. if the surrender is not signed.

At this crucial moment, Hácha goes dizzy and faints. Now it's the two Nazis who are terrified, standing there over his inert body. He absolutely must be revived: if he dies, Hitler will be accused of murdering him in his own office. Thankfully, there is an expert injecter in the house: Dr Morell, who will later inject Hitler with amphetamines several times a day until his death—a medical regime that probably had some link with the Führer's growing dementia. So Morell suddenly appears and sticks a syringe into Hácha, who wakes up. A telephone is shoved into his hand. Given the urgency of the situation, the paperwork can wait. Ribbentrop has taken care to install a special direct line to Prague. Gathering what is left of his strength, Hácha informs the Czech cabinet in Prague of what is happening in Berlin, and advises them to surrender. He is given another injection and taken back to see the Führer, who presents him once again with that wretched document. It is nearly 4:00 a.m. Hácha signs. 'I have sacrificed the state in order to save the nation,' he believes. The imbecile. It's as if Chamberlain's stupidity was contagious . . .


81

Berlin, March 15, 1939:

At their request, the Führer received today in Berlin Dr Hácha, the president of Czechoslovakia [the Germans, it seems, still hadn't officially ratified Slovakia's independence, even though it was they themselves who'd orchestrated it], and Dr Chvalkovsky, the foreign minister of Czechoslovakia, in the presence of Mr von

Ribbentrop, the foreign minister. During this meeting, there was a very frank discussion of the serious situation created by events of recent weeks in Czechoslovakian territory.

Both parties said they were convinced that all efforts must be made to maintain calm, order, and peace in this region of central Europe. The president of the Czechoslovakian state said that, in order to attain this objective and to create a definitive peace, he had put the destiny of the Czech people and country in the hands of the Führer of the German Reich. The Führer acknowledged this declaration and expressed his intention of placing the Czech people under the protection of the German Reich and of guaranteeing the autonomous development of their ethnic life.

## 82

Hitler is jubilant. He kisses all his secretaries and tells them: 'My children, this is the most beautiful day of my life! My name will go down in history. I will be considered the greatest German who ever lived!'

To celebrate, he decides to go to Prague.

## 83

The most beautiful city in the world is disfigured by outbreaks of violence. The local Germans are spoiling for a fight. Protesters march along Václavské náměstí, the wide avenue overshadowed by the imposing Museum of Natural History. They are trying to spark a riot, but the Czech police have been told not to intervene. Acts of violence, pillage, and vandalism perpetrated by Germans awaiting the arrival of their Nazi brothers are war cries that find no echo in the silence of the capital.

Night swoops upon the city. An icy wind sweeps the streets. Only a handful of adolescent hotheads hang around to yell insults at the police on guard duty outside the Deutsches Haus. Beneath the Astronomical Clock in the Old Town Square, the little skeleton pulls its cord as it has done every hour for centuries. The bells toll midnight. The creaking of the wooden shutters is heard, but tonight, I bet no one bothers to watch the little figures march around the tower. They quickly go back inside: perhaps they will be safe there. I imagine clouds of crows flying around the sinister watchtowers of the dark Týn Church. Under the Charles Bridge flows the Vltava. Under the Charles Bridge flows the Moldau. The peaceful river that crosses Prague has two names—one Czech, the other German. It is one too many.

The Czechs toss and turn in their beds. They hope that if they make more concessions, the Germans will be merciful—but what concessions have they not already made? They hope President Hácha's servility will move the Germans to pity. Their will to resist was broken at Munich by the betrayal of the French and the British. Now they have only their passivity to protect them from the Nazis' bellicosity. What is left of Czechoslovakia has no greater aim than to be a small and peaceful nation. But the gangrene that infected the country in the time of Premysl Ottokar II has spread—and the amputation of the Sudetenland didn't change anything. Before dawn, the radio broadcasts the terms of the agreement concluded between Hitler and Hácha. It is annexation, pure and simple. The news explodes like a bombshell in every Czech home. Day has still not risen when the streets begin to buzz with this rumour, and gradually the noise turns from a murmur to a clamour. People leave their houses. Some carry small suitcases: they will go to the doors of the embassies to ask for asylum and protection, which will generally be refused. The first suicides are reported.

At 9:00 a.m., the first German tank enters the city.

84

Actually I don't know if it was a tank that first entered Prague. The most advanced troops seem largely to have driven motorbikes with sidecars.

So: at 9:00 a.m., German soldiers on motorbikes enter the Czech capital. Here they discover local Germans welcoming them as liberators, which makes them relax a little after several days of high tension. But they also see Czechs shaking their fists, shouting hostile slogans, and singing their national anthem, which is more worrying.

A dense crowd has gathered on Václavské náměstí, the Czech equivalent of the Champs-Élysées, and in the city's main thoroughfares Wehrmacht trucks are soon blocked by the vast numbers of people. The German troops don't know where they stand.

But this is far from an insurrection. Acts of resistance are limited to throwing snowballs at the invaders.

The main strategic objectives are achieved without a shot being fired: control of the airport and of the War Ministry. Above all the Germans control Hradčany—the castle perched high on its hill, the seat of power. Before 10:00 a.m., artillery batteries are ranged on the battlements, aimed at the city below.

The only real problems are logistical: the most difficult test faced by German vehicles is the blizzard, and here and there we find broken-down trucks, tanks immobilized by mechanical troubles. The Germans also have problems finding their way in Prague's maze of streets: we see them asking directions from Czech policemen, who answer obligingly—out of Pavlovian respect for the uniform, I suppose. Nerudova, the beautiful street decorated with banners that leads up to the castle, is blocked by a lost armoured car. While the driver gets out to ask the way from a delegation of Italian diplomats, the soldier remains alone on his gun turret, his finger tensed on the machine-gun trigger, watched by the silent, gawking crowd that surrounds him. But nothing happens. The general in command of the German vanguard has nothing worse to complain about than acts of minor sabotage: a few slashed tyres.

Hitler can prepare for a peaceful visit. Before the end of day, the city is 'secured'. Troops on horseback move calmly along the banks of the Vltava. A curfew is decreed, forbidding Czechs to go outside after 8:00 p.m. The doors of hotels and official buildings are patrolled by German guards carrying long rifles with bayonets. Prague has fallen without a fight. The cobblestones of the city are stained with dirty snow. This is the beginning of a long, dark winter for the Czechs.

Passing the endless, serpentine line of soldiers marching along the icy road, a convoy of Mercedes cars makes its way laboriously towards Prague. All the most eminent members of Hitler's clique are here: Göring, Ribbentrop, Bormann. And in the Führer's own car, next to Himmler, sits Heydrich.

What goes through his mind when, after this long journey, they finally arrive at their destination? Is he struck by the mazelike beauty of the city of a hundred towers? Or is he too busy savouring the importance of his position? Does he grow irritated when the convoy gets lost in the city conquered by the Führer that very morning? Or is there, in his calculating brain, the first glimmer of an idea that his career will one day take him back to the former Czech capital?

Today, the future Hangman of Prague, whom the Czechs also nicknamed 'the Butcher', sees for the first time the Bohemian city of kings: the streets are deserted because of the curfew; the tyre tracks of the German army are visible in the mud and snow on the roads; an impressive calm reigns. The windows on the high street reveal expensive glassware boutiques and delicatessens; in the heart of the Old Town stands the Opera House, where Mozart created *Don Giovanni*; the cars drive on the left, as in Britain. For the first time, Heydrich sees the snaking road that leads to the castle, gloriously isolated on its hill, and the beautiful and disturbing statues that decorate the main entrance, guarded by the SS.

The convoy enters what was until yesterday the presidential palace. A swastika flag flies over the castle, signalling the presence of its new masters. When Hácha returns from Berlin—his train still hasn't arrived, having been conveniently delayed in Germany—he will use the servants' entrance. I suppose he will feel the full ironic weight of the situation, having been so thrilled by the presidential welcome he received in Berlin. The president is now nothing but a puppet, and they're making sure he knows it.

Hitler and his followers settle into their rooms in the castle. The Führer climbs the stairs to the first floor. There is a famous photo of him, hands leaning on the sill of an open window, contemplating the city below. He looks pleased with himself. Afterward he goes back downstairs and enjoys a candlelit dinner in one of the dining rooms. Heydrich can't help noticing that the Führer eats a slice of ham and drinks a Pilsner Urquell, the most famous Czech beer—Hitler, who is a teetotaller and vegetarian. He keeps saying that Czechoslovakia has ceased to exist, and no doubt he wishes to mark the historic importance of this day—March 15, 1939—by departing from his usual eating habits.

## 86

The next day, Hitler makes this proclamation:

> For a thousand years, the provinces of
> Bohemia and Moravia have been part of the
> German people's living space. Czechoslovakia
> has shown its inability to survive, and today it
> is reduced to a state of complete dissolution.
> The German Reich cannot tolerate continual
> difficulties in this region. So, out of self-
> preservation, the German Reich is now
> determined to intervene. We will take decisive
> measures in order to establish the basis of
> a rational order in central Europe. Over a
> thousand years of its history, the Reich has
> proved—with the greatness and qualities of
> the German people—that it alone is qualified
> to undertake this task.

In early afternoon, Hitler leaves Prague. He will
never set foot in the country again. Heydrich goes
with him, but *he* will be back.

## 87

'For a thousand years, the provinces of Bohemia
and Moravia have been part of the German people's
living space.'

It's true that in the tenth century—that is, a
thousand years earlier—Václav I, the famous Saint

Wenceslaus, swore allegiance to the no-less-famous Henry I, the Fowler, at a time when Bohemia was not yet a kingdom, and when the king of Saxony was not yet head of the Holy Roman Empire. However, Václav was able to keep his sovereignty, and it wasn't until three centuries later that German settlers came to Bohemia on a large scale—and even then, their arrival was peaceful.

So it's true that the Czech and German countries have always been closely linked. It's also true that Bohemia has been almost continuously part of the German sphere of influence. But it seems to me utterly wrong to talk about German *Lebensraum* with regard to Bohemia.

It was also Henry the Fowler—Nazi icon, idol of Himmler—who began the *Drang nach Osten*, the drive towards the east, which Hitler would claim as his inspiration in order to legitimize his desire to invade the Soviet Union. But Henry the Fowler never sought to invade or colonize Bohemia. He contented himself with an annual tribute. Even after this, there has never, as far as I know, been any German colonization forcibly imposed on Bohemia. The flow of German settlers in the fourteenth century was a response to the Czech sovereign's demand for specialized labour. Finally, no one had ever before considered ridding Bohemia and Moravia of their Czech inhabitants. So it's safe to say that the Nazis, once more, are political innovators. And Heydrich, of course, is in the thick of it.

How can you tell the main character of a story? By the number of pages devoted to him? I hope it's a little more complicated than that.

Whenever I talk about the book I'm writing, I say, 'My book on Heydrich.' But Heydrich is not supposed to be the main character. Through all the years that I carried this story around with me in my head, I never thought of giving it any other title than *Operation Anthropoid* (and if that's not the title you see on the cover, you will know that I gave in to the demands of my publisher, who didn't like it: too SF, too Robert Ludlum, apparently). You see, Heydrich is the target, not the protagonist. Everything I've written about him is by way of background. Though it must be admitted that in literary terms Heydrich is a wonderful character. It's as if a Dr Frankenstein novelist had mixed up the greatest monsters of literature to create a new and terrifying creature. Except that Heydrich is not a paper monster.

I'm all too aware that my two heroes are late making their entrance. But perhaps it's no bad thing if they have to wait. Perhaps it will give them more substance. Perhaps the mark they've made in history and on my memory might imprint itself even more profoundly in these pages. Perhaps this long wait in the antechamber of my brain will restore some of their reality, and not just vulgar plausibility. Perhaps, perhaps . . . but nothing could be less sure! I'm not scared of Heydrich anymore. It's those two who intimidate me.

And yet I can see them. Or let's say that I am beginning to discern them.


## 89

On the borders of eastern Slovakia is a city I know well—Košice. This is where I did my military service: I was the sublieutenant responsible for teaching French to the Slovakian air force's young future officers. Košice is also the town where Aurélia—the beautiful Slovak woman with whom I had a passionate five-year relationship, nearly ten years ago now—was born. And incidentally, it is, of all the world's cities I've ever visited, the one with the highest concentration of pretty girls. And when I say pretty, I mean exceptionally beautiful.

I don't see any reason why this should have been any different in 1939. The pretty girls stroll eternally on Hlavná ulica—the long main street that is the heart of the town, lined by gorgeous pastel-coloured Baroque houses, with a magnificent Gothic cathedral at its centre. Except that, in 1939, you also see German soldiers, who greet the pretty girls discreetly as they pass. Slovakia has indeed gained its independence—the prize for its betrayal of Prague—but it is an independence surveyed by the friendly, searching eyes of Germany.

Jozef Gabčík sees all of this, walking up the grand main street: the pretty girls and the German soldiers. He's been thinking it over for several months now.

Two years ago he left Košice to work in a chemical factory in Žilina. He has come back today to meet up with his friends from the 14th Infantry regiment, in which he served for three years. Spring is late and the stubborn snow whispers under his boots.

The cafés in Košice rarely open onto the street. Normally, you have to go under a porch, then either up or down a staircase, in order to reach a well-heated room. Gabčík meets his former comrades in such a café that very evening. Reunited over pints of Zlatý Bažant (a Slovak beer whose name means 'Golden Pheasant'), everyone is very happy. But Gabčík hasn't come just to make a social visit. He wants to know where the Slovak army is, and its position with regard to Tiso, the collaborator.

'The field officers have fallen in with Tiso; you know, Jozef, for them, the break with the Czech staff, it's a chance to get promoted more quickly...'

'The army hasn't protested: neither the officers nor the troops. It's a new Slovak army, so they've got to obey the new Slovak government. That's understandable, isn't it?'

'We've wanted independence for years, so who cares how we get it! Tough shit for the Czechs! If they'd treated us better, maybe we wouldn't be in this situation now! You know as well as I do that the Czechs always got the best jobs. In the government, the army, everywhere! It was a scandal!'

'Anyway, we had no choice: if Tiso hadn't said yes to Hitler, we'd have been flattened like they were. And yeah, I know it's a bit like being occupied, but in the end we've still got more autonomy than we had with the Czechs.'

'In Prague, you know, German is now the official

116

language! They're closing all the Czech universities. They're censoring all Czech culture. They've even shot at students! Is that what you want? Believe me, this was the best solution . . .'

'It was the only solution, Jozef!'

'Why should we have fought when it was Hácha himself who told us to surrender? All we were doing was obeying orders.'

'Beneš? Yeah, yeah, but he's fighting the war from London—that's much easier. Us poor bastards are stuck here.'

'And all of this is his fault. He signed the Munich Agreement, didn't he? He didn't send us to fight for the Sudetenland, remember? At the time, our army might have been able to put up a fight—I say might have been!—with the Germans . . . But now, what could we do? Have you seen the numbers of the Luftwaffe? You know how many bombers they've got in service? They'd cut through us like butter. We'd be massacred!'

'I don't want to die for Hácha—or for Beneš!'

'I don't want to die for Tiso either!'

'All right, so there are a few German soldiers hanging around the city. So what? I'm not going to pretend I like it, but it's not as bad as a real military occupation. Go and ask your Czech friends!'

'I've got nothing against the Czechs but they've always treated us like peasants. I went to Prague once and they pretended they couldn't understand me because of my accent! They've always despised us. Now let's see how they get on with their new compatriots! We'll see if they prefer the German accent!'

'Hitler got what he wanted. He said he wouldn't make any more territorial claims. And us, we've never been part of the German zone. Anyway, if it wasn't for him, Hungary would have swallowed us up, Jozef! You have to see things how they are.'

'What do you want? A coup d'état? No general would have the balls to do that. And even if one did, what would happen afterward? We take on the German army on our own? You think France and England would suddenly rush to our aid? We spent a whole year waiting for them!'

'Listen, Jozef, you've got a steady job: go back to Žilina, find yourself a nice girl, and forget about all this. We didn't come out of it too badly in the end.'

Gabčík has finished his beer. It's already late, and he and his comrades are slightly drunk. Outside, it's snowing. He stands up, waves goodbye to his friends, and goes to retrieve his coat from the cloakroom. While a young girl is serving him, one of his companions comes over. He whispers:

'Listen, Jozef, if you want to know, when the Czechs were demobilized after the Germans arrived, some refused to return to civilian life. Perhaps out of patriotism or perhaps because they didn't want to find themselves unemployed, I don't know. But anyway, they went to Poland and they've formed a Czechoslovak liberation army. I don't think there are many of them, but I know there are some Slovaks involved. They're based in Kraków. You see, if I did that, I'd be considered a deserter, and I can't leave my wife and kids. But if I were your age, and if I were single . . . Tiso is scum, that's what I think, and most of the other guys too. We haven't all turned into Nazis, you know. But we're shit-scared. What's happening in Prague is terrible—they're executing anyone who shows the slightest sign of protesting. Me, I'm going to try to

118

live with the situation. I won't overdo it, but I'll go along with them. As long as they don't start telling us to deport the Jews . . .'

Gabčík smiles at his friend. He puts on his coat, thanks him, and leaves. Outside, night has fallen. The streets are deserted and the snow crunches beneath his feet.


## 90

On his way back to Žilina, Gabčík makes his decision. At the end of his working day at the factory, he says goodbye to his friends as though nothing is going on. But he doesn't accompany them, as he usually does, to the bar on the corner. Instead he rushes home, where he takes not a suitcase but a little canvas bag, puts on two coats (one on top of the other) and his soldier's boots (the most solid boots he owns), then leaves, locking the door behind him. He calls on one of his sisters—the one he's closest to—and leaves her his keys. She's one of the few who knows about his plans. She makes him tea and he drinks it in silence. He stands up. She holds him tightly in her arms and cries. Then he heads for the bus station, where he waits for a bus that will take him north, towards the border. He smokes a few cigarettes. He feels perfectly calm. He's not the only one waiting on the platform, so nobody takes any notice of him despite the fact that he's dressed too warmly for May. The bus arrives. Gabčík dives inside and grabs a seat. The doors close again. The bus moves off with a roar. Through the window, Gabčík watches Žilina grow smaller. He will never see the town again. The Baroque and Romanesque towers of the old town stand out against the dark horizon that fades away behind him. When Gabčík casts one last glance at Budatín Castle, located at the confluence of two of the three rivers that flow through the town, he cannot know that it will be almost totally destroyed in the years that follow. Nor can he know that he is leaving Slovakia forever.

## 91

That scene, like the one before it, is perfectly believable and totally made up. How impudent of me to turn a man into a puppet—a man who's been dead for a long time, who cannot defend himself. To make him drink tea, when it might turn out that he liked only coffee. To make him put on two coats, when perhaps he had only one. To make him take the bus, when he could have taken the train. To decide that he left in the evening, rather than the morning. I am ashamed of myself.

But it could be worse. I spared Kubiš a similarly fanciful treatment, probably because Moravia, where he's from, is less familiar to me than Slovakia. It was June 1939 when Kubiš went to Poland, from where he reached France—I don't know how—and enrolled in the Foreign Legion. That's all I have to say. I don't know if he went via Kraków, the main rallying point for Czech soldiers who refused the surrender. I suppose he joined the Legion in Agde, in the south of France, with the first infantry battalion of exiled Czechoslovak

120

armed forces. Or had the battalion, whose ranks were swelling daily, already become a regiment? A few months later it will be practically a whole division and will fight alongside the French army during the war. I could write quite a lot about the Czechs in the French army: the 11,000 soldiers, made up of 3,000 volunteers and 8,000 expatriate Czech conscripts, along with the brave pilots, trained at Chartres, who will shoot down or help to shoot down more than 130 enemy planes during the Battle of France . . . But I've said that I don't want to write a historical handbook. This story is personal. That's why my visions sometimes get mixed up with the known facts. It's just how it is.

## 92

Actually, no: that's not how it is. That would be too simple. Rereading one of the books that make up the foundation of my research—a collection of witness accounts assembled by a Czech historian, Miroslav Ivanov, under the title *The Attack on Heydrich*—I become aware, to my horror, of the mistakes I've made concerning Gabčík.

First of all, Košice had since November 1938 been part of Hungary, not Czechoslovakia, and the town was occupied by Admiral Horthy's army, so it's highly unlikely that Gabčík would have been able to visit his comrades from the 14th Infantry. Second, by May 1, 1939, when he left Slovakia for Poland, he had been working for almost two years in a factory near Trenčín, so in all likelihood he no longer lived in Žilina. The passage where I recount his last glance at the castle seems suddenly ridiculous. In fact, he never quit the army, and it was as a noncommissioned officer that he was working in the chemical factory, whose products were destined for military use. I also forgot to mention that before he left his job, he perpetrated an act of sabotage: he poured acid into some mustard gas, which apparently harmed (how, I've no idea) the German army. What a thing to forget! Not only do I deprive Gabčík of his first act of resistance—a minor one, admittedly, but still courageous—but I also omit a link in the great causal chain of human destiny. Gabčík himself explains, in a biographical note written in England when he put himself forward as a candidate for special missions, that he left the country straight after this act of sabotage because he would inevitably have been arrested if he'd stayed.

On the other hand, he did go through Kraków, as I'd supposed. After fighting alongside the Poles during the German attack that started the Second World War, he fled. Perhaps via the Balkans, like a great number of Czechs and Slovaks who went to France, crossing Romania and Greece, then reaching Istanbul, Egypt, and finally Marseilles. Or perhaps he went through the Baltic, which would seem more practical: leaving the port of Gdynia and arriving at Boulogne-sur-Mer, then travelling south. Whatever, I'm sure that this journey is an epic deserving of a whole book to itself. For me, the crowning moment would be his first meeting with Kubiš. How and when did they meet? In Poland? In France? During the journey between the two? Or later, in England? That's what I would love to know. I'm not sure yet if I'm going to 'visualize'

122

(that is, invent!) this meeting or not. If I do, it will be the clinching proof that fiction does not respect anything.

93

A train pulls into the station. In the immense hall of Victoria Station, Colonel Moravec waits on the platform, accompanied by a few other exiled compatriots. A man gets off the train: a serious-looking little man with a moustache and a receding hairline. It's Beneš, the former president who resigned the day after Munich. But today—July 18, 1939, the date of his arrival in London—he is above all the man who declared, the day after Hácha's surrender, that the First Czechoslovak Republic still existed, in spite of the attack it had suffered. 'The German divisions,' he said, 'swept up the concessions torn from us by our enemies and by our allies in the name of peace, justice, and good sense, the gentle reasons invoked at the time of the 1938 crisis. Now the Czechoslovak territory is occupied. But the Republic is not dead. It will continue to fight, even from beyond its own borders.' Beneš, seen by Czechoslovak patriots as the only legitimate president, wants to form a provisional government-in-exile as quickly as possible. A year before the Appeal of June 18, Beneš is a bit like a combination of de Gaulle and Churchill. The spirit of the Resistance is in him.

Unfortunately, it is not yet Churchill who guides the destiny of Britain and the world but the vile Chamberlain, a man whose spinelessness

123

is equalled only by his blindness. He has sent a lowly Foreign Ministry employee to welcome the former president. And the pen pusher's welcome is not particularly warm either. Barely is Beneš off the train before he is notified of the conditions of his exile: Great Britain agrees to grant him political asylum only on the express condition that he promises to refrain from all political activity. Beneš, who is recognized as the de facto head of the liberation movement both by his friends and his enemies, takes the insult with his customary dignity. He, more than anyone else, will have to put up with Chamberlain's contemptuous stupidity—and he will do it with absolutely superhuman stoicism. If for this reason only, his historical reputation is almost more imposing than de Gaulle's.

## 94

It's now fourteen days since the SS-Sturmbannführer Alfred Naujocks arrived incognito in the little town of Gleiwitz, on the German–Polish border in German Silesia. The operation has been meticulously planned; now he waits. Heydrich called him yesterday at midday to ask him to check the final details with 'Gestapo' Müller, who came in person, and who is staying in the neighbouring village of Oppeln. Müller is supposed to provide him with what they call the *Konserve* ('canned goods').

It's 4:00 a.m. when the phone rings in his hotel room. He answers, and is told to call back to Wilhelmstrasse. At the other end of the line,

Heydrich's shrill voice tells him: 'Grandmother is dead.' This is the signal: Operation Tannenberg can begin. Naujocks rounds up his men and goes to the radio station that he plans to attack. But before the action starts, he must give each member of the expedition a Polish uniform. He must also receive the *Konserve*: a prisoner expressly freed from a concentration camp. This man, too, is dressed as a Polish soldier—unconscious but still alive, although Müller, following orders, has given him a lethal injection.

The attack begins at 8:00 a.m. The employees are easily neutralized, and a few gunshots are fired in the air as a matter of form. The *Konserve* is left lying across the doorway, as evidence of the Polish attack, and it is almost certainly Naujocks who finishes him off with a bullet in the heart (a bullet in the back of the neck smacks too much of execution, and a bullet in the head risks delaying identification), even if he will never admit it at his trial. Now they have to broadcast the speech in Polish, prepared by Heydrich. One of the SS guards, chosen for his linguistic abilities, is given the job of reading it out. The trouble is that no one knows how to work the radio. Naujocks gets a bit panicky, but in the end they manage to transmit it. The announcement is read out in a feverish Polish. It's a short speech declaring that Poland, provoked by Germany, has decided to launch an attack. The transmission lasts less than four minutes. In any case, the transmitter is not powerful enough and, save for a few small border towns, nobody hears it. Who cares? Naujocks does, having been warned beforehand by Heydrich: 'If you fail, you die. And me, too, perhaps.'

But Hitler has what he needs, and he couldn't care less about the technical difficulties. A few hours later he makes a speech to the Reichstag deputies: 'Last night, Polish soldiers opened fire for the first time on German soil. This morning, Germany retaliated. From now on, bombs will be met by bombs.'

The Second World War has just begun.

## 95

It is in Poland that Heydrich unveils his most devilish creation. The Einsatzgruppen are special SS troops, made up of SD and Gestapo members, whose job is to clean up the zones occupied by the Wehrmacht. Each unit is given a little booklet containing the necessary information: in tiny characters, on extra-thin paper, is a list of all those who must be liquidated as the country is occupied. Not only Communists but also teachers, writers, journalists, priests, industrialists, bankers, civil servants, merchants, wealthy farmers . . . everyone of any note. Thousands of names are listed, with their addresses and telephone numbers, plus a list of known acquaintances—in case these subversive elements attempt to take refuge with parents or friends. Each name is accompanied by a physical description and sometimes even a photo. Heydrich's information services have already achieved an impressive level of efficiency.

However, this meticulousness is probably a bit superfluous considering the behaviour of the troops, who shoot first and ask questions later.

Among the first victims of the Polish campaign are a group of Scouts, aged twelve to sixteen. They are lined up against a wall in the market square and shot. The priest who sacrifices himself to perform their last rites is also executed. Only afterward do the Einsatzgruppen take care of their real objectives: the merchants and local notables, who are, in their turn, lined up and shot. Essentially, the work of the Einsatzgruppen—a detailed written account of which would take up thousands of pages—can be summed up in three terrible letters: *etc*. Until they reach the USSR, at least: at that point, even *et cetera*'s suggestion of infinity will not be enough.

96

It's incredible. Almost anywhere you look in the politics of the Third Reich, and particularly among its most terrifying aspects, Heydrich is there—at the centre of everything.

On September 21, 1939, he sends a personally signed letter to all the relevant services about the 'Jewish problem in the occupied territories'. This letter concerns the roundup of Jews into ghettos, and orders the creation of Jewish councils—the infamous Judenräte—under the direct authority of the RSHA. The Judenrat is undoubtedly inspired by Eichmann's ideas as Heydrich saw them applied in Austria: the key is to make the victims collaborate in their own murder. Despoiled yesterday, destroyed tomorrow.

On September 22, 1939, Himmler's creation of the RSHA becomes official.

The RSHA—the central office of Reich security (Reichssicherheitshauptamt)—brings together the SD, the Gestapo, and the Kripo in one monstrous organization whose powers are beyond imagining. The head of this organization, nominated by Himmler, is Heydrich. Espionage, political police, and criminal police, all placed in the hands of one man. They may as well just have named him officially 'the most dangerous man in the Third Reich'. In any case, this quickly became his nickname. Only one police force is not controlled by him: the Ordnungpolizei, the uniformed police whose task is to maintain order, is given to a nobody called Dalüge, directly answerable to Himmler. It is a trifle compared with the rest, but Heydrich, in his thirst for power, is not the type of man to ignore it. All the same, it *is* a trifle, in my opinion—although it's true that I don't have Heydrich's aptitudes or experience in these matters. Anyway, the RSHA hydra has enough heads to keep him busy. So now he has to delegate. He gives each of the RSHA's seven divisions to a colleague who is selected first and foremost for his abilities rather than his politics—and this is rare enough to be worth mentioning in the lunatic asylum that is the Nazi regime. Heinrich Müller, for example, who is put in charge of the Gestapo—and who identifies so completely with his job that hereafter he is known simply as 'Gestapo' Müller—is a former Christian Democrat: an affiliation that does not prevent him from becoming one of the Nazis' most devastating weapons. The other RSHA offices are given to brilliant intellectuals: youngsters such as Ohlendorf (Inland-SD) and Schellenberg (Ausland-SD), or experienced academics like Six (Written Records). Such men contrast strongly with the cohort of cranks, illiterates, and mental degenerates who populate the Party's higher echelons.

One minor branch of the Gestapo—a status that does not reflect its true importance, but it's always better to remain discreet with such sensitive subjects—is devoted to Jewish affairs. Heydrich already knows who he wants to run it: that little Austrian Hauptsturmführer who did such good work before, Adolf Eichmann. At the moment he's working on a particularly original dossier: the Madagascar Plan. The idea is to deport all the Jews there. An idea worth pursuing. First, it is necessary to defeat Britain, because sending the Jews by sea will otherwise be impossible. Afterward . . . we'll see.

## 98

Hitler has decided to invade Britain. For a landing on the English coastline to succeed, Germany must first control the skies. Yet, in spite of Göring's promises, the RAF's Spitfires and Hurricanes are still flying over the Channel. Day after day, night after night, the heroic British pilots repulse the attacks of the German bombers and fighters.

Operation Sea Lion, planned for September 11, 1940, is postponed first until the fourteenth, and then until the seventeenth. But on September 17, a Kriegsmarine report states: 'The enemy air force is still not beaten, in any way. In fact, it is increasingly active. On the whole, atmospheric conditions do not allow us to hope for a period of calm.' So the Führer decides to delay Sea Lion indefinitely.

That same day, however, Heydrich—told by Göring to organize repression and purification in the immediate aftermath of the invasion—gives orders to one of his colleagues, Standartenführer Franck Six, former head of economics at the University of Berlin, now redeployed in the SD. This is the man Heydrich has chosen to settle in London and to command the specially formed Einsatzgruppen: six small units to be based in London, Bristol, Birmingham, Liverpool, Manchester, and Edinburgh—or Glasgow, if the Forth Bridge is destroyed before then. 'Your task,' Heydrich tells him, 'is to fight, by any means necessary, all opposition groups, organizations, and institutions.' In concrete terms, the work of these Einsatzgruppen will be as it was in Poland, and as it will later be in Russia: they are death squads, ordered to exterminate everything in their path.

But at this point the mission is complicated by the Sonderfahndungliste GB, the special search list for Great Britain better known as the Black Book. It is a list of some 2,300 people to be found, arrested, and delivered to the Gestapo as quickly as possible. At the head of the list, unsurprisingly, is Churchill. Among the other politicians, British and foreign, are Beneš and Masaryk, representatives of the Czech government-in-exile. So far, so logical.

130

But the list also contains the names of writers such as H. G. Wells, Virginia Woolf, Aldous Huxley, and Rebecca West. Freud is there, despite having died in 1939. And Baden-Powell, too, the founder of the Scout movement. In retrospect, the execution of the young Scouts in Poland is more than an excess of zeal: it's a mistake because the Scouts are considered by the German secret services to be among the best potential sources of information. This is, altogether, a fairly weird collection of names. Apparently it was drawn up not by Heydrich but by Schellenberg. If the work seems rather botched, that might be due to the fact that Schellenberg was very busy preparing the attempted kidnapping of the Duke of Windsor in Lisbon.

So the list is rather comical, the duke's kidnapping will fail, the Luftwaffe will lose the Battle of Britain, and Operation Sea Lion will never be launched. A few stray stones in the garden of German efficiency.


# 99


I'm still not sure about the veracity of all the Heydrich anecdotes I'm collecting, but this one is particularly unreliable: the witness and protagonist of the scene I'm about to describe isn't even certain himself about what happened to him. Schellenberg is Heydrich's right-hand man in the SD. He is a fierce, unscrupulous bureaucrat, but also a brilliant, cultivated, elegant young man whom Heydrich sometimes invites not only on regular trips to brothels but to spend evenings with himself and Lina, at the theatre or the opera. So he counts almost as a close friend of the couple. One day when Heydrich has a meeting out of town, Lina calls Schellenberg to suggest they take a stroll around a lake. They drink coffee, talk of literature and music. That's as much as I know. Four days later, after work, Heydrich takes Schellenberg and 'Gestapo' Müller for a night on the town. The evening begins in a chic restaurant on Alexanderplatz. Müller pours the drinks. The atmosphere is relaxed, everything seems normal. Then Müller says to Schellenberg: 'So, did you have a good time the other day?' Schellenberg understands immediately. Heydrich, whitefaced, says nothing. 'Do you wish to be informed of what happened on the outing?' Schellenberg asks him, speaking like a bureaucrat almost in spite of himself. And suddenly the evening plunges into strangeness. Heydrich hisses: 'You have just drunk poison. It will kill you within six hours. If you tell me the whole, absolute truth, I will give you the antidote. But I want the truth.' Schellenberg's heartbeat races. He starts to describe the afternoon while trying to keep his voice from trembling. Müller interrupts him: 'After the coffee, you went for a walk with the boss's wife. Why are you hiding this? You do understand that you were being watched, don't you?' But if Heydrich already knew everything, what would be the point of this drama? Schellenberg confesses to a fifteen-minute walk and gives an account of the subjects touched upon during their conversation. Heydrich remains pensive for a long time. Then he delivers his verdict: 'All right, I suppose I must believe you. But give me your word of honour that you will never do anything like this again.' Schellenberg, sensing that the greatest danger is over, manages to conquer his fear and to reply in an aggressive voice that he will give his word after drinking the antidote because an oath extorted in such circumstances would be worthless. He even dares to ask: 'As a former naval officer, would you consider it honourable to proceed in any other way?' Bearing in mind how Heydrich's naval career ended, you have to admit that Schellenberg has balls. Heydrich stares at Schellenberg. Then he pours him a dry martini. 'Perhaps I was imagining it,' Schellenberg writes in his memoirs, 'but it seemed to taste more bitter than normal.' He drinks, apologizes, gives his word of honour, and the evening begins again.


## 100

During one of his many brothel visits, Heydrich has an inspired idea: open his own.

His closest collaborators—Schellenberg, Nebe, and Naujocks—are given the task of carrying out this venture. Schellenberg finds a house in a chic district of suburban Berlin. Nebe, who has worked for years in fashionable society, recruits the girls. And Naujocks takes care of fitting out the premises: each room bristles with microphones and cameras. They're behind paintings, inside lamps, under armchairs, on top of wardrobes. A listening post is installed in the cellar. The idea is brilliant in its simplicity: instead of going out to spy on people in their homes, get them to come to you. So it has to be a high-class brothel to attract a prestigious clientele.

When all is ready, Kitty's Salon opens its doors and, thanks to word of mouth, is soon famous in diplomatic circles. The bugs work twenty-four hours a day. The cameras are useful for blackmailing clients.

Kitty, the boss, is an ambitious madam from Vienna: distinguished, competent, and devoted to her work. She loves being able to boast about her famous clients. The visit of Count Ciano, the Italian foreign minister and Mussolini's son-in-law, drives her mad with happiness. I suppose there is also a fascinating book to be written about her.

Quite quickly, Heydrich starts giving visits of inspection. He turns up late, usually drunk, and goes upstairs with one of the girls.

One morning, Naujocks happens upon a recording of his boss. Out of curiosity he listens—I don't know if there was a film—and, having had a good chuckle, prudently decides to erase the recording. I don't have the details, but evidently Heydrich's performance is laughable.

## 101

Naujocks stands in Heydrich's office—he has not been invited to sit down—beneath an enormous chandelier whose point hangs ominously over his head like the sword of Damocles. His fate, he knows, hangs by a thread this morning. Heydrich sits before the vast wall tapestry embroidered with a gigantic eagle clasping a swastika. He bangs his fist on the solid wood table and the impact makes the photo of his wife and children jump.

'How the devil could you decide to record my visit to Kitty's Salon last night?'

Even if he'd already guessed the reason for this morning's summons, Naujocks turns pale.

'Record?'

'Yes. Don't deny it!'

Naujocks makes a quick calculation: Heydrich has no material proof, because he took care to erase the tape. So he adopts what seems to him the most profitable strategy. Knowing his boss as he does, however, he is aware that he's risking his life.

'But I do deny it! I don't even know which room you were in! Nobody told me!'

There follows a long, unnerving silence.

'You're lying! Either that or you're getting careless.'

Naujocks wonders which of these hypotheses is, in his boss's eyes, the most unforgivable. In a calmer and thus more disturbing voice, Heydrich begins to speak again:

'You should have known where I was. It's part of your job. It is also your duty to switch off the microphones and tape recorders when I'm there. You didn't do that last night. If you think you can make a fool of me, Naujocks, you'd better think again. Leave.'

Naujocks—the jack of all trades who, at Gleiwitz, started the war—is sidelined. It is thanks only to his remarkable survival instinct that he is not simply liquidated. After this regrettable incident, he will spend most of his time trying to keep his head down. In the end, this is not a very high price to pay for fucking with Heydrich: his boss, Himmler's right-hand man, the SS number two, supreme leader of the RSHA, master of the SD and the Gestapo. Heydrich, the Blond Beast, who, through his ferocity but also through his sexual performances, is doubly deserving of his nickname. Or not, as Naujocks must snigger to himself in those moments of calm between the surges of fear.

## 102

The dialogue in the preceding chapter is the perfect example of the difficulties I'm facing. Certainly Flaubert didn't have the same problems with *Salammbô*, because nobody recorded the conversations of Hamilcar, father of Hannibal. But when I make Heydrich say:

'If you think you can make a fool of me, Naujocks, you'd better think again,' all I am doing is repeating the words as reported by Naujocks himself. You could hardly hope for a better witness, for reporting a phrase, than the only other person in the room, who heard it and to whom it was addressed. That said, I doubt whether Heydrich really formulated his threat in that way. It's not his style. What we have here is Naujocks recalling a phrase years after the event, which is rewritten by whoever's taking down his dictation, and then again by the translator. But Heydrich, the most dangerous man in the Reich, saying, 'If you think you can make a fool of me, Naujocks, you'd better think again' . . . . well, it's a bit lame. It is surely much more likely that Heydrich—a coarse man on a power trip, and angry too—said something along the lines of: 'You want to fuck with me? Watch it,

136

I'll rip your balls off!' But what is my opinion worth compared with an eyewitness account?

If it were up to me, I'd write:

'Tell me, Naujocks, where did I spend the night?'

'I beg your pardon, General?'

'You heard me.'

'Well . . . I don't know, General.'

'You don't know?'

'No, General.'

'You don't know that I was at Kitty's?'

' . . .'

'What have you done with the recording?'

'I don't understand, General.'

'Stop fucking with me! I want to know if you kept the recording!'

'General . . . I didn't know that you were there! . . . Nobody warned me! Of course, I destroyed the recording as soon as I recognized you . . . I mean, as soon as I recognized your voice! . . .'

'Stop bullshitting, Naujocks! You're paid to know everything, and especially where I am, because I'm the one who pays you! The instant I take a room at Kitty's, you switch off the microphones! The next time you try to fuck with me, I'll send you to Dachau, where they'll hang you up by the balls! Am I making myself clear?'

'Perfectly clear, General.'

'Now fuck off!'

That would, I think, be a bit livelier and more realistic, and probably closer to the truth. But it's impossible to know for sure. Heydrich could be foulmouthed, but he also knew how to play the icy bureaucrat when the need arose. So, all in all, between Naujocks's version, however corrupted, and mine, it is undoubtedly better to choose that

137

of Naujocks. But I still think Heydrich would have wanted to rip his balls off.

compared with an example
If it were up to me, I'd write:
"Tell me, Naujocks, where did I spend the night?"
"I beg your pardon, General?"
"You heard me."
"Well . . . I don't know, General.

## 103

From one of the high windows in the north tower of Wewelsburg Castle, Heydrich contemplates the plain of Westphalia. In the middle of the forest, he can just make out the huts and the barbed-wire fences of Germany's smallest concentration camp. But his gaze is probably focused on the parade ground, where the troops of his Einsatzgruppen are being drilled. Operation Barbarossa will be launched within a week. Within two, these men will be in Byelorussia, in Ukraine, in Lithuania, and will be seeing action. They've been promised that they'll be home again by Christmas, once their job is done. In reality, Heydrich has no idea how long this war will last. Within the Party and the army, everyone who knows about the operation is highly optimistic. The Red Army's performances on the battlefield—mediocre in Poland, frankly rubbish in Finland—lead the Nazis to believe that the still-invincible Wehrmacht can achieve a rapid victory. Based on what he's seen in the SD reports, however, Heydrich is more circumspect. The enemy's forces—the number of their tanks, for example, or of their reserve divisions—seem to him to have been dangerously underestimated. But the high command of the armed forces has its own information service, the Abwehr, and it has chosen to ignore Heydrich's warnings and to put its faith instead in the more encouraging conclusions of Admiral Canaris, Heydrich's former boss. Heydrich, whose expulsion from the navy remains an unhealed wound, must be choking with rage. Hitler has declared:

'The beginning of a war is always like opening a door onto a darkened room. You never know what's hiding in there.' Implicitly, it is admitted that the SD's warnings might not be baseless. But the decision to attack the Soviet Union has been taken, all the same. Heydrich watches with concern as the clouds gather over the plain below.

Behind him, he hears the voice of Himmler talking to his generals.

For Himmler, the SS is an order of knights. He considers himself a descendant of Henry the Fowler, the Saxon king who, by repelling the Magyars in the tenth century, laid the foundations of the Germanic Holy Roman Empire, and who then spent most of his reign exterminating Slavs. With his claims to such a lineage, the Reichsführer needed a castle. When he found this one, it was a ruin. He had to bring four thousand prisoners from Sachsenhausen, nearly a third of whom died during the renovations. Now, however, it towers imperiously over the Alme, which flows through the valley. Its two towers and its dungeon, connected by battlements, form a triangle whose point, turned towards the mythical land of Thule, birthplace of the Aryans, represents the *axis mundi*, the symbolic centre of the world.

Here in the heart of the dungeon, in a former chapel renamed Obergruppenführersaal, Himmler is holding a meeting that Heydrich has been unable to get out of. In the middle of this great circular room, the highest SS dignitaries are gathered around an enormous oak table. It is round and seats twelve, of course, because Himmler wanted to reproduce the symbolism of the Arthurian legend. But the Reich's quest for the Grail in 1941 is a little different from Perceval's. 'The final confrontation between two ideologies . . . the need to seize new *Lebensraum* . . .' Heydrich knows this mantra by heart, as do all Germans at the time. 'A question of survival . . . pitiless racial struggle . . . twenty to thirty million Slavs and Jews . . .' At this point Heydrich, who is fond of numbers, pricks up his ears: 'Twenty to thirty million Slavs and Jews will perish through military actions and the problems of food supply.'

Heydrich does not let his irritation show. He stares at the magnificent black sun inlaid with runes on the marble floor. Military actions . . . problems of supply . . . could they be any more evasive? Heydrich is well aware that with certain sensitive subjects one must not be too explicit, but a moment always comes when you have to call a spade a spade—and it seems reasonable to think that this moment has now arrived. Otherwise, through a lack of clarity in their orders, there is a risk that the men will mess things up. And he is the one who's responsible for this mission.

When Himmler ends the meeting, Heydrich hurries through corridors cluttered with suits of armour, coats of arms, and paintings. He knows that there are alchemists, occultists, and magi here working full-time on esoteric problems, but he pays no mind to any of this. Two days he's been stuck in this lunatic asylum! He wants to get back to Berlin as soon as possible.

But outside the clouds are massing in the valley,

and if he waits too long his airplane won't be able to take off. They escort him to the parade ground, where he has the honour of reviewing the troops. He dispenses with the long speech and dashes past the assembled ranks, hardly even glancing at the gang of assassins chosen to go and exterminate subhumans in the East. There are nearly three thousand of them and they are turned out impeccably. Heydrich dives into the plane that idles at the end of the runway. It takes off just before the storm breaks. In the sudden downpour, the troops of the four Einsatzgruppen start to march.


## 104

In Berlin, there is no round table and no black magic. The atmosphere is bureaucratic, and Heydrich studiously writes his directives. Göring has asked him to keep them short and simple. On July 2, 1941, two weeks after the launch of Barbarossa, the following note is sent to SS commanders behind the front line:

'To be executed: all Komintern functionaries, Party functionaries, people's commissars, Jews occupying positions in the Party or the State, other radical elements (saboteurs, propagandists, irregular soldiers, murderers, agitators).'

Simple indeed, but also quite cautious—curiously so. Why specify that Jews occupying positions in the Party or the State should be executed when all such functionaries were to be executed anyway, Jewish or otherwise? Heydrich didn't know then how ordinary soldiers would react to the demands of his

Einsatzgruppen. It's true that the famous directive signed by Keitel on June 6, 1941, and thus approved by the Wehrmacht, authorizes the massacres, but officially this is limited to political enemies. In other words, Soviet Jews are targeted only because of their politics. The redundant meaning in this note is like a trace of one final scruple. Naturally, if the local people want to organize pogroms, that will be discreetly encouraged. But at the beginning of July, there is still no question of openly pursuing the extermination of Jews simply because they are Jews.

Two weeks later, swept along by the euphoria of their victories, this embarrassment will have disappeared. While the Wehrmacht routs the Red Army on all fronts, while the invasion progresses even more easily than the most optimistic forecasts, and while 300,000 Soviet soldiers are taken prisoner, Heydrich rewrites his directive. The main points are reprised, the list lengthened, and a few details added (former Red Army commissars are now included, for instance). And finally Heydrich replaces 'Jews occupying positions in the Party or the State' with 'all the Jews'.

## 105

Hauptmann Heydrich is on board a Messerschmitt 109 whose cabin is embossed with the initials *RH* in runic lettering: this is his private plane and it is flying over Soviet territory at the head of a formation of Luftwaffe fighters. Whenever the German pilots spot columns of slowly retreating Russian soldiers below, they swoop on them like tigers and, lining up the columns of men in their sights, massacre them with machine guns.

Today, however, what Heydrich sees below him is not a column of foot soldiers but a Yak. The Soviet plane's plump silhouette is easily recognized. In spite of the enormous number of enemy planes destroyed on the ground by German bombers at the beginning of the offensive, the Soviet air force has not been completely eliminated, and there are still pockets of resistance: this Yak is proof of that. But the German planes are obviously superior, both in quality and quantity. No Soviet fighter in the current situation can hope to hold its own against the Me109. Imperious and vain, Heydrich orders his squadron to remain in formation. He wants to give his men a demonstration by shooting down the Russian plane on his own. He descends to the Yak's height and glides along in its vapour trail. The Yak's pilot hasn't seen him. The object of the manoeuvre is to get closer to the target so that he can open fire at a distance of about five hundred feet. The German plane is much faster. The gap closes. When he can clearly make out the Russian's tail in his sights, Heydrich shoots. The Yak beats its wings like a terror-stricken bird. But the first salvo hasn't touched it, and in truth the pilot is not terror-stricken. He sends the plane into a dive. Heydrich tries to follow, but his turn is hopelessly wide in comparison. That idiot Göring claimed Soviet aviation was obsolete, but in that, as in almost all the Nazis' assumptions about the Soviet Union, he was wrong. Admittedly, the Yak doesn't measure up to the German fighters in terms of speed, but its relative slowness is balanced by an astonishing manoeuvrability. The little Russian plane keeps descending while continuing to twist and turn ever more tightly. Heydrich follows but can't fix the enemy in his sights. It's like a hare being pursued by a greyhound. Heydrich wants to claim a victory and paint a little plane on the fuselage of his aircraft, so he persists. What he doesn't realize is that the Yak, while constantly changing direction to evade his pursuer's salvoes, is not flying randomly but heading towards a precise location. Only when the explosions echo all around him does Heydrich understand: the Russian pilot has led him over a Soviet anti-aircraft battery and he—the imbecile—has thrown himself into the trap.

A violent impact shakes the cabin. Black smoke pours from the tail. Heydrich's plane crashes.

## 106

Himmler looks like someone's just smacked him in the face. The blood rises to his cheeks and he feels his brain swell inside his skull. He's just heard the news: during an air battle over the Berezina, Heydrich's Messerschmitt 109 has been shot down. If Heydrich is dead, it is of course a terrible loss for the SS: brilliant man, dedicated colleague, et cetera. But the real worry is if he's still alive: that could spell catastrophe. Because the plane crashed *behind* Soviet lines. Himmler imagines having to inform the Führer that his security chief has fallen into enemy hands. That would not be a pleasant meeting. He makes a mental inventory of all the information Heydrich possesses that is likely to interest Stalin.

The answer makes him dizzy. And then there are things Heydrich knows of which the Reichsführer is unaware. Politically, strategically, if Heydrich talks, the consequences could be incalculable. Himmler can't even begin to measure the potential magnitude of the disaster. Behind his little round glasses and his little moustache, he is sweating.

To tell the truth, that isn't even the most urgent problem. If Heydrich is dead or a prisoner of the Russians, the absolute priority is to get hold of his dossiers. God only knows what they might contain, and about whom. All his files must be seized, in his office and at his home. To deal with Prinz Albert Strasse, he must warn Müller, who looks after the RSHA, along with Schellenberg. For Heydrich's home, deal politely with Lina, but everything must be searched. Meanwhile, as Heydrich is reported missing, the only thing to do is wait. Go see Lina, to prepare the ground, and send orders to the front that he must be found, dead or alive.

One might reasonably ask what the hell the head of the Nazi secret services was doing in a German fighter plane above a Soviet combat zone. The answer is that, along with his SS duties, Heydrich was a reserve officer in the Luftwaffe. In readiness for the war, he had taken flying lessons, and when the invasion of Poland began, he absolutely wanted to answer the call of duty. As prestigious as his post as head of the SD was, he regarded it as a bureaucrat's job—and since the country was at war, he had to behave like a true Teutonic Knight: he had to fight. Thus he found himself, first of all, as a machine gunner in a bomber. But unsurprisingly he wasn't keen on this secondary role, so he took command of a Messerschmitt

145

110 on reconnaissance flights over Great Britain, and then of a Messerschmitt 109 (the German equivalent of the Spitfire) in which he broke an arm taking off during the Norwegian campaign. I got hold of a slightly hagiographic book that describes admiringly how he flew planes with his arm in a sling. Afterward, he fought in battles against the RAF.

While this was happening, Himmler was already worrying about him like a father. I have before me a letter dated May 15, 1940, written from his private train (the Sonderzug *Heinrich*) and addressed to his 'very dear Heydrich,' which shows just how solicitous Himmler was towards his right-hand man: 'Give me your news every day if you can.' Knowing all he knew, Heydrich was a very valuable man.

Only two days later, Heydrich was picked up by a German 'patrol'—his own men from Einsatzgruppen D—who had just liquidated forty-five Jews and thirty hostages. He'd been shot down by Soviet anti-aircraft fire, crash-landed, spent two days and two nights in hiding, and finally crossed the German lines on foot. Returning home filthy and unshaven, he was also, according to his wife, quite unnerved by his misadventure, although it did give him what he'd wanted: the Iron Cross, first class—a highly respected medal in the German military. Following this glorious feat, however, he was never allowed to take part in any more aerial battles. Hitler himself, horrified in hindsight by the story of the Berezina, appears to have officially forbidden this. So, in spite of his efforts and his undeniable impetuosity, Heydrich never scored a single kill. His career as a pilot ended on this disappointing note.

146

Natacha reads the chapter I've just written. When she reaches the second sentence, she exclaims: 'What do you mean, "The blood rises to his cheeks and he feels his brain swell inside his skull"? You're making it up!'

I have been boring her for years with my theories about the puerile, ridiculous nature of novelistic invention, and she's right, I suppose, not to let me get away with this skull thing. I thought I'd decided to avoid this kind of stuff, which has, a priori, no virtue other than giving a bit of colour to the story, and which is rather ugly. And even if there are clues to Himmler's panicked reaction, I can't really be sure of the symptoms of this panic: perhaps he went red (that's how I imagine it), but then again, perhaps he turned white. This is quite a serious problem.

I defend myself halfheartedly: it's more than likely that Himmler had some kind of headache, and anyway, this thing about the swelling brain is just a cheap metaphor with which to express his fear. But even I'm not convinced by this. The next day, I delete the sentence. Unfortunately, that creates an emptiness that I don't like. I'm not sure why, but I'm not at all keen on the segue from 'smacked him in the face' to 'He's just heard the news.' Too abrupt: I miss the link provided by my skull metaphor. So I feel obliged to replace the deleted sentence with another, more prudent one. I write something like: 'I imagine that his face, like a bespectacled little rat's, must have turned red.'

It's true that Himmler's fat cheeks and moustache made him rather rodentlike, but obviously this phrase lacks gravitas. I decide to remove 'bespectacled'. The effect of 'little rat's', even without the spectacles, still bothers me. You can see the advantage of this option, however, with its cautious qualifications: 'I imagine . . . ,' 'must have . . .' With a hypothesis openly presented as such, I avoid the clash with reality. I don't know why I feel the need to add: 'His face is flushed.'

I had this vision of Himmler red-faced and with a blocked nose (perhaps because I've had a nasty cold myself for the past four days) and my tyrannic imagination wouldn't budge from this idea: I wanted a detail of this kind for the Reichsführer's face. But clearly I wasn't happy with the result: I got rid of it once again. I contemplated this nothingness between the first and third sentence for a long time. And, slowly, I began to type: 'The blood rises to his cheeks and he feels his brain swell inside his skull.'

As usual, I think of Oscar Wilde. It's the same old story: 'I was working on the proof of one of my poems all the morning, and took out a comma. In the afternoon I put it back again.'

108

Heydrich, who I imagine settled comfortably in the back of his black Mercedes, presses his briefcase tightly to his knees. It contains probably the most important document of his career, and of the Third Reich's history.

The car zooms through the suburbs of Berlin.

Outside, it's a pleasant summer evening, and it's difficult to imagine that the sky will soon be filled with black shapes dropping bombs. But a few damaged buildings, a few destroyed houses, a few hurrying passersby, is all it takes to bring to mind the extraordinary relentlessness of the Royal Air Force.

It's already more than four months since Heydrich asked Eichmann to write the first draft of this document in order to get Göring's approval. But they also needed the agreement of Rosenberg, the minister in charge of the eastern territories. And this nonentity is the one who made things difficult! Since then, Eichmann has worked hard on revising the text and all the problems seem to have been ironed out.

We are in the heart of the forest, north of Berlin. The Mercedes stops at the gates of a villa guarded by heavily armed SS men. This is Karinhall, the little baroque palace that Göring had built to console himself after the death of his first wife. The guards salute, the gates open, and the car sweeps up the driveway. Göring stands waiting on the steps, his expression jolly, his body squeezed into one of those eccentric uniforms that have earned him the nickname 'Perfumed Nero.' He greets Heydrich effusively, happy to meet the fearsome head of the SD in person. Heydrich is well aware that everyone considers him the most dangerous man in the Reich, and it's a source of vanity for him, but he also knows that if all the Nazi dignitaries court him so insistently, it is above all to try to weaken Himmler, his boss. Heydrich is an instrument for these men, not yet a rival. It's true that in the devilish duo he forms with Himmler, he is thought to be the brains ('HHhH,' they say in the SS: *Himmlers Hirn heisst Heydrich*—Himmler's brain is called Heydrich), but he is still only the right-hand man, the subordinate, the number two. Heydrich is so ambitious that he will not be satisfied with this situation forever. But when he studies how the balance of power within the Party has evolved, he congratulates himself for having stayed faithful to Himmler, whose power continues to grow while Göring mopes in his mansion, half in disgrace since the Luftwaffe's failure in England.

Yet Göring is still officially in charge of the Jewish question, and that's why Heydrich is here tonight.

Before they get to the matter in hand, Heydrich must first suffer his host's childish enthusiasms. Fat Hermann wants to show him his electric train set, a gift from the Prussian National Theatre. He is very proud of it and plays with it every evening. Heydrich bears this patiently. After going into raptures over the private cinema, the Turkish baths, a room with a pharaonic ceiling, and even a lion called Caesar, he finally manages to sit down with Göring in a wood-panelled office. Now he can take out his precious paper, which he gives to the Reichsmarschall to read:

The Marshal of the Reich of Greater
Germany
Delegate of the four-year plan
President of the council of ministers for the
defence of the Reich
For the attention of:
Head of the Gestapo and the SD
SS-Gruppenführer Heydrich

150

Berlin

Supplementary to the task that has been
entrusted to you by the edict of January
24, 1939, to solve the Jewish problem by
means of migration or evacuation in the best
possible way according to present conditions,
I hereby assign you the task of making all
the necessary organizational, practical, and
financial preparations in order to facilitate
a total solution of the Jewish question in
all the territories of Europe under German
occupation.
  As far as these matters fall within the
domain of other central organizations, those
organizations should be involved.

Göring stops and smiles. Eichmann added this
paragraph to satisfy Rosenberg. Heydrich smiles,
too, though unable to hide his contempt for these
bureaucratic ministers. Göring begins to read again:

Furthermore, I charge you to submit to me
as soon as possible an overall plan of the
preliminary organizational, practical, and
financial measures necessary for the execution
of the final solution of the Jewish question
such as it is envisaged.

In silence, Göring dates and signs what
will become for history the *Ermächtigung*: the
authorization. Heydrich can't suppress a contented
grin. He tidies away the precious paper in his
briefcase. It's July 31, 1941, and we are present at

151

the birth of the Final Solution. Heydrich will be its principal architect.

## 109

In the first draft, I'd written: 'squeezed into a blue uniform.' I don't know why, I just imagined it being blue. It's true that in photos Göring often sports a pale blue uniform, but I don't know what he was wearing on that particular day. He might just as easily have been in white, for example.

I'm not sure if this kind of scruple still makes much sense at this stage.

## 110

Bad Kreuznach, August '41. The second German fencing championships have just taken place. The twelve best fencers of the Reichsonderklasse [literally 'elite class of the Reich'] have been chosen and will receive a gold or silver medal from the NSRL (National Socialist Society for Gymnastics). In fifth place comes an Obergruppenführer [did the magazine editors make a mistake, or are they toadying up to Heydrich by giving him an anticipated promotion?] of the SS and general of police: it's Reinhard Heydrich, the head of the Gestapo and the SD. He joyfully received the congratulations of the public, but his whole attitude breathed the modesty of a true victor. Those who know him know that rest is, for him, an alien concept. No rest and no relaxation: that is his first principle, whether with regard to sport or to service.

(ARTICLE APPEARING IN THE SPECIALIST MAGAZINE *GYMNASTICS AND PHYSICAL EDUCATION*)

Those who know him know that, above all, it's better not to skimp on praise for this tremendous thirty-six-year-old athlete, nor to dwell on how stressed the judges might have been feeling when they had to decide whether to validate a strike against the head of the Gestapo. Nor is it a good idea to mention Commodus or Caligula, both of whom fought in the arena against gladiators who knew perfectly well that it was not in their interests to win against the emperor.

During the tournament, though, Obergruppen-führer Heydrich seems to have behaved quite well. One day, when he cursed a judge's decision, the tournament director put him curtly in his place by telling him, in front of everyone: 'In fencing, the only laws are those of sport, and nothing else!' Stunned by the man's courage, Heydrich didn't even protest.

He kept his fits of hubris for other circumstances. For it was at the time of this tournament in Bad Kreuznach that he would tell two friends (since when did Heydrich have friends?), in vivid terms, that he would not hesitate to neutralize Hitler himself 'if the old man gives me any shit.'

What exactly did he mean by that? I would like to know.

This summer, at the zoo in Kiev, a man entered the lion's enclosure. When another visitor tried to stop him, he said, stepping over the barrier, 'God will save me.' And he was eaten alive. If I'd been there, I'd have said to him: 'Don't believe everything you're told.'

God was no help at all to the people who died at Babi Yar.

In Russian, *yar* means 'gully'. Babi Yar, or 'Grandmother's Gully', was a huge natural ravine just outside Kiev. Today, all that's left is a grassed-over depression, not very deep, at the centre of which is an impressive, Socialist-style sculpture commemorating those who died there. But when I went, the taxi driver showed me the place where Babi Yar had been. He took me to a kind of wooded gorge where, he explained through a young Ukrainian woman who acted as my translator, the bodies had been thrown. Then we went back to the taxi and he dropped me off at the memorial, *nearly a mile away*.

Between 1941 and 1943, the Nazis made of Grandmother's Gully what is probably the largest mass grave in the history of humanity. As the commemorative plaque makes clear—in three languages (Ukrainian, Russian, and Hebrew)— more than 100,000 people perished here, victims of fascism.

More than a third of them were executed in less than forty-eight hours.

That morning in September 1941, the Jews of

Kiev turned up in the thousands to the meeting point where they'd been summoned, carrying their personal effects. They were resigned to being deported. Little did they suspect the kind of exit the Germans had in mind for them.

They realized too late—some on their arrival, others not until they reached the ditch's edge. The process was quick: the Jews gave up their suitcases, their valuable objects, and their identity papers, which were torn up in front of them. Then they had to walk between two lines of SS guards who beat them with truncheons and clubs. If a Jew fell, they let the dogs loose on him. Either that or he was trampled underfoot by the panic-stricken crowd. At the end of this infernal corridor, emerging into a hazy landscape, the stunned Jews were ordered to undress completely, then conducted naked to the lip of a gigantic ditch. There, even the most obtuse or the most optimistic must have abandoned all hope. They screamed with terror: at the bottom of the ditch was a pile of corpses.

But the story of these men, women, and children does not end above this chasm. Because, with a very German concern for efficiency, the SS—before shooting them—first made them descend to the bottom of the ditch, where a 'crammer' was waiting for them. The job of this 'crammer' was similar to that of an usher at a theatre. He led each Jew to a pile of bodies and, having found a suitable place, made him or her lie facedown, naked and alive, on top of naked corpses. Then another guard, walking on the dead bodies, put a bullet in the back of the neck. A remarkable customization of mass killing. On October 2, 1941, the officer in charge of the Einsatzgruppe at Babi Yar wrote in his report:

'Sonderkommando 4a, in collaboration with group staff and two commandos of Police Regiment South, executed 33,771 Jews in Kiev on September 29 and 30, 1941.'

## 112

I've just learned of an extraordinary story that took place in Kiev during the war. It happened in 1942 and none of the main characters of Operation Anthropoid is involved, so theoretically it has no place in my novel. But one of the great advantages of the genre is the almost unlimited freedom it gives the author.

In the summer of 1942, Ukraine is governed by the Nazis with characteristic brutality. However, they wish to organize soccer matches between the various occupied and satellite countries of the East. Now, it happens that one team soon distinguishes itself with a series of victories over Romanian and Hungarian opponents: FC Start, a team hastily assembled from the bones of the defunct Dynamo Kiev, which has been banned since the beginning of the occupation but whose ex-players are reassembled for these matches.

Rumours of the team's success reach the Germans, who decide to organize a match in Kiev between the local side and the Luftwaffe's team. The Ukrainian players are told they must make a Nazi salute when the teams line up.

The day of the match, the stadium is full to bursting. The two teams come out on the pitch, and the German players lift their arms and shout 'Heil

Hitler!' The Ukrainian players also lift their arms, no doubt a disappointment to the crowd, who see the match as an opportunity to show some symbolic resistance. But instead of shouting 'Heil Hitler!', they close their fists, bang them against their chests, and yell: 'Long live physical culture!' This slogan, with its Soviet connotations, sends the crowd wild.

The match has hardly begun when one of the Ukrainian strikers has his leg broken by a German player. At the time there were no substitutes, so FC Start have to play on with only ten men. Thanks to their numerical superiority, the Germans open the score. Things are going badly. But the Kiev players refuse to give up, and they equalize to loud cheers. When they score a second goal, the supporters explode with joy.

At halftime, General Eberhardt, the superintendent of Kiev, goes to see the Ukrainian players in their changing room and tells them: 'Bravo, you've played an excellent game and we've enjoyed it. But now, in the second half, you must lose. You really must! The Luftwaffe team has never lost before, certainly not in any of the occupied territories. This is an order! If you do not lose, you will be executed.'

The players listen in silence. Back on the pitch, after a brief moment of uncertainty, and without discussing it, they make their decision: they will play to win. They score a goal, then another, and end up winning 5–1. The Ukrainian fans go crazy. The German supporters mutter angrily. Shots are fired in the air. But none of the players is worried yet, because the Germans believe they can avenge the insult on the pitch.

Three days later, a return match is organized,

and promoted by a poster campaign. The Germans send urgently for reinforcements: some professional footballers come from Berlin to strengthen their team.

The second match kicks off. The stadium is full to bursting again, but this time it's patrolled by SS troops. Officially, they are there to maintain order. As before, the Germans score first. But the Ukrainians never lose faith, and they win the match 5–3. At the final whistle, the Ukrainian supporters are ecstatic but the players look pale. The pitch is invaded, and in the confusion three Ukrainian players disappear: they will survive the war. The rest of the team is arrested and four of them are sent immediately to Babi Yar, where they are executed. On his knees at the edge of the ditch, Nikolai Trusevich—the captain and goalkeeper—manages to yell, before getting a bullet in the back of the neck: 'Communist sport will never die!' The other players are murdered one by one. Today, there is a monument to them in front of Dynamo's stadium.

There are an unbelievable number of different versions of this legendary 'death match.' Some say there was actually a third game, won by the Ukrainians—with a score of 8–0—and that it was only after this that the players were arrested and killed. But the version I've recounted seems the most credible to me, and in any case all the versions share the same broad outline. I'm worried that there are some errors in what I've written: since this subject has no direct link with Heydrich, I haven't had time to investigate more deeply. But I didn't want to write about Kiev without mentioning this incredible story.

The SD reports are piling up on Hitler's desk, denouncing the scandalous leniency of the Protectorate's government. Acts of sabotage; a still-active Resistance; seditious conversations overheard in public; an expanding black market; an 18 per cent fall in production; the Czech prime minister's relations with London . . . according to Heydrich's men, the situation is explosive. With the opening of the Russian front, the productivity of Czech industry—one of the best in Europe—is now becoming crucial for the Reich. The Škoda factories must work flat out to support the war effort.

Despite being paranoid, Hitler is not a complete fool. He must know that Heydrich has a vested interest—coveting, as he does, Neurath's position as Protector of Bohemia and Moravia—in discrediting the old baron by making things look as black as possible. At the same time, Hitler loathes weakness. He isn't too keen on barons either, for that matter. The latest news is the straw that breaks the camel's back. A call to boycott the occupation newspapers, made by Beneš and his clique in London, has been taken up to a remarkable extent by the local population for a whole week now. In itself, this isn't a big deal, but it shows how much influence the Czech government-in-exile still exerts. And what it says about the local population's overall state of mind is not very comforting for the occupying forces. When you bear in mind Hitler's sworn hatred of Beneš, you can guess at how angry this must make him.

Hitler knows that Heydrich is a rising star ready to do anything to further his own ambitions. This doesn't shock him, though, and for a good reason. Couldn't the same thing have been said about Hitler himself? Hitler respects Heydrich because he combines fierceness with efficiency. If you add to this his loyalty towards the Führer, you get the three elements that make the perfect Nazi. And that's without even mentioning his pure Aryan appearance. Try as Himmler might to be 'faithful Heinrich', he can't compete with this blueprint. So it's likely that Hitler admires Heydrich. Along with Stalin, that would make him one of the few living people to have had this honour. What's more, Hitler seems not to have been afraid of Heydrich— surprising, for a paranoiac like him. Perhaps he wanted to stoke the fires of competition between Heydrich and Himmler? Perhaps he believed, as he confided to his Reichsführer, that the dossier on Heydrich's supposed Jewishness was a guarantee of his devotion? Or perhaps the Blond Beast was such a perfect incarnation of the ideal Nazi that Hitler couldn't imagine him capable of betrayal?

In any case, he must have called Bormann to organize an emergency meeting in his Rastenburg HQ. Summoned immediately: Himmler, Heydrich, Neurath, and his assistant Frank, the Sudeten bookseller.

Frank is the first to arrive. He's about fifty and has a deeply wrinkled mafioso's face. Over lunch with Hitler, he paints a picture of the Protectorate that confirms the SD reports in every detail. Himmler and Heydrich arrive next. Heydrich makes a brilliant speech in which he outlines the problems and proposes solutions. Hitler is

160

impressed. Neurath, delayed by bad weather, gets there the next day—but by then his fate is already sealed. Hitler uses the same tactics as when he wishes to strip a general of his command: enforced sick leave. The position of Protector is now up for grabs.

## 114

On September 27, 1941, the Czech press agency, controlled by the Germans, sends out the following press release:

> The Protector of the Reich of Bohemia and Moravia, Reich minister and honourable citizen Herr Konstantin von Neurath, has decided that it was his duty to ask the Führer for prolonged leave due to reasons of health. Given that the present war situation means the Protector must work full-time, Herr von Neurath has asked the Führer to temporarily relieve him of his duties, and to name a replacement for the whole length of his absence. In view of the circumstances, the Führer could not refuse this request, and he has named Obergruppenführer and police general Heydrich as Protector of Bohemia and Moravia for the entire duration of Reichsminister von Neurath's illness.

## 115

In order to occupy such a prestigious post, Heydrich is promoted to Obergruppenführer, the second-highest rank in the SS hierarchy— subordinate only to Himmler's title of Reichsführer. The only rank that surpasses that is Oberstgruppenführer, and in September 1941 nobody has reached that level yet. (There will be only four Oberstgruppenführers by the end of the war.)

So Heydrich savours this decisive step in his irresistible if somewhat meandering rise. He phones his wife, who is not very taken by the idea of moving to Prague. (She claims to have said to him: 'Oh, if only you'd become a postman!' But she is so conceited and complacent that it is hard to imagine her ever having such a regret.) Heydrich replies: 'Try to understand what this means to me. It'll be a change from doing all the dirty work! Finally, I will be something more than the Reich's dustbin!' The Reich's dustbin: so that's how he defined his duties as head of the Gestapo and the SD. Duties, by the way, that he would continue to fulfil with the same efficiency as before.

## 116

Heydrich arrives in Prague the day that his appointment is announced to the Czech people. His airplane, a three-engined Junkers 52, lands at

Ruzyne Airport around noon.

He goes to the Esplanade Hotel, one of the most beautiful in town, but he obviously doesn't spend long there, because that same evening Himmler is able to read his colleague's report, sent by teleprinter:

At 15:10, ex-prime minister Eliáš was arrested, as arranged.
At 18:00, also as arranged, the arrest of ex-minister Havelka took place.
At 19:00, Czech radio announced my appointment by the Führer.
Eliáš and Havelka are being interrogated now. For diplomatic reasons, I must convene a special assembly in order to bring Eliáš to justice before a popular tribunal.

Eliáš and Havelka are the two most important members of the Czech government that is collaborating with the Germans under Hácha's presidency. They have nonetheless maintained regular contact with Beneš in London—a fact known to Heydrich's spies. This is why they are immediately condemned to death. Although, after thinking about it, Heydrich decides not to execute the sentence straightaway. It is, of course, only a temporary reprieve.

117

The next morning, at eleven o'clock, Heydrich's investiture takes place in Hradčany Castle, or

Hradchine, as the Germans call it. The vile Karl Hermann Frank—the Sudeten bookseller turned SS general and secretary of state—greets Heydrich amid great pomp in the castle courtyard. An orchestra, summoned for the occasion, plays the Nazi hymn 'Horst Wessel Lied.' Then Heydrich inspects the troops while a second banner is hoisted next to the swastika that flies above the castle and the town: a black flag embossed with two runic *S*s, signalling that another rung has been climbed on the ladder of terror. From now on, Bohemia and Moravia are, almost officially, the first SS state.

### 118

That same day, two great leaders of the Czech Resistance are executed: General Josef Bilý and Major General Hugo Vojta. They were found guilty of fomenting an armed uprising. Before his death, General Bilý shouts: 'Long live the Czechoslovak Republic! Now shoot me, you dogs!' These two men—yes, two more—do not really have a role to play in my story. But I felt it would be disrespectful not to even mention their names.

Along with Bilý and Vojta, nineteen former Czech army officers are killed, four of them generals. The crackdown begins in the days that follow. A state of emergency is declared throughout the country. All gatherings, indoors or out, are forbidden in accordance with martial law. The courts now have only two options, whatever the charges: acquittal or death. Czechs are sentenced to death for distributing pamphlets, selling goods on the black market, or simply listening to foreign radio stations. Each new law is announced by a red poster in two languages, and soon the town's walls are filled with them. The Czechs learn quickly who their new master is.

And the Jews, of course, learn even more quickly. On September 29, Heydrich closes all the synagogues and announces the arrest of any Czechs who, in protest against the recent law forcing Jews to wear a yellow star, decide to sport them in sympathy. In France, a year later, there will be similar shows of solidarity, and anyone imprudent enough to take part will be deported 'with their Jewish friends.' In the Protectorate, however, all of this is only a prelude.


# 119


On October 2, 1941, at Czernin Palace—now the Savoy Hotel—situated at the end of the castle's enclosure, Heydrich sets out his political creed as interim Protector of Bohemia and Moravia. Standing with his hands on a wooden pulpit, his iron cross hanging over his heart, his wedding ring visible on his left hand, he addresses the leaders of the occupation forces. He wishes to educate his compatriots:

'For tactical reasons relating to the war, we should not provoke the Czechs into action, nor push them to the point where revolt seems their only option.'

This is the first aspect of his policy. There are only two: the carrot and the stick. The stick comes next, although the dialectical balance between the two is uncertain:

'The Reich will not be mocked, and the Reich is master in its own house. This means that no German should let a Czech get away with anything, in the same way that no Jew should be allowed to get away with anything in the Reich. No German should say that a Czech is a decent person. If someone says that, we should expel them. If we don't form a united front against Czechness, the Czech will find a way to cheat us.'

After that, Heydrich—who is unaccustomed to making public speeches, and is certainly no Cicero—moves to the *illustratio*:

'No German can allow himself to be seen smashed in public. Let's be frank about this: we can get drunk, and we can relax—nobody has anything against that—but we must do it within four walls or in the officers' mess. The Czech must see that the German holds himself straight, in both military and civil life. He must see that we are the master, the lord, from head to toe.'

After this odd example, the speech becomes more specific—and more threatening.

'I want to make the citizens of this country understand, without any ambiguity and with an unshakable firmness, that they are part of the Reich—and, as such, owe their allegiance to the Reich. This is an absolute priority dictated by the imperatives of war. I want to be certain that each Czech worker gives his all to help the German war effort. To be clear, this means that the Czech worker will be provided for according to how well he works.'

Having dealt with the social and economic

166

aspects, the new interim Protector now moves on to the racial question. He can, after all, justifiably claim to be one of the Reich's first specialists on this subject:

It is obvious that our approach to the Czech people must be completely different to that of other races, such as the Slavs. The Czechs of Germanic origin should be treated firmly but with justice. We must guide them with the same humanity we show our own people if we wish to keep them in the Reich for good, and to make them mix with us. In order to decide who is fit for Germanization, I need to make a racial inventory.

We have all kinds of people here. For those who are of a good race and are well-disposed towards us, things are simple: they will be Germanized. At the other end of the spectrum—those of inferior races with hostile intentions—we must get rid of them. There's plenty of room for them in the East.

Between these two extremes, there are others whose cases we must look at more carefully. There are racially inferior people who are favourably disposed towards us. This type can be moved, whether in the Reich or elsewhere, but we must ensure that they do not reproduce, as we have no interest in their development. In the long term, these non-Germanizable elements—who we estimate at about half the population—can be transferred later to the Arctic, where we are building concentration camps for the Russians.

That leaves us with one group: those who

are racially acceptable but ideologically hostile. These are the most dangerous, because they belong to a race of leaders. We should ask ourselves very seriously what should be done with them. Some can be rehoused within the Reich, in a purely German environment, in order to re-educate and Germanize them. If that proves impossible, we must put them up against the wall. We cannot allow them to be sent to the East, where they might form a class of leaders who could turn against us.

I think he's covered all the bases there. Notice, by the way, this discreet and euphemistic metonymy: 'to the East'. Although his audience doesn't know it, what Heydrich means by this is 'to Poland', and more specifically 'to Auschwitz'.

## 120

On October 3 in London, the free Czechoslovak press formally records a change of politics in Prague with this headline:

'Mass Murders in the Protectorate.'

## 121

One of Heydrich's men was already running things there two years before. In 1939, Eichmann—having done such a good job in Austria—found himself in charge of the central office for Jewish emigration in Prague before being promoted to head of Jewish affairs at the RSHA in Berlin. Today, he returns to Prague at his master's summons. But in two years things have really changed. From now on, when Heydrich organizes a conference, it is no longer to discuss 'emigration' but 'the Final Solution of the Jewish question' in the Protectorate. These are the facts: 88,000 Jews live in the Protectorate, of whom 48,000 are in Prague, 10,000 in Brno, and 10,000 in Ostrava. Heydrich decides that Terezín will be the ideal transportation camp. Eichmann takes notes. Transportation will be quick—two or three trains a day, with a thousand people on each train. Following the tried-and-tested method, each Jew will be allowed to take one piece of luggage (without padlock) containing up to fifty kilos of personal belongings. In order to simplify the Germans' task, he should also carry enough food to last him between two and four weeks.

## 122

Newspaper and radio reports relay developments in the Protectorate to London. Sergeant Jan Kubiš listens as a parachutist friend tells him about the situation in his homeland. Murders, murders, murders. What else? Since Heydrich's arrival, every day is a day of mourning. People are deported, tortured, hanged. What monstrous new details have plunged Kubiš into this state of shock today? He shakes his head and, like a stuck record, repeats: 'How is it possible? How is it possible?'

I went to Terezín once. I wanted to see the place where the poet Robert Desnos died. Coming from Auschwitz, and passing through Buchenwald, Flossenburg, and Flöha, he ended up—on May 8, 1945—at the liberated camp of Terezín. But during the long, exhausting death marches that preceded this, he caught the typhus that would kill him. He died on June 8, 1945—in death as he was in life: free—in the arms of two young Czech nurses, a man and a woman, who loved surrealism and admired his works. Another story I could write a whole book about: the two young nurses were called Josef and Alena . . .

Terezín—Theresienstadt in German—was 'a fortified town built by the Empress of Austria to defend the Bohemian quarter from the grasp of the Prussian king Frederick II.' Which empress? I don't know. I'm borrowing this sentence—because I like it—from Pierre Volmer, Desnos's companion and the witness of his final days. Maria Theresa? Of course—Theresienstadt, the town of Theresa.

In November 1941, Heydrich turns the town into a ghetto—and the barracks into a concentration camp.

But this is not all there is to say about Terezín. Far from it.

Terezín was not like the other ghettos.

It was used as a transportation camp: the Jews there were waiting to be deported eastward, to Poland or the Baltic countries. The first convoy left for Riga on January 9, 1942: a thousand people, of whom 105 would survive. The second convoy, a week later, also went to Riga: a thousand people, 16 survivors. The third, in March: a thousand people, 7 survivors. The fourth: a thousand people, 3 survivors. There is nothing unusual in this dreadful numerical progression towards 100 percent. It is just another sign of the Germans' famous efficiency.

But while the deportations continue, Terezín has to function as a *Propagandalager*—a showcase ghetto for the eyes of foreign observers. The ghetto's inhabitants must put on a good show during visits from the International Red Cross.

At Wannsee, Heydrich announces that German Jews decorated in the First World War, German Jews over the age of sixty-five, and certain famous Jews—the *Prominenten*, too famous to disappear overnight without a trace—should be kept at Terezín, in decent conditions. This is done out of consideration for German public opinion, somewhat aghast by 1942 at the politics of the monster it has nurtured since 1933.

In order for Terezín to work as an alibi, the Jews must appear well treated. This is why the Nazis allow them to have a relatively well developed cultural life, with art and theatre encouraged—under the vigilant control of the SS, which asks everyone to wear their most winning smiles. And it works. The Red Cross representatives, impressed by their visits, report very positively on the ghetto, its culture, and the treatment of prisoners. Of the 140,000 Jews who will live in Terezín during the war, only 17,000 will survive. Kundera writes of them:

171

They were under no illusions: they were living in death's antechamber; their cultural life was exhibited by Nazi propaganda as an alibi; but should that be a reason to refuse freedom, however precarious and fraudulent? Their response was utterly clear: their creations, their art shows, their concerts, their loves, the whole array of their lives were incomparably more important than their jailers' macabre theatrics. That was their wager.

In conclusion, he adds: 'It should be ours, too.'

124

You don't need to be head of the secret services to see that President Beneš is extremely worried. London constantly evaluates the contribution to the war effort made by the various underground movements in the occupied countries. And while France—thanks to Operation Barbarossa—is benefiting from the input of Communist groups, the Czech Resistance is practically nonexistent. Since Heydrich took control, the Czech underground movements have fallen one by one, and the few that remain have largely been infiltrated by the Gestapo. This ineffectiveness puts Beneš in a very uncomfortable position: as it stands, even if the Allies are victorious, Britain will not want to listen to a discussion about revoking the Munich Agreement. This means that, even in victory, Czechoslovakia would be restored only to its

September 1938 frontiers, with the Sudetenland amputated, leaving it far from its original territorial integrity.

Something must be done. Colonel Moravec listens as his president moans bitterly. This humiliating insistence with which the British compare Czech apathy with the patriotism of the French, the Russians, even the Yugoslavs! It can't go on.

But what to do? There's no point ordering the internal Resistance to intensify its activities, given its disordered state. So the solution lies here, in Britain. Beneš's eyes must have shone, and I imagine his fist banging the table as he explained to Moravec what he was thinking. A spectacular attack on the Nazis—an assassination prepared in the greatest secrecy by his parachute commandos.

Moravec understands Beneš's reasoning. The Resistance is dying, so reinforcements must be sent from abroad—armed men, well trained and motivated, who will accomplish a mission that sends out shock waves, nationally and internationally. It must impress the Allies by showing them that Czechoslovakia cannot be counted out, and at the same time it must stimulate Czech patriotism so that the Resistance can rise once again from the ashes. I say 'Czech patriotism', but I'm pretty sure that Beneš said 'Czechoslovak'. I'm also pretty sure that he was the one who insisted that Moravec choose a Czech and a Slovak to carry out the operation. Two men to symbolize the indivisible unity of the two peoples.

But we're getting ahead of ourselves. First they must decide on a target. Moravec thinks straightaway of his namesake—Emanuel Moravec, the most collaborationist minister in the Protectorate, a sort of Czech Quisling. But his resonance is too local—no one beyond the country's borders would care. Karl Hermann Frank is better known: his ferocity and his hatred of the Czechs is legendary—and besides, he's a German, and a member of the SS. He could make a good target. Then again, if you're going to choose a German, and a member of the SS . . .

I can imagine what it must have meant—especially to Colonel Moravec, head of the Czech secret services—the idea of assassinating Obergruppenführer Heydrich: interim Protector of Bohemia and Moravia, Hangman of his people, Butcher of Prague . . . and also head of the German secret services, thus in some ways his opposite number.

Yes. If you're going to do something, do it properly. Why not Heydrich?

125

I read a brilliant book set against the backdrop of Heydrich's assassination. It's a novel written by a Czech, Jiří Weil, entitled *Mendelssohn Is on the Roof*.

The title is taken from the first chapter, which reads almost like a joke. Some Czech workmen are on the roof of the Opera House in Prague in order to take down a statue of Mendelssohn, the composer, because he's a Jew. The order has come directly from Heydrich, recently named Protector of Bohemia and Moravia, and a connoisseur of classical music. But there's a whole row of statues on the roof, and Heydrich hasn't specified which is Mendelssohn. Now, apart from Heydrich, it seems that nobody—even among the Germans—is capable of recognizing the Jewish composer. But nobody dares disturb Heydrich just for that. So the SS guards supervising the operation decide to point out the statue with the biggest nose. Well, they're looking for a Jew, aren't they? But—disaster!— the statue the workmen start to remove is actually Wagner!

The mistake is narrowly avoided, and—ten chapters later—the statue of Mendelssohn is finally pulled down. In spite of their efforts not to damage it, the Czech workmen break one of its hands when they're laying it on the ground. This comic story is based on fact: the statue of Mendelssohn really was knocked over in 1941, and (as in the novel) one of its hands was broken. I wonder if they stuck it back on again? In any case, the peregrinations of the poor SS guards in charge of removing the statue— imagined by a man who lived through this period— are an apex of burlesque typical of Czech literature, which is always imbued with this very particular kind of humour, sugarcoated yet subversive. Its patron saint is Jaroslav Hašek, immortal author of the adventures of the good soldier Švejk.

## 127

Moravec watches the parachute commandos being trained. Soldiers in combat fatigues run, jump, and shoot. He notices an agile, energetic little man who brings down all his opponents in hand-to-hand combat. He asks the instructor—an old Englishman who has served in the colonies—what this soldier is like with explosives. 'An expert,' the Englishman replies. And with firearms? 'An artist!' His name? 'Jozef Gabčík.' A Slovak-sounding name. He is summoned immediately.

127

Colonel Moravec talks to the two parachutists selected for Operation Anthropoid: Sergeant Jozef Gabčík and Sergeant Anton Svoboda—a Slovak and a Czech, just as President Beneš wished.

'You will know, from newspapers and the radio, about the insane murders being committed in our homeland. The Germans are killing the best of us. This state of affairs, however, is part and parcel of war, so there's no point moaning or crying about it. We must fight.

'In our homeland, our people have fought. But now they find themselves in a situation that limits their ability to do so anymore. It's our turn to help them, from the outside. One of the tasks that must be performed as part of this outside help will be entrusted to you. October is the month of our national holiday—the saddest since we won our independence. We must commemorate this anniversary in a dazzling, devastating way. It has been decided that this will be done by an act that will go down in history—just as the murders committed against our people have done.

'In Prague, there are two men who personify

this mass extermination: Karl Hermann Frank and Heydrich, the new arrival. In our opinion, and in the opinions of our bosses, you must see to it that one of these two pays for everything— to show them that we'll fight back, an eye for an eye. This is your mission. You must go back to our homeland, the two of you, so that you can support each other. This will be necessary because, for reasons that will become clear, this is a task you must complete without the collaboration of our compatriots. I mean to say that you won't receive any real help until your mission has been accomplished. Afterward, you will get plenty of assistance from them. You must decide yourselves how to accomplish your mission, and how long it will take you to do so. You will be equipped with everything we are able to give you. But, for your part, you must act with prudence and consideration. I don't need to repeat that your mission is of great historic importance and that the risks are high. To succeed, you must rely on your own skill. We'll talk more about this when you come back from your special training. As I've said, the task is serious. You should therefore consider it with an open and loyal heart. If you have any doubts about what I've said, tell me.'

Gabčík and Svoboda have no doubts. And if the high command was perhaps still hesitating over the choice of target (as Moravec's speech would suggest), the two of them already know which way their hearts incline them. It's the Hangman of Prague—the Butcher, the Blond Beast—who must pay.

Captain Sustr is talking to Gabčík. 'The news isn't good.' Following a parachute accident that occurred during a training jump, Svoboda—the second man of Operation Anthropoid, the Czech—is still suffering from persistent migraines. He's been sent to London to be examined by a doctor. Gabčík must complete his preparation alone, but he already knows that Anthropoid has been postponed. His partner will not go with him. 'Do you know anyone among the men here capable of replacing him?' the captain asks.

'Yes, Captain, I know someone,' Gabčík replies.

Jan Kubiš can now make his entry upon the great stage of history.

I'm now going to paint a portrait of the two heroes with much less hesitation than before, as all I need to do is quote directly from the British Army's personnel reports:

JOZEF GABCIK:
A smart and well-disciplined soldier.
Not the brain of some others, slow at acquiring knowledge.
Thoroughly reliable and very keen, with plenty of common sense.
Self-confidence in practical work but lacks it

as far as brain is concerned.

Good leader when sure of his ground and obeys orders to the last detail. He is surprisingly good at signalling.

Also appears to have technical knowledge, perhaps of use (worked in poison gas factory).

Physical training: very good
Fieldcraft: good
Close combat: very good
Weapon training: good
Explosives: good 86%
Communication: very good 12 words/min in Morse code
Reports: very good
Map reading and sketching: fair 68%
Driving:
bike yes
motorbike no
car yes

JAN KUBIS:
A good reliable soldier, quiet, comes in for a certain amount of good-natured teasing.

Physical training: very good
Fieldcraft: good
Close combat: very good
Weapon training: good
Explosives: good (90%, slow in practice and instructions)
Communication: good
Reports: good
Map reading and sketching: very good (95%)
Driving: bike motorbike car

You can't imagine my joy at discovering this

document at the army museum in Prague. Natacha is the only one who could describe it to you, as she saw me feverishly copy down these precious notes.

These reports allow us to sketch the contrasts in style and personality between the two friends: Gabčík, the small one, is a fiery ball of energy, while Kubiš, the tall one, is more thoughtful and easygoing. All the witness accounts I've found support this view. What it meant in concrete terms is that they were allocated different tasks: Gabčík got the machine gun, and Kubiš the explosives.

Other than that, what I know of Gabčík leads me to believe that the officer who wrote the report scandalously underestimated his intellectual capacities. And my feeling is corroborated by Gabčík's boss, Colonel Moravec, who writes in his memoirs:

> During the training, he showed himself to be talented, clever and cheerful, even in the most difficult situations. He was open, warm-hearted, enterprising and resourceful. A natural born leader. He overcame all the difficulties of training without ever complaining and with excellent results.

> About Kubiš, on the other hand, Moravec confirms that he was slow in his movements, but with great stamina and perseverance. His instructors noted his intelligence and imagination. He was very disciplined, discreet and reliable. He was also very calm, reserved and serious—the complete opposite of Gabčík's merry, outgoing personality.

180

This book, *Master of Spies*—picked up at the clearance sale of a bookshop in Illinois—is one of my most cherished possessions. Colonel Moravec had a real story to tell. If I'd followed my instincts, I'd have copied out the whole thing. Sometimes I feel like a character in a Borges story. But no, I'm not a character either.

## 130

'If you're lucky enough to escape death during the assassination attempt, you will have two options: try to survive inside the country, or attempt to cross the border and make your way back to the base in London. Both possibilities are extremely risky, considering the likely reaction of the Germans. But to be perfectly honest, the most probable outcome is that you will be killed on the spot.'

Moravec summons the two men separately, in order to give them the same speech. Neither shows any emotion.

For Gabčík, the mission is a war operation, and the risk of being killed goes with the job.

Kubiš thanks the colonel for having chosen him for such an important mission.

Both men say they would rather die than fall into the hands of the Gestapo.

You are Czech or Slovak. You do not like it when they tell you what to do, nor when they hurt people—that's why you decide to leave your country and join up elsewhere with your compatriots who are resisting the invader. You go north or south, through Poland or the Balkans, and—after numerous complications—you reach France by sea.

When you get there, things become even more complicated. The French make you join the Foreign Legion and send you to Algeria or Tunisia. But you do finally end up with a Czechoslovak division formed in a town full of Spanish refugees, and you fight alongside the French when they in turn are attacked by the Nazis. You fight courageously and take part in all the retreats and defeats. You cover the never-ending retreat while planes roar through the skies. You suffer through this long agony, which the French call La Débâcle, and for you it is both the first defeat and the last. In the conquered south of France everything is in chaos, but you manage to take off again and this time you land in England. In recognition of your courage in heroically resisting the invader and redeeming March 1939, President Beneš decorates you in the middle of a field. You are exhausted, and your uniform is crumpled, but you are standing next to your friend when Beneš pins a medal to your coat. And then it's Churchill himself, leaning on his walking stick, who inspects you and your comrades. You have fought the invader and in doing so saved your country's honour. But you are eager for more.

You join the special forces and are trained in various grandly named castles all over Scotland and England. You jump, you shoot, you fight, you throw grenades. You're good. You are extremely charming. You're a good soldier and the girls love you. You flirt with the young women. You drink tea at their parents' houses, and their parents think you're wonderful. You continue to train for the most important mission that any country has ever entrusted to only two men. You believe in justice and you believe in vengeance. You are brave, willing, and gifted. You are ready to die for your country. You are becoming something that grows inside you, and that begins, little by little, to be bigger than you, but at the same time you remain very much yourself. You are a simple man. You are a man.

You are Josef Gabčík or Jan Kubiš, and you are going to make history.


## 132


Each London-based government-in-exile has its own reconstituted army, and each army its own football team, and these teams play regular friendly matches. Today it's France versus Czechoslovakia. As always, there is a large crowd, made up of soldiers of all ranks from many different countries. The atmosphere is relaxed; men in coloured uniforms shout encouragements. On the terraces, in the middle of this noisy crowd, we can see Gabčík and Kubiš, wearing brown army hats and talking animatedly. Their lips move quickly, as do their hands. Their conversation, you guess, is technical and complicated. Only half watching the match, they stop talking whenever a dangerous move gets the crowd on its feet. They follow the action to see what happens, then resume their discussion with the same gusto as before, surrounded by shouting and singing.

France opens the score. The French supporters celebrate noisily.

Perhaps our two heroes' behaviour contrasts so markedly with the engrossed spectators around them that people take notice of them. In any case, they are already the subject of gossip among the soldiers of the free Czechoslovak forces. Their special mission, prepared in the greatest secrecy, gives Gabčík and Kubiš a mysterious prestige that is intensified by their refusal to answer any questions about it—even when the questioners are their oldest comrades from the evacuation of Poland or the French Foreign Legion.

Gabčík and Kubiš undoubtedly discuss their mission. On the pitch, Czechoslovakia presses for an equalizer. The number 10 gets the ball near the penalty spot and pulls his foot back to shoot, but is blocked by a French defender. The centre forward, lying in wait on the left, picks up the loose ball and fires a powerful drive under the bar. The beaten goalkeeper rolls in the dust. Czechoslovakia has equalized—the stadium explodes. Gabčík and Kubiš stop talking. They are happy. The two teams leave the pitch after the game ends in a draw.

## 133

On November 19, 1941, at a ceremony that takes place amid the golden splendour of St Vitus cathedral in the heart of Prague's Hradčany district, President Hácha solemnly presents the seven keys of the city to his new master, Heydrich. These grand, finely worked keys are kept in the same room as St Wenceslas's crown, the Czech nation's most precious jewel. There is a photo of Heydrich and Hácha standing in front of the crown, which sits on a finely embroidered cushion. It's said that on this occasion, Heydrich couldn't resist placing the crown on his head. And according to an old legend, whoever wrongfully wears the crown will die within the year, along with his eldest son.

If you look carefully at the photo, though, you'll see that Hácha, resembling an old bald owl, is staring at the crown mistrustingly, while Heydrich appears to be putting on a show of somewhat forced respectfulness. I suspect that he's not really awed by what he might very well regard as a quaint ornament of little value. In short, I wonder if this ceremony isn't a bit of a bore for him.

There is no proof that Heydrich really did put the crown on his head. I think people wanted to believe this story because it suggested, restrospectively, an act of hubris that could not go unpunished. But I doubt whether Heydrich suddenly believed himself to be in the middle of a Wagnerian opera. As evidence, I offer the fact that Heydrich handed three of the seven keys back to Hácha: a show of friendship designed to give the illusion that the Germans were prepared to share the government of the country with the Czechs. An empty symbolic gesture, to be sure, but the half-hearted nature of this exchange means that the scene loses its potential outrageousness. This is diplomacy at its most formal and least meaningful. Heydrich probably can't wait for the ceremony to be over so he can go back home and play with his kids or work on the Final Solution.

And yet . . . if you look more closely at the photo, you'll see Heydrich's right hand, partially masked by the cushion on which the crown rests. Heydrich has removed his glove—his right hand is bare, while his left is still gloved. The right hand is moving towards something. In front of the crown, half concealed by the cushion, is a sceptre. Now, even if we can't see it clearly, there are strong reasons to believe that his hand is touching, or about to touch, the sceptre. And this leads me to reinterpret the expression on Heydrich's face. Perhaps it is not boredom but covetousness. I don't believe he put the crown on his head, because we're not in a Charlie Chaplin film, but I'm equally sure that he did pick up the sceptre—to weigh it casually in his hand. A less demonstrative gesture, but symbolic all the same. And Heydrich, though pragmatic, also had a pronounced taste for the trappings of power.


## 134


Josef Gabčík and Jan Kubiš dunk biscuits in the tea made for them by their landlady, Mrs Ellison. The English all want to help with the war effort in any way they can. So when it was suggested to Mrs Ellison that she put up these two boys, she agreed with pleasure. Particularly as they're so charming. I don't know how or where he learned the language, but Gabčík is fluent in English. Talkative and outgoing, he leads the conversation, and Mrs Ellison is enchanted. Kubiš is more reserved and less at ease with the language, but his good-natured smile and his kindness go down well with the hostess. 'You'll have a bit more tea?' The two men, seated side by side on the same sofa, accept politely. They've suffered so many hardships in the past that they never pass up the opportunity to eat and drink. They let the biscuits melt in their mouths. Suddenly, the doorbell rings. Mrs Ellison gets up, but the door opens before she can get there and two young women appear.

'Come in, darlings, I'll introduce you!' Gabčík and Kubiš stand up. 'Lorna, Edna, this is Josef and Jan—they're going to live here for a while.' The two young girls move forward, smiling. 'Gentlemen, allow me to introduce my daughters.' At this moment the two soldiers must say to themselves that sometimes, after all, there is a bit of justice in this mean, cruel world.


135


My mission involves being sent to my native country with another member of the Czechoslovak army in order to commit an act of sabotage or of terrorism in a place and according to methods which will depend upon the circumstances that we find there. I will do all that is in my power to obtain the results desired, not only in my native country but also beyond it. I will work with all my heart and soul to be able to successfully complete this mission, for which I have volunteered.

On December 1, 1941, Gabčík and Kubiš sign what looks like a standard document. I wonder if it was used for all the parachutists of all the armies based in Great Britain.

## 136

Albert Speer, Hitler's architect and the minister of armaments, should have been Heydrich's kind of man. Refined, elegant, charming, intelligent, he operates at a cultural level markedly higher than most Nazi dignitaries. He is neither a chicken farmer like Himmler, nor a crank like Rosenberg, nor a fat pig like Göring and Bormann.

Speer is passing through Prague. Heydrich shows him around the city in his car. He takes him to the Opera House, where Mendelssohn's statue is no longer on the roof. Speer shares his taste for classical music. In spite of this, the two men don't like each other. Speer, a distinguished intellectual, sees Heydrich as a cultivated thug who unblinkingly carries out Hitler's dirty work. As for Heydrich, he regards Speer as a competent man whose qualities he admires but who is nonetheless a snobbish, pampered civilian. What bothers him about Speer is that he *doesn't* get his hands dirty.

Speer, in his capacity as minister of armaments, has been sent by Göring to demand that Heydrich supply sixteen thousand extra Czech workers for the German war effort. Heydrich does his best to fulfil this request as quickly as possible. He explains to Speer that the Czechs have already been tamed—in contrast with France, for example, which is overrun by Communist Resistance fighters and saboteurs.

The line of official Mercedes cars crosses the Charles Bridge. Speer goes into raptures over the tracery on the Gothic and Baroque buildings. While the streets rush past, the architect in Speer gets the upper hand over the minister. He dreams of various urban developments: this vast unexploited area in the Letna district, for instance, could be used to build a new headquarters for the German government. Heydrich doesn't say a word, but he's not keen on the idea of being forced to leave the castle, where he can think of himself as a monarch. In Strahov, near the monastery, which houses one of the most beautiful libraries in Europe, Speer envisions a great German university rising from the earth. He has many ideas for completely redeveloping the banks of the Moldau, and he recommends that the replica of the Eiffel Tower—which sits imposingly on Petřín, the highest hill in Prague—be demolished. Heydrich tells Speer of his desire to make Prague the cultural capital of the German Reich. He can't resist mentioning, with pride, the piece of music he has chosen to open the coming musical season: an opera composed by his father. 'Excellent idea,' Speer says politely. (He's never heard any of Papa Heydrich's works.) 'And when will that happen?' May 26. Speer's wife, in the second car, examines Lina's appearance. The two spouses give each other the cold shoulder, apparently. For two hours, the black Mercedes continue to criss-cross the city's main streets. By the end of his visit, Speer has already forgotten the date of Heydrich Senior's opera.

It's May 26, 1942. The day before . . .

## 137

Gabčík the Slovak and Kubiš the Moravian have never been to Prague, and in fact this is one of the reasons they were chosen. If they don't know anyone, they won't be recognized. But their lack of local knowledge is also a handicap, so part of their intensive training involves studying maps of their beautiful capital.

Gabčík and Kubiš pore over a map of Prague, memorizing the main squares and streets. At this point, they have never set foot upon the Charles Bridge or the Old Town Square, the hills of Petřín and Strahov, the banks of the Vltava, Wenceslas Square or Charles Square, the courtyard of Hradčany Castle, or the cemetery of Vyšehrad Castle, where Vitezslav Nezval—author of the immortal collection of poems *Prague with Fingers of Rain*—is not yet buried. They have never laid eyes on the sad islands in the river with their swans and ducks, nor the bluish towers of Týn Church, nor the Astronomical Clock on City Hall with its little automated figures that move every hour. They still haven't drunk a hot chocolate in the Café Louvre or a beer in the Café Slavia. They have not been

190

eyed scornfully by the statue of the iron man in Platnéřská Street. For now, the lines on the map evoke nothing more than names learned as children or military objectives. To see them studying the city's topography, you might easily believe them—were it not for the uniforms—to be vacationers, planning their trip with particular care.

## 138

Heydrich receives a delegation of Czech yokels. He is not very welcoming. He listens in silence to their grovelling promises of cooperation, then explains to them that Czech farmers are saboteurs. They fiddle with their inventories of livestock and grain. To what end? For the black market, obviously. Heydrich has already begun executing butchers and wholesalers, but to have any real effect in combating this scourge that starves the people he must gain total control of agricultural production. So Heydrich threatens them: all farmers who fail to give a precise account of their production will have their farms confiscated. The yokels are stunned. They know that if Heydrich decided to burn them alive in the Old Town Square, no one would come to their aid. To be complicit in the black market is to take food from the mouths of the people, and on this point the people support Heydrich's laws. The Hangman of Prague thus achieves a political masterstroke: creating a reign of terror and applying a popular law *at the same time*.

As soon as the yokels have gone, Karl Hermann Frank—his secretary of state—wants to start drawing up a list of farms to be confiscated. Heydrich tells him to calm down. The only farms that will be confiscated are those run by farmers judged unfit for Germanization.

Come on—this isn't the Soviet Union, you know!

## 139

Perhaps the scene took place in Heydrich's wood-panelled office. Heydrich is busying himself with his dossiers, when there's a knock at the door. A man in uniform enters the room—an expression of terror on his face, a piece of paper in his hand.

'Herr Obergruppenführer, the news has just arrived! Germany has declared war on the United States!'

Heydrich doesn't blink. The man hands him the message. He reads it in silence.

A long moment passes.

'What are your orders, Herr Obergruppen-führer?'

'Take a detachment of men to the train station and remove the statue of Wilson.'

'...'

'I don't expect to see that piece of crap there tomorrow morning. Do it, Major Pomme!'

## 140

President Beneš knows that he will have to face up to his reponsibilities. Come what may, he must prepare for the mass reprisals that the Germans will undoubtedly unleash if Operation Anthropoid succeeds. To govern is to choose, and the decision has been made. But making a decision is one thing; taking responsibility for it is something else. And Beneš—who founded Czechoslovakia with Tomáš Masaryk in 1918 and who, twenty years later, was unable to avoid the disaster of Munich—knows that the pressure of history is enormous, and that the judgement of history is the most terrible of all. All his efforts from now on are aimed at restoring the integrity of the country he created. Unfortunately, the liberation of Czechoslovakia is not in his hands. The RAF and the Red Army will decide its fate. Admittedly, Beneš has been able to provide seven times more pilots for the RAF than the French have. And the record for the highest number of enemy planes shot down is held by Josef František: the ace of British aviation is a Czech. Beneš is more than a little proud of this. But he also knows that in times of war, the power of a head of state is measured only by the numbers of his divisions. For this reason, his activities have been almost entirely reduced to a humiliating diplomacy: he must give pledges of goodwill to the only two powers still resisting the Germans, without any certainty that those two powers will end up victorious. It's true that, confronted by German bombardments in 1940, Britain was able to ride the blow and win the air battle—for the moment at least. It's also true that the Red Army, having been pushed all the way back to Moscow, was able to stop the enemy advance just before it reached its goal. Britain and the USSR, having each barely avoided collapse, are today in a position to fight back against the

Reich. But this is late 1941. The Wehrmacht is almost at the zenith of its power. It still hasn't suffered any significant defeat to dent the myth of its invincibility. Stalingrad is still far off—we are a long way from seeing images of defeated German soldiers, eyes lowered to the snow. All Beneš can do is gamble on an uncertain outcome. The entry of the United States into the war is naturally a source of great hope, but the GIs have yet to cross the Atlantic and they are still so busy fighting the Japanese that they pay no attention to the fate of a small country in central Europe. Thus Beneš makes his own version of Pascal's wager: his god is a god with two heads—Britain and the USSR—and he bets on their survival. But to keep two heads happy at the same time is not easy. Britain and the USSR are, of course, allies. And Churchill, despite his inborn anticommunism, will show an indestructible loyalty to the Soviet Union, in military terms, throughout the war. As for what happens after the war—*if* the war ends and *if* the Allies win —well, that is obviously another story.

With Anthropoid, Beneš is attempting a great coup to impress these two European giants. London has given logistical backing and collaborated closely. But Beneš has to be careful not to offend the Russians' pride: that's why he has decided to inform Moscow of the launch of the operation. So the pressure is now at its height: Churchill and Stalin are waiting. The future of Czechoslovakia is in their hands; best not disappoint them. Above all, if it's the Red Army that liberates his country, Beneš wants Stalin to regard him as a credible representative—all the more so given his fears of the Czech Communists' influence.

194

Beneš is probably thinking about all this when his secretary comes to warn him:

'Mr President, Colonel Moravec is here with two young men. He says he's got an appointment, but there's nothing in today's schedule about it.'

'Let them in.'

Gabčík and Kubiš have been brought by taxi through the streets of London without any idea where they were going, and now they are received by the president himself. On his desk, the first thing they notice is a little tin replica of a Spitfire. They salute and stand to attention. Beneš wanted to meet them before their departure but didn't want to leave any official record of their visit—because to govern is also to take precautions. The two men stand before him. While he talks to them of their mission's historic importance, he observes them carefully. He's struck by how young they look—Kubiš especially, although he's only one year younger than Gabčík—and by the touching simplicity of their determination. For several minutes, he forgets all the geopolitical considerations. He no longer thinks of Britain and the USSR, nor of Munich, or Masaryk, or the Communists, or the Germans. He hardly even thinks of Heydrich. He is completely absorbed in the contemplation of these two soldiers, these two boys whom he knows—whatever the outcome of their mission—haven't got a chance in hell of getting out alive.

I don't know what his last words to them are. 'Good luck,' or 'God keep you,' or 'The free world is counting on you,' or 'You carry in your hands the honour of Czechoslovakia' . . . something like that, probably. According to Moravec, the president has tears in his eyes when Gabčík and Kubiš leave his office. Perhaps he has a premonition of the terrible future. The impassive little Spitfire keeps its nose in the air.

## 141

Since joining her husband in Prague, Lina Heydrich is in heaven. She writes in her autobiography: 'I am a princess and I live in a fairy-tale land.'

How come?

First, because Prague really is a fairy-tale city. Not for nothing did Walt Disney take his inspiration for the queen's castle in *Sleeping Beauty* from Týn Church.

Next, because in Prague she really is the queen. Overnight her husband has become almost a head of state. In this fairy-tale land, he is Hitler's viceroy and his wife shares all the honours of his rank. As the Protector's spouse, Lina enjoys an esteem that her parents—the von Ostens—never dreamed of, for her or for themselves. How long ago it seems that her father wanted to break off her engagement because Reinhard had been kicked out of the navy. Now, thanks to him, Lina's life is an endless series of receptions, inaugurations, and official events where everyone shows her the greatest deference. I see her in a photo taken at a concert at the Rudolfinum to celebrate the anniversary of Mozart's birth. Dolled up in a white evening dress, weighed down with rings, bracelets, and earrings, surrounded by men in smoking jackets all currying favour with her husband, who stands by her side . . .

smiling, relaxed, and sure of herself, she stands with one hand resting chastely on top of the other and with a look of ecstatic happiness on her face.

But it's not only Prague. From now on, her husband's position allows her to mix with the Reich's high society. Himmler is a longstanding friend, but she also knows the Goebbelses and the Speers, and she's even had the supreme honour of meeting the Führer, who, seeing her on her husband's arm, remarked: 'What a handsome couple!' Oh yes, she's part of the upper crust now. And Hitler pays her compliments!

And she has her own castle: a palace confiscated from a Jew, twelve miles north of Prague, surrounded by a vast estate. Wildly enthusiastic, she gets to work on doing it up. She is the lady of the manor but, like the queen in *Sleeping Beauty*, she is also a nasty piece of work. She treats her staff harshly, and insults everyone when she's in a bad mood—and when she's in a good mood, she doesn't speak to anyone. In order to perform the enormous amount of work required for her princely home, she makes use of the abundant manpower supplied by the concentration camps. She doesn't treat these workers any better than the camps do. She supervises the renovation work dressed as a horsewoman, a riding crop in her hand. Hers is a reign of terror, sadism, and eroticism.

Apart from all that, she looks after her three children and congratulates herself on how affectionate Reinhard is with them. He particularly adores the youngest one, Silke. So much so that he impregnates his wife for the fourth time. Long gone are the days when she would sleep with Schellenberg, his right-hand man. Long gone the days when he was never home. Here in Prague, her husband returns almost every evening. He makes love to her, goes horse riding, and plays with the children.

Gabčík and Kubiš are going home in a Halifax bomber. But before that there are certain formalities to be taken care of. From behind his desk, a British NCO asks them to undress. No matter where in the Czech countryside they land, it's not a good idea to look like British parachutists. They take off their uniforms. 'Completely,' adds the NCO as they stand there in their underwear. Used to discipline, the two men obey. So they're stark naked when a choice of clothing is spread out before them. Without losing any of his very British, very military dryness, the NCO makes his pitch like a sales assistant at Harrods, proudly presenting his products: 'Suits made in Czechoslovakia. Shirts made in Czechoslovakia. Underwear made in Czechoslovakia. Shoes made in Czechoslovakia. Please check your size. Ties made in Czechoslovakia. Choose a colour. Cigarettes made in Czechoslovakia. Several brands available. Matches made in . . . Toothpaste made in . . .'

Once they're dressed, the two men are given false papers with all the necessary stamps.

Now they are ready. Colonel Moravec waits for them next to the Halifax, whose engines are already running. There are five other parachutists in the plane with them, but they are going to different places on different missions. Moravec shakes Kubiš's hand and wishes him good luck. But when he turns towards Gabčík, the little Slovak asks if they can have a quick word in private. Moravec cringes inwardly. He fears a last-minute withdrawal and suddenly regrets what he said to the two boys when he first chose them that they shouldn't hesitate to tell him frankly if they didn't feel up to the task. He'd even added that there was nothing shameful in changing your mind. He still believes this, but standing next to the waiting airplane is not the ideal time to hear it. He'd have to get Kubiš off the plane and delay the departure while he found a replacement for Gabčík. The mission would be postponed till God knows when. Gabčík begins with a few carefully phrased words that don't bode well: 'Colonel, I'm very embarrassed to ask this . . .' But what comes next allays his boss's fears: 'I've left an unpaid bill for ten pounds at our restaurant. Could you possibly pay it for me?' Moravec is so relieved that he says in his memoirs he could do nothing more than nod. Gabčík shakes his hand. 'You can count on us, Colonel. We'll fulfil our mission exactly as ordered.' Those were his last words before disappearing into the cabin.

143

The two men wrote down their final wishes just before they took off, and I have these magnificent, hastily scribbled documents in front of me now. Covered in inkstains and crossings-out, they are almost identical. Both are dated December 28,

1941; both are divided in two parts; both have a few extra lines added to them, written diagonally across the page. Gabčík and Kubiš ask that their families be looked after in the event of their deaths. To that end, each gives an address—in Slovakia, in Moravia. Both men are orphans, and neither has a wife or child. But I know Gabčík has sisters, and Kubiš brothers. Both ask that their English girlfriends be informed if they die. Lorna Ellison is named in Gabčík's will, and Edna Ellison in Kubiš's. The two men had grown as close as brothers, so they went out with sisters. A photo of Lorna has reached us, slipped inside Gabčík's military records—a young woman with dark curly hair. He will never see her again.

### 144

I have no evidence that Gabčík and Kubiš's clothes were provided by the British SOE (Special Operations Executive). In fact, it's more likely that this was dealt with by Moravec's Czech services. So there's no reason why the NCO who looks after them should be British. Oh, what a pain . . .

### 145

The general kommissar of Byelorussia, based in Minsk, complains about the actions of Heydrich's Einsatzgruppen. He deplores the fact that the systematic extermination of the Jews is depriving him of much-needed manpower. He also protests to Heydrich about decorated Jewish war veterans being deported to his ghetto in Minsk. He submits a list of Jews to be freed while denouncing the Einsatzgruppen's indiscriminate killings. This is the reply he receives:

> You will agree with me that, in the third year of the war, there are more important tasks for the war effort—both for the police and the security services—than running around trying to look after the needs of the Jews, wasting time drawing up lists, and distracting all my colleagues from more urgent business. If I ordered an inquiry into the people on your list, it would only be to prove—once and for all, and in writing—that such attacks are baseless. I regret still having to provide this kind of justification, six and a half years after the decree of the Nuremberg racial laws.

Well, you can't accuse him of not being clear.

## 146

That night, at an altitude of two thousand feet, the huge Halifax aircraft roared out of the sky above the winter countryside of Czechoslovakia. The four airscrews churned through the drifts of low broken cloud, flailing them back against the wet black flanks of the machine, and in the cold fuselage Jan Kubis and Josef Gabchik stared down at their homeland through the open, coffin-shaped exit hatch cut in the floor.

This is the opening paragraph of Alan Burgess's novel *Seven Men at Daybreak*, written in 1960. And from those first lines, I know that he hasn't written the book I want to write. I don't know how much of their homeland Gabčík and Kubiš could see at an altitude of more than two thousand feet in that black December night. As for the image of the coffin, I'd prefer to avoid such obvious metaphors.

Automatically they checked the release boxes and static lines of their parachute harnesses. Within minutes they were to plunge down through that darkness to the earth below, knowing that they were the first parachutists to come back to Czechoslovakia, and knowing also that their mission was as unique and hazardous as any that had yet been conceived.

I know everything it's possible to know about this flight. I know what Gabčík and Kubiš had in their backpacks: a pocketknife, a pistol with two magazines and twelve cartridges, a cyanide pill, a piece of chocolate, meat-extract tablets, razor blades, a fake ID card, and some Czech currency. I know they were wearing civilian clothes made in Czechoslovakia. I know that, following orders, they didn't say anything to their fellow parachutists during the flight apart from 'Hello' and 'Good Luck.' I know that their fellow parachutists suspected they were being sent to kill Heydrich. I know that it was Gabčík who most impressed the air dispatcher during the voyage. I know that they had to quickly make their wills before takeoff. I know the names of each member of the two other teams who accompanied them, along with their respective missions. And I also know each man's fake identity. Gabčík and Kubiš, for example, were called Zdenek Vyskocil and Ota Navratil, and according to their false papers they were, respectively, a locksmith and a labourer. I know pretty much everything that can be known about this flight and I refuse to write a sentence like:

'Automatically they checked the release boxes and static lines of their parachute harnesses.' Even if, without a doubt, they did exactly that.

'The taller of the two, Jan Kubiš, was twenty-seven years old and nearly six foot tall. He had blond hair and deep-set grey eyes that watched the world steadily . . .' et cetera. I'll stop there. It's a shame that Burgess wasted his time with clichés like this, because his book is undeniably well researched. I found two glaring errors—concerning Heydrich's wife, whom he called Inga rather than Lina, and the colour of his Mercedes, which he insists is dark green rather than black. I also spotted two dubious stories that I suspect Burgess of having invented, including a dark tale of swastikas branded on buttocks with a hot iron. But in other respects I learned a great deal about Gabčík and Kubiš's life in Prague during the months before the assassination. It must be said that Burgess had an advantage over me: only twenty years after the events, he was able to talk to living witnesses. Yes, a few of them did survive.

So, to cut a long story short, they jumped.

According to Eduard Husson, a reputable academic who is writing a biography of Heydrich, everything went wrong right from the beginning.

Gabčík and Kubiš are dropped a long way from the target area. They should have landed near Pilsen but actually end up a few miles from Prague. Now, you may say: well, that's where the operation will take place, so in a way they've actually gained time. But such thinking just goes to show how little you know about secret operations. Their contacts in the Resistance are waiting for them in Pilsen. They don't have an address in Prague. The people in Pilsen are supposed to make the introductions for them. So they are close to Prague, where they need to get to, but only after they've passed through Pilsen. They feel the absurdity of this roundabout journey every bit as much as you do, but they know it's necessary all the same.

They feel it once they know where they are, but at this precise moment they don't have the faintest idea. They land in a graveyard. They don't know where to hide the parachutes, and Gabčík is limping badly because he's fractured a toe landing on his native soil. They walk blindly and leave tracks. They bury the parachutes quickly under a snowdrift. The sun, they know, will soon rise: they are dangerously exposed and must find somewhere to hide.

They find a rocky shelter in a quarry. Protected from the snow and the cold but not from the Gestapo, they know they can't stay here—but they don't know where else to go. Strangers in their own land, lost, injured, and undoubtedly already the subject of a search—the Germans couldn't have failed to hear the plane's engines—the two men decide to wait. What else can they do? They consult the map, but it's hard to imagine what they're hoping for. To pinpoint the location of this tiny quarry? Their mission, hardly even begun, is already under threat of being aborted. Or, if we assume that they will never be discovered (which is a ridiculous supposition), of never getting started at all.

Anyway, they are discovered.

It's a gamekeeper who finds them, early that morning. He heard the plane in the night, he found the parachutes in the graveyard, he followed their tracks in the snow. Now he enters the quarry. And, coughing, says to them: 'Hello, lads!'

According to Eduard Husson, everything went wrong from the beginning, but they also had some good luck. The gamekeeper is a decent man. He knows he's risking his life by doing so, but he's going to help them.

149

This gamekeeper is the first link in a long chain of Resistance fighters who will lead our two heroes to

Prague, and to the Moravecs' apartment.

The Moravec family consists of the father, the mother, and the youngest son, Ata. The eldest son is in England, flying a Spitfire. They are namesakes of Colonel Moravec, but not blood relations. Like him, however, they are resisting the German occupation.

And they're not the only ones. Gabčík and Kubiš will meet lots of ordinary people ready to risk their lives in order to help them.

## 150

I'm fighting a losing battle. I can't tell this story the way it should be told. This whole hotchpotch of characters, events, dates, and the infinite branching of cause and effect—and these people, these real people who actually existed. I'm barely able to mention a tiny fragment of their lives, their actions, their thoughts. I keep banging my head against the wall of history. And I look up and see, growing all over it—ever higher and denser, like a creeping ivy—the unmappable pattern of causality.

I examine a map of Prague, marking the locations of the families who helped and sheltered the parachutists. Almost all of them paid with their lives—men, women, and children. The Svatoš family, a few feet from the Charles Bridge; the Ogoun family, near the castle; the Novak, Moravec, Zelenka, and Fafek families, all farther east. Each member of each of these families would deserve his or her own book—an account of their involvement with the Resistance until the tragic dénouement of

Mauthausen. How many forgotten heroes sleep in history's great cemetery? Thousands, millions of Fafeks and Moravecs, of Novaks and Zelenkas...

The dead are dead, and it makes no difference to them whether I pay homage to their deeds. But for us, the living, it does mean something. Memory is of no use to the remembered, only to those who remember. We build ourselves with memory and console ourselves with memory.

No reader could possibly retain this list of names, so why write it? For you to remember them, I would have to turn them into characters. Unfair, but there you go. I know already that only the Moravecs, and perhaps the Fafeks, will find a place in my story. The Svatošes, the Novaks, the Zelenkas—not to mention all those whose names or existence I'm unaware of—will return to their oblivion. But in the end a name is just a name. I think of them all. I want to tell them. And if no one hears me, that doesn't matter. Not to them, and not to me. One day, perhaps, someone in need of solace will write the story of the Novaks and the Svatošes, of the Zelenkas and the Fafeks.

## 151

On January 8, 1942, Gabčík (limping) and Kubiš walk upon Prague's sacred earth for the first time. I'm sure they marvel at the city's Baroque beauty. First, though, they must deal with the three great problems facing any secret mission: accommodation, provisions, and identification. London has equipped them with fake ID cards, but it's not enough—far from it. In the Protectorate of Bohemia and Moravia in 1942, you must be able to produce a work permit. And, above all, if you are stopped in the daytime hanging around in the streets—which will often be the case for Gabčík and Kubiš during the coming months—you must have a very good reason not to be working. The Resistance talks to the doctor who treats Gabčík's foot: he diagnoses an ulcer in Gabčík's duodenum, and for Kubiš an inflamed gallbladder, thus establishing the two men's inability to work. So their papers are in order and they've got money. Now they must find a place to stay. But as they will soon discover to their pleasure, there is no shortage of people willing to help them even in these dark times.

## 152

Don't believe everything you're told—especially when the Nazis are telling you. They tend to be wrong in one of two ways. Either, like big fat Göring, they are guilty of wishful thinking, or—like Goebbels Trismegistus (called 'the human loudspeaker' by Joseph Roth)—they lie shamelessly for propagandist ends. And quite often they do both at the same time.

Heydrich is not immune to this Nazi trait. When he claims to have decapitated and neutralized the Czech Resistance, he probably believes what he's saying—and it's not completely false. Even so, it's a somewhat hollow boast. On the night of December 28, 1941, when Gabčík injures himself in a clumsy collision with his native soil, the state of the Resistance in the Protectorate is worrying but not entirely hopeless. They still have a few cards up their sleeve.

For a start, Tri kralové ('the Three Kings'—the unified organization of Czech Resistance movements) is still operational, despite taking some heavy blows. The three kings are the heads of this organization: three former Czechoslovak army officers. On Heydrich's arrival in January 1942, two of them are put out of action: one is shot, the other tortured in a Gestapo jail. But that leaves one—Václav Morávek (with a *k* at the end, thankfully, so he can't be confused with Colonel Moravec, nor with the Moravec family, nor with Emanuel Moravec, the minister of education). He wears gloves all year round because one of his fingers was severed sliding down a lightning conductor to avoid a Gestapo patrol. The last of the three kings is intensely active in coordinating what remains of his network, and continues to risk his life. He is waiting for what his organization asked for months before—the arrival of the parachutists from London.

Morávek is also the conduit for the incredible information sent to London by one of the greatest spies of the Second World War—a high-level German Abwehr officer called Paul Thümmel (code name A54; alias René). He alone was able to warn Colonel Moravec of the Nazi invasions of Czechoslovakia, of Poland, of France (in May 1940), of Great Britain (planned for June 1940), and of the USSR (in June 1941). Unfortunately, the countries in question were not always able or willing to heed such warnings. But the quality of the information greatly impressed London, and it was only through Morávek that it could arrive—because A54 was based in Prague and, prudently, wanted to deal with only one Allied agent. So he is one of Beneš's trump cards, and the president spends whatever it takes to keep him onside.

At the other end of the chain are the ordinary Resistance fighters—little people like you or me, except that they are willing to risk death by hiding comrades, storing materials, and delivering messages. They form a significant Czech shadow army, which can still be counted upon.

Gabčík and Kubiš may only be two men, charged with fulfilling a daunting mission. But they are not alone.

## 153

In a Prague apartment in the Smichov district, two men wait. They jump when the bell rings. One of them gets up and opens the door. A man walks in, quite tall for the time. It's Kubiš.

'I am Ota,' he says.

'And I'm Jindra,' one of the men replies.

Jindra is the name of one of the most active internal Resistance groups, organized by a sport and physical culture association, the Sokols.

They pour tea for the newcomer. A heavy silence is finally broken by the man who introduced himself in the organization's name:

'I would like you to notice that the house is guarded, and that we each have something in our pocket.'

Kubiš smiles and takes a pistol from his jacket.

(In fact, he's got another one up his sleeve.)

'I like toys too,' he says.

'Where have you come from?'

'I can't tell you.'

'Why?'

'Our mission is secret.'

'But you've already told lots of people that you've come from England.'

'So what?'

A silence, presumably.

'Don't be surprised that we don't trust you. There are many double agents in this country.'

Kubiš says nothing. He doesn't know these people. He may need their help, but he's clearly decided that he's not answerable to them.

'Do you know any Czech officers in England?'

Kubiš agrees to name a few. He responds more or less graciously to some other potentially embarrassing questions. The second man intervenes. He shows Kubiš a photo of his son-in-law, who's gone to London. Kubiš recognizes him, or doesn't recognize him, but he seems at ease because he is. The man who called himself Jindra speaks again:

'Are you from Bohemia?'

'No, from Moravia.'

'What a coincidence—me too!'

Another silence. Kubiš knows he's being tested.

'Could you tell me whereabouts?'

'Near Třebíč,' Kubiš replies grumpily.

'I know that area. What would you say is unusual in the train station at Vladislav?'

'There's a beautiful clump of rosebushes. I guess the station boss likes flowers.'

The two men start to relax. Kubiš adds:

211

'Don't be offended by my silence. All I can tell you is the mission's code name: Anthropoid.'

What's left of the Czech Resistance tends to be guilty of wishful thinking. For once, it's not wrong.

'You've come to kill Heydrich?' asks Jindra. Kubiš is stunned:

'How do you know that?'

The ice is broken. The three men drink more tea. Now everyone who's anyone in the Prague Resistance will be at the service of the two parachutists from London.

## 154

For fifteen years, I hated Flaubert. I held him responsible for a certain kind of French literature— devoid of grandeur and imagination, content to portray mediocrity, wallowing in the most boring sort of realism, revelling in the very petit bourgeois universe it claims to denounce. And then I read *Salammbô*, which immediately became one of my ten favourite books.

When I had the idea of going back to the Middle Ages to sketch the origins of Czech–German hostilities, I wanted to find a few examples of historical novels whose action takes place before the modern era. I thought again of Flaubert.

While composing *Salammbô*, Flaubert worries in his letters: 'It's History, I know that. But if a novel is as boring as a scientific book . . .' He also felt that he was writing 'in a deplorable academic style,' and then 'what bothers [him] is the psychological aspect of [his] story,' all the more so as he must 'make people think *in a language in which they never thought!* ' Regarding research: 'When I research a word or an idea, I let my mind wander into infinite daydreams . . .' This problem goes hand in hand with that of veracity: 'As for my archaeology, it will be "probable", that's all. As long as no one can *prove* that what I've written is nonsense, that's all I ask.' There I'm at a disadvantage: it's easier to be proved wrong about the registration number of a Mercedes in the 1940s than the harnessing of an elephant in the third century before Christ.

Even so, I am comforted by the idea that Flaubert, long before me, writing his masterpiece, felt this same anguish and asked himself these same questions. I am also reassured when he writes:

'Our worth should be measured by our aspirations more than our works.' That means I'm allowed to make a mess of my book. Everything should come together more quickly now.

## 155

Unbelievable—I've just found another novel about the assassination! It's called *Like a Man*, and it's by a certain David Chacko. The title is supposed to be a rough translation of the Greek word *anthropoid*. The book is extremely well researched. I get the impression the author has utilized everything currently known about Heydrich and the attack—even some fairly obscure (and sometimes questionable) theories such as the hypothesis that the bomb contained poison. I was greatly impressed by the mass of details he's gathered and I'm inclined to think they're authentic, as I haven't found a single one that I know to be false. This has forced me to qualify my opinion of *Seven Men at Daybreak*, the Alan Burgess novel I had previously thought rather fanciful. I had been particularly sceptical about the swastika branded on Kubiš's ass. I also condescendingly picked up on a glaring error regarding the colour of Heydrich's Mercedes, which the author claimed was green. But David Chacko's novel agrees with Burgess's on both points. And since I haven't otherwise been able to spot a single mistake in his book—even with very specific details that I had imagined, in a fit of slightly delirious pride, were perhaps known only to me—I am bound to trust what he writes. Suddenly I start questioning myself. But this Mercedes—it was black, I'm sure. Not only in the army museum at Prague, where the car was exhibited, but also in the numerous photos that I checked. Obviously, in a black-and-white photo, it would be easy to confuse black with dark green. And admittedly there is some controversy over the exhibited Mercedes: the museum claims it's the original, but certain people dispute this, saying that it's been re-created (with the blown tyre and the smashed rear right door) as an exact replica. But even if it is a replica, surely they would have made sure they got the colour right! Anyway, I'm probably attaching too much importance to what is, at the end of the day, just a background detail. I know that. In fact it's a classic symptom of neurosis. I must be anal-retentive. Let's move on . . .

When Chacko writes: 'The castle could be entered in several ways, but Heydrich, the showman, always came and went by the main

214

gate, where the guard was,' I am fascinated by his certainty. I wonder: 'How does he know? How can he be so sure?'

Another example. This is a dialogue between Gabčík and Heydrich's Czech chef. The chef is telling Gabčík about the security surrounding Heydrich in his own house. 'Heydrich scorns protection, but the SS take their job seriously. He's their leader, you know. They treat him like a god. He looks like they say they all want to look. The Blond Beast. They actually call him that in the service. You won't be able to truly understand Germans until you realize they mean it as a compliment.'

Chacko's art resides in his skill at integrating historical fact—Heydrich really was nicknamed the Blond Beast—into psychologically acute dialogue. It is through dialogue that he turns history into fiction. And I must say, loath as I am to use this method, that he does it very successfully: I was really gripped by several passages. When Gabčík replies to the chef, who has just given him a terrifying description of Heydrich, 'Don't worry. He's human. There's one way to prove that,' I cheered as if I were watching a Western.

Obviously, the scenes in which he describes Gabčík being given a blow job in the middle of the living room, or Kubiš jerking off in the bathroom, are probably invented. I *know* that Chacko *doesn't know* if Gabčík was given a blow job, nor (if he was) in what circumstances, and he certainly doesn't know where or when Kubiš jerked off: this kind of scene, by its very nature, has no witnesses— well, with a few rare exceptions—and Kubiš had no reason to tell anyone about his little jerk-off

215

sessions, and he didn't keep a diary. But the author deals perfectly with the psychological dimension of his novel, which is full of interior monologues, and makes no claims to exact historical accuracy. Indeed, the book opens with the formula: 'Any similarity of characters or events to real persons or actual events is coincidental.' In other words, Chacko wanted to write a novel—well researched, admittedly, but without being a slave to the facts. So he bases his tale on a true story, fully exploiting its novelistic elements, blithely inventing when that helps the narration, but without being answerable to history. He's a skilful cheat. A trickster. Well . . . a novelist, basically.

Now that I look at the photos more carefully, I'm unsure about the colour. The exhibition was several years ago, so perhaps my memory is betraying me. But I really see it black, that Mercedes! Maybe my imagination is playing games with me? When the time comes, I'll just have to decide. Or verify the truth. One way or the other.


# 156

I asked Natacha about the Mercedes. She remembers it being black as well.


# 157

The more powerful Heydrich grows, the more he behaves like Hitler. Now, like the Führer, he tortures his colleagues with long, impassioned speeches on the destiny of the world. Frank, Eichmann, Böhme, Müller, and Schellenberg listen quietly to their boss's delirious commentaries as he bends over a map of the world:

'The Scandinavians, the Dutch, and the Flemish belong to the Germanic race . . . the Middle East and Africa will be shared with the Italians . . . the Russians will be driven back beyond the Urals and their country will be colonized by peasant soldiers . . . the Urals will be our eastern border. Our new recruits will do their national service there and they'll be trained in guerrilla warfare as border guards. If anyone's not willing to fight tooth and nail, I'll let them go, I won't do anything to them . . .'

Intoxicated by his own power, Heydrich—like his master—already imagines himself master of the world. But there's still a war to be won, Russia to be conquered, and a long list of heirs to supplant. Heydrich's star may still be rising through the black night of the Reich, but even looking at it optimistically, all of this is very premature.

The battle between Hitler's potential successors has always been ferocious. Where does Heydrich fit in, stuck out here in this backwater? Many people, fascinated by his evil aura and using his meteoric rise as evidence, argue that he would have ended up succeeding (or deposing) the Führer.

But in 1942, the road to the highest peak is still long. More than ever, Heydrich is being wooed by the first rank of pretenders. Göring, Bormann, Goebbels—all try to lure him away from Himmler, who jealously watches over his right-hand man. Even if his new role in Prague and his responsibility for the Final Solution have given him an added dimension, Heydrich is not yet quite at their level. Göring is still officially the regime's number two and Hitler's designated successor, even if he's fallen well behind in the race to succeed Hitler. Bormann has replaced Rudolf Hess at the head of the Party and by Hitler's side. The propaganda machine controlled by Goebbels is, more than ever, propping up the regime. Himmler is in charge of the Waffen SS, whose combat divisions are covering themselves in glory on every front, and he is also in total control of the system of concentration camps—two areas where Heydrich has no power.

Even if his position as Protector now allows him to short-circuit the hierarchy above him by appealing directly to Hitler, Heydrich still hasn't decided to supplant Himmler. However insignificant Himmler may look, Heydrich knows his boss should not be underestimated. And besides, his position as number two in the SS means he can hide behind Himmler if the need arises, allowing him to bide his time until he becomes so powerful that he need fear no one.

So Heydrich's direct rivals are, for the moment, of a lowlier kind. There is Alfred Rosenberg, minister for the Occupied Eastern Territories and the theorist behind the idea of colonizing these countries. There is Oswald Pohl, in charge of the organization of concentration camps, and—like Heydrich—the head of a 'central office' (Haupt Amt, the *HA* in 'RSHA') within the SS. There is Hans Frank, the governor-general of Poland, Heydrich's counterpart in Warsaw. And there is also Canaris, head of the Abwehr—Heydrich's counterpart in the Wehrmacht. Having accumulated so many offices, Heydrich's power is

218

admittedly far superior to any of these men, taken one by one. But each has enough control over his own domain to prevent Heydrich really spreading his wings. Actually, looking at it that way, I should add Dalüge, head of the general police—another 'central office' answering directly to Himmler in the hierarchy of the SS. His power is limited to ordinary police tasks, the maintenance of order and the enforcement of common law, but the Orpo, the Schupo, and the Kripo—while lacking the power and dark prestige of the Gestapo—are still police forces beyond Heydrich's control.

So the road is long. But Heydrich, as he has already amply demonstrated, is not a man easily discouraged.

## 158

I've come across this anecdote in lots of books: Himmler, attending an execution at Minsk, fainted when two young girls were shot just in front of him and he was spattered with their blood. Following this unpleasant scene he realized the need to find another method, less hard on the executioners' nerves, for continuing the extermination of the Jews and other *Untermenschen*.

But according to my notes, the end of this type of execution coincides with a similar realization on Heydrich's part. He was also making an inspection visit, accompanied by his subordinate 'Gestapo' Müller.

The Einsatzgruppen always carried out their work in more or less the same way: they dug a gigantic ditch, and—having gathered together hundreds or even thousands of Jews (or other supposed opponents) from the surrounding towns and villages—lined them up at the edge of the ditch and machine-gunned them. Sometimes they made them kneel down so they could put bullets in the backs of their necks. But most of the time, they didn't even bother to check whether everyone was dead, so some were buried alive. A few survived: sheltered beneath a corpse, half-dead themselves, they waited for nightfall before digging through the earth that covered them until they reached the surface. But such cases are the miraculous exceptions. Several witnesses have described seeing pits filled with bodies piled on top of one another and hearing the groans of the dying emitted by the seething mass. Afterward, the pits were filled in. Using such primitive methods, the Einsatzgruppen exterminated a total of about one and a half million people, the vast majority Jews.

Heydrich attended quite a few of these executions, sometimes in the company of Himmler, sometimes Eichmann, sometimes Müller. One time, a young woman held out her baby so that he could save it. Mother and child were shot right in front of him. Heydrich, who was thicker-skinned than Himmler, did not faint. But the cruelty of the scene made an impression on him, and he wondered about the suitability of this method of execution. Like Himmler, he was worried about the effects of such scenes on the morale of his brave SS guards. Having voiced his doubts, he reached for his hip flask and swallowed a mouthful of slivovitz. Slivovitz is a Czech spirit distilled from plums—it's very strong and, in the opinion of many Czechs, not very nice. Heydrich, who was a heavy drinker, must have picked up a taste for it after his arrival in Prague.

However, it took him some time to conclude that the Einsatzgruppen were not the ideal solution to the Jewish question. Because in July 1941, when he undertook his first inspection with Himmler—at Minsk, where the two men arrived on the Reichsführer's special train—Heydrich, just like his boss, could find no fault with the slaughter he witnessed. It must have taken several months for the two of them to understand that such a procedure implicated the Third Reich in a realm of barbarism likely to be condemned by future generations. They had to do something to remedy this. But the process of extermination was already so advanced that the only remedy they found was Auschwitz.

## 159

Surprisingly, in this dark and horrible period, the number of Czech marriages keeps rising. But there is a reason for this. In early 1942, compulsory work service applies only to single men. Suddenly, there is a marked increase in the number of Czech citizens marrying in haste. This does not escape the watchful eye of Heydrich's secret services. So it's decided that forced labour be extended to all male Czech citizens, with no exceptions. Thus tens of thousands of Czech workers, married and single, are sent to all four corners of the Reich to serve as manpower wherever they're needed—which means everywhere, because German workers are being swallowed by the Wehrmacht in their millions. It's not only Czechs either: the same law applies to the Poles, Belgians, Danes, Dutch, Norwegians, French, and others.

This policy does produce some interesting side effects, though. In one of the many RSHA reports to land on Heydrich's desk, we read:

> From various places in the Reich, where millions of foreign workers are employed, there is talk of them having sexual relations with German women. The danger of biological weakening is constantly rising. There are more and more complaints concerning young women of German blood seeking out Czech workers for amorous relations.

I suppose Heydrich pulls a face when he reads this. Screwing foreigners has never bothered him, personally. But for Aryan women in heat to mate with those filthy subhumans . . . that surely must disgust him. It's also an added reason not to trust women in general. There is no danger that Lina would ever do such a thing—not even to avenge her husband's infidelities. Lina is a true German, of pure and noble blood, who would kill herself rather than go to bed with a Jew, a black, a Slav, an Arab, or anyone of an inferior race. Not like those shameless bitches who don't deserve to be German. He'd send the whole damn lot to a whorehouse, quick as you like, or to those Aryan breeding grounds, those stud farms where the young blonde women line up to mate with SS stallions. Let them complain then.

I wonder how the Nazis reconciled their racial doctrine with the Slavs' beauty: not only are the prettiest women on the continent to be found in eastern Europe, but on top of that they're often blonde and blue-eyed. Anyway, when Goebbels had his affair with the gorgeous Czech actress Lida Baarova, he didn't ask too many questions about her racial purity. He probably thought her beauty made her suitable for Germanization. When you consider the physical degeneracy of most of the Nazi high command—and Goebbels, with his clubfoot, is a prime specimen—you have to laugh at this idea of 'weakening the race' that so exercised them. It's different for Heydrich. He's no brown midget: his appearance marks him out as a true Germanic standard-bearer. Did he believe this? I think so. People are always quick to believe whatever suits and flatters them. I think of what Paul Newman said: 'If my eyes should ever turn brown, my career is shot to hell.' I wonder if Heydrich thought the same thing.

## 160

Once again, I've chanced upon a work of fiction relating to Heydrich. This time, it's the made-for-TV movie of Robert Harris's novel *Fatherland*, shown in France as *Twilight of the Eagles*. The lead role is played by Rutger Hauer, the Dutch actor famous for his immortal performance as the replicant in Ridley Scott's *Blade Runner*. Here, he plays an SS officer working for the Kripo.

The story takes place in the 1960s. The Führer

still rules Germany. Berlin has been rebuilt according to Albert Speer's plans, and the resulting city is a stylistic mix of Baroque, Art Nouveau, and Futurist. The war against Russia rumbles on, but the rest of Europe is under Third Reich domination. There is, however, a thaw in relations with the United States. Kennedy is about to meet Hitler to sign a historic agreement. In this fictional history, it's the father, Joseph Patrick—rather than his son, John Fitzgerald—who has been elected president. And JFK's father never hid his Nazi sympathies. So, as in other 'What if . . .?' stories, an alternative history is built upon a hypothesis: in this case, that Germany won the war and Hitler's regime endured.

In the plot of *Fatherland*, Nazi dignitaries are being murdered; with the help of a female American journalist (in Germany to cover Kennedy's visit), the SS inspector played by Rutger Hauer discovers the link between these murders. Bühler, Stuckart, Luther, Neumann, Lange . . . all were present at a mysterious meeting that took place twenty years before—at Wannsee, in January 1942, organized by Heydrich himself. In the 1960s Heydrich has taken Göring's place as Reichsmarshall, and is more or less the regime's number two. Afraid that the agreement with Kennedy might be compromised if the truth ever comes out, Hitler intends to make everyone who attended the meeting permanently disappear. Because it was at this meeting, on January 20, 1942, that the Final Solution was officially ratified by all the relevant ministers. Here, led by Heydrich, the Nazis planned the extermination by gas of eleven million Jews.

However, one of the participants does not want to die. Franz Luther, who represented Ribbentrop on behalf of the Foreign Ministry, has irrefutable proof of the genocide of the Jews and he intends to offer it to the Americans in exchange for political asylum. Because the world is unaware of the genocide: officially, Europe's Jews have been deported—to Ukraine, where the proximity of the Russian front makes it impossible for any international observer to go and verify their presence. Just before being murdered, Luther contacts the American journalist, who manages *in extremis*—as Hitler is about to welcome Kennedy amid great pomp—to deliver the precious documents to the American president. The meeting between Kennedy and Hitler is cancelled, the United States goes back to war against Germany, and the Third Reich ends up collapsing, twenty years late.

In this fiction, the Wannsee Conference is in some way *the* crucial moment of the Final Solution. Now, it's true that the decision wasn't made at Wannsee. And it's also true that Heydrich's Einsatzgruppen had already killed hundreds of thousands of Jews on the Eastern Front. But it was at Wannsee that the genocide was rubber-stamped. No longer need the task be given, more or less on the quiet (if you can really talk of killing millions of people 'on the quiet'), to a few death squads; now the entire political and economic infrastructure of the regime is at their disposal.

The meeting lasted barely two hours. Two hours to settle what were essentially legal questions: What should be done with half-Jews? And with quarter-Jews? With Jews who'd been decorated

225

in the First World War? With Jews married to German women? Should these men's Aryan widows be compensated by giving them a pension? As in all meetings, the only decisions that are really made are those decided beforehand. In fact, for Heydrich, it was just a question of informing all the Reich ministries that they were going to have to work together with one objective in mind: the physical elimination of all Europe's Jews.

I have in front of me a list distributed by Heydrich to all the participants at the conference that details the number of Jews to be 'evacuated', country by country. The list is divided in two parts. The first includes all the countries of the Reich, among which we notice that Estonia is already *judenfrei*, while the Government General (that is, Poland) still has more than two million Jews. The second part, giving an idea of how optimistic the Nazis still were in early 1942, brings together the satellite countries (Slovakia: 88,000 Jews; Croatia: 40,000 Jews) and allied countries (Italy, including Sardinia: 58,000 Jews), but also neutral countries (Switzerland: 18,000; Sweden: 8,000; Turkey: 55,500; Spain: 6,000) or even enemies (the only two remaining in Europe at this time: the USSR— already invaded to a great extent—with five million Jews, more than half of them in occupied Ukraine; and Britain, with 330,000 Jews, which was a long way from being invaded). So the plan was that every country in Europe would be forced or persuaded to deport its Jews. The total was written at the bottom of the page: more than eleven million. The mission would be half accomplished.

Eichmann has described what happened after the conference. The ministerial representatives

226

having left, he and Heydrich were alone with 'Gestapo' Müller. They moved through to an elegant wood-panelled drawing room. Heydrich poured himself a brandy, which he sipped while listening to classical music (Schubert, I believe), and the three men each smoked a cigar. According to Eichmann, Heydrich was in an excellent mood.


## 161

Raul Hilberg died yesterday. He was the leader of the 'functionalists', those historians who believe the extermination of the Jews was not premeditated but dictated by circumstances. This school of thought is in direct opposition to the 'intentionalists', who maintain it was all clearly and definitely planned from the beginning—that is, from the writing of *Mein Kampf* in 1924.

To mark Hilberg's death, *Le Monde* published extracts from an interview he gave in 1994, in which the broad outlines of his theory are recapitulated:

I believe that the Germans did not know, at the beginning, what they were doing. It's as if they were driving a train whose general direction was toward a growing violence against Jews, but whose precise destination was uncertain. Let's not forget that Nazism was more than a political party: it was a movement that had to keep going forward, without ever stopping. Confronted with a completely unprecedented task, German bureaucracy didn't know what to do. And that's where Hitler's role is important. Someone at the top had to give the green light to the naturally conservative bureaucrats.

One of the intentionalists' main pieces of evidence is this phrase of Hitler's, taken from a public speech made in January 1939: 'If the international Jewish financiers in and outside Europe should succeed in plunging the nations once more into a world war, the result will not be the Bolshevization of the earth, and thus the victory of Jewry, but the annihilation of the Jewish race in Europe.' Conversely, the most revealing clue in support of the functionalists is that, for a long time, the Nazis were genuinely seeking out territories to which they might deport the Jews: Madagascar, the Arctic Ocean, Siberia, Palestine. On more than one occasion, Eichmann even met with some militant Zionists. But the hazards of war would force them to abandon all these plans. Most notably, the transportation of the Jews to Madagascar could not take place until the Germans had control of the seas—in other words, until the war with Great Britain was over. The search for more radical solutions would finally be precipitated by the turning of the war in the East. Even if they didn't admit it, the Nazis knew their eastern conquests were in peril. They did not fear the worst—because nobody in 1942 imagined that the Red Army would one day invade Germany and penetrate all the way to Berlin—but the powerful Soviet resistance forced them to acknowledge that they might lose the occupied territories. Consequently, they had to move quickly. So it was, one thing leading to another, that the Jewish question took on an

228

industrial dimension.

## 162

A freight train screeches to a halt. At the end of the tracks is a gate surmounted by a tower, with a brownstone wing on either side. Above, you hear the cawing of crows. The gate opens. You are now entering Auschwitz.

## 163

This morning, Heydrich receives an indignant letter from Himmler. It concerns some five hundred young Germans arrested by the Hamburg police because they were fans of swing, that degenerate foreign dance accompanied by Negro music.

> I will oppose any half measures in this matter. All the ringleaders are to be sent to a concentration camp. First of all, these youths will get a good thrashing there. They will stay in the camp quite a long time—two or three years. Obviously they will no longer have the right to study. Only through brutal actions can we stop the spread of these dangerous Anglophile trends.

Heydrich will actually deport about fifty of these youngsters. Just because the Führer has entrusted him with the historic task of getting rid of every single Jew in Europe does not mean he's going to neglect his other duties.

## 164

Goebbels's diary, January 21, 1942:

Heydrich has now installed his new government of the Protectorate. Hacha has made the declaration of solidarity with the Reich that was requested of him. Heydrich's policy in the Protectorate is truly a model one. He mastered the crisis there with ease. As a result, the Protectorate is now in the best of spirits, quite in contrast to other occupied or annexed areas.

## 165

Hitler is giving another of his interminable political soliloquies to a servile, silent audience. His diatribe touches on the situation in the Protectorate:

The Czechs were taking Neurath for a ride! Another six months of that regime and production would have fallen by twenty-five percent! Of all the Slavs, the Czech is the most dangerous—because he's a worker. He is disciplined, methodical; he knows how to conceal his intentions. But they will knuckle down now because they know we are violent and merciless.

It's his way of saying that he is very pleased with the job Heydrich is doing.

## 166

Not long afterward, Heydrich goes to see Hitler in Berlin. So Heydrich finds himself in the presence of the Führer—or perhaps it's the other way around. Hitler declares: 'We will clean up the Czech mess if we stick to a consistent policy with them. A lot of Czechs have Germanic origins, so it's not impossible to re-Germanize them.' This speech, too, is a way of complimenting Heydrich on his work. The Blond Beast is—along with Speer (though for very different reasons)—the colleague Hitler most respects.

With Speer, the Führer can talk of things other than politics, war, Jews. He can discuss music, painting, literature, and he can give substance to Germania—the future Berlin whose plans they've drawn up together, and which his brilliant architect is responsible for building. For Hitler, Speer is a breath of fresh air, a window in the National Socialist labyrinth (the Führer's creation and now his prison), giving him a view of the outside world. True, Speer is a card-carrying and utterly devoted Nazi. Since being named minister of armaments (in addition to his title of official architect), he uses all his intelligence and talent to improve production. His loyalty and efficiency are above suspicion. But that's not why Hitler prefers him. If it were

231

only a matter of loyalty, then Himmler would be unbeatable. In fact, he'd be unbeatable if it were just a matter of efficiency too. But Speer, in his well-cut suits, has so much more class and style. He is one of those intellectuals whom Hitler, the failed artist and former Munich tramp, ought to loathe. But Speer gives him something that no one else has given him: the friendship and admiration of a brilliant man at ease in any social situation.

Hitler likes Heydrich for very different reasons. Just as Speer is the embodiment of the 'normal' elite world to which Hitler has never belonged, Heydrich is the perfect Nazi prototype: tall, blond, cruel, totally obedient, and deadly efficient. It is an irony of fate that, according to Himmler, he has Jewish blood. But the violence with which he fights against and triumphs over this corrupt part of himself is proof—in Hitler's eyes—of the superiority of the Aryans over the Jews. And if Hitler really believes in these Jewish origins, then it is all the more satisfying for him to turn Heydrich into the Angel of Death for the people of Israel by making him responsible for the Final Solution.

167

The images are well-known: Himmler and Heydrich, wearing civilian clothes, conversing with the Führer on the terrace of his eagle's nest, the Kehlsteinhaus—the gigantic luxury bunker built on the side of an Alpine peak in Bavaria. What I didn't know was that they had been filmed by Hitler's mistress. I learn this during an 'Eva Braun evening' organized by a cable TV station. This is a real treat for me. I like to delve as deeply as possible into the private lives of my characters. So I take pleasure in rewatching these images of Hitler welcoming the blond, hook-nosed Heydrich, a head taller than everyone around him, smiling and relaxed in his beige suit with its too-short sleeves. Frustratingly, there is no sound. But the producers have done things properly: they've hired the services of lip-reading experts. So now we know what Himmler said to Heydrich, standing by the low stone wall that overhangs the sunlit valley: 'Nothing must divert us from our task.' So there you go. Clearly they had the next step in mind. I'm a bit disappointed by this, but happy at the same time. It's better than nothing. And besides, what was I hoping for? He was hardly going to say: 'You know, Heydrich, I reckon little Lee Harvey Oswald is going to make a very fine recruit.'

## 168

Despite being increasingly weighed down by the enormous responsibilities of organizing the Final Solution, Heydrich does not neglect the Protectorate's internal affairs. In January 1942, he finds time for a ministerial reshuffle of his Czech government, effectively suspended since his sensational arrival in Prague last September. On the nineteenth, the day before the conference at Wannsee, he names a new prime minister— although that doesn't mean much, since this position no longer carries any real power. The two key posts in this puppet government are those of finance minister, given to a German whose identity is irrelevant to this story, and minister of education, given to Emanuel Moravec. By appointing a German as finance minister, Heydrich imposes German as the language of government. By naming Moravec as the head of education, he assures himself of the services of a man he recognized as an eager collaborator. The two ministers are united by the same objective: to maintain and develop an industrial production that satisfies the Reich's needs. The role of finance minister consists in forcing all Czech companies to help the German war effort. As for Moravec, his role is to create an education system whose sole aim is to train workers. Consequently, Czech children will now learn only what is necessary for their future profession. Mostly this means manual abilities, with a bare minimum of technical knowledge.

On February 4, 1942, Heydrich gives a speech that interests me because it concerns my own honourable profession:

It is essential to sort out the Czech teachers because the teaching profession is a breeding ground for opposition. It must be destroyed, and all Czech secondary schools must be shut. The Czech youth must be torn away from this subversive atmosphere and educated elsewhere. I cannot think of a better place for this than a sports ground. With sport and physical education, we will simultaneously guarantee their development, their education, and their re-education.

I think that covers all the main points.

The possibility of reopening the Czech universities—hit by a three-year ban in November 1939 for political agitation—is not even considered. It's up to Moravec to find an excuse for prolonging their closure when the three years are up.

Reading Heydrich's speech, I have three comments:

1. In the Czech state, as elsewhere, the feeblest defender of the values of national education is the responsible minister. Having been a virulent anti-Nazi, Emanuel Moravec became, after Munich, the most active collaborator in Heydrich's Czech government and the Germans' preferred Czech representative—much more so than senile old President Hácha. Local history books tend to call him 'the Czech Quisling'.
2. The staunchest defenders of the values of national education are teachers because, whatever we might otherwise think of them, they have the authority and the will to be subversive. And they deserve praise for that.
3. Sport? What a load of fascist rubbish it is.

169

Once again I find myself frustrated by my genre's constraints. No ordinary novel would encumber itself with three characters sharing the same name—unless the author were after a very particular effect. Me, I'm stuck not only with Colonel Moravec, the brave head of Czech secret services in London, but with the heroic Moravec family who are part of the internal Resistance, *and* with Emanuel Moravec, the infamous collaborationist minister. And that's without even counting Captain Václav Morávek, the head of the Tri kralové Resistance network. This must be tiresome and confusing for the reader. In a fiction, you'd just do away with the problem: Colonel Moravec would become Colonel Novak, for instance, and the Moravec family would be transformed into the Svigar family—why not?— while the traitor might be rebaptized with a fanciful name like Nutella or Kodak or Prada. But of course I am not going to play that game. My only concession to the reader's convenience consists in not declining the proper nouns: so, even if the feminine form of 'Moravec' ought logically to be 'Moravcova', I will nevertheless keep the basic form when talking about Aunt Moravec. I do this in order not to add one complication (the homonyms of real people) to another (the declension of feminine or plural proper nouns in the Slav languages). Well, I'm not writing a Russian novel, am I? Anyway, it's worth noting that in the French translation of *War and Peace*, Natasha Rostova becomes (or remains) Natasha Rostov.

170

Goebbels's diary, February 6, 1942:

Gregory gave me a report on the Protectorate. The atmosphere is very good. Heydrich has worked brilliantly. He has shown such prudence and political intelligence that there is no more talk of crisis. Heydrich wanted to replace Gregory with an SS-Führer. I don't agree. Gregory has an excellent knowledge of the Protectorate and the Czech population, and Heydrich's staff is not always very intelligent. Above all, it does not show much leadership. That's why I keep faith with Gregory.

Sorry, I don't have the faintest idea who this Gregory could be. And just so my falsely off hand tone doesn't give you the wrong idea: I have tried to find out!

## 171

Goebbels's diary, February 15, 1942:

I had a long conversation with Heydrich about the situation in the Protectorate. Sentiment there is now much more favourable to us. Heydrich's measures are producing good results. It is true that the intelligentsia is still hostile to us, but the danger to German security from Czech elements in the Protectorate has been completely neutralized. Heydrich is clever. He plays cat and mouse with the Czechs and they swallow everything he tells them. He has carried out a number of extremely popular measures, first and foremost the almost total conquest of the black market. It is absolutely staggering to see how much food people have hidden away. He is successfully Germanizing a large number of Czechs. He proceeds in this matter with great caution but he will undoubtedly achieve good results in the long term. The Slavs, he emphasized, cannot be educated as one educates a Germanic people. One must either break them or humble them constantly. At present he does the latter. Our task in the Protectorate is perfectly clear. Neurath completely misjudged it, and that's how the first crisis in Prague arose.

Heydrich is building a security service for all the occupied sectors. The Wehrmacht is causing him problems in this regard, but these difficulties tend to smooth themselves out. The longer this goes on, the more the Wehrmacht shows itself incapable of dealing with these questions.

Heydrich has experience with certain parts of the Wehrmacht: they are not sympathetic to National Socialist politics, nor to a National Socialist war. As for leading the people, they understand nothing at all.

## 172

On February 16, Lieutenant Bartos, head of Operation Silver A, sends a message to London. The message is sent via the transmitter Libuse, the machine his group parachuted into the country the same night as Gabčík and Kubiš. Reading this message gives us a good idea of the difficulties encountered by the parachutists in the fulfilment of their secret mission:

The groups that you send should be given plenty of money and dressed suitably. A small-calibre pistol and a towel—difficult to find here—are very useful. The poison should be carried in a smaller tube. Depending on the circumstances, you should send the groups to areas away from those where they have to report. This makes it more difficult for the German security services to find them. The biggest problem here is finding work. Nobody will hire you unless you have a work permit. Anyone who does have one is given a job by the Work Office. The danger of forced labour increases greatly in the spring, so we can't commit a greater number of men to secret missions without also increasing the risk that the entire system will be discovered. That's why I consider it more beneficial to use those already here to the maximum, and to limit the arrival of new men to an absolute minimum. Signed, Ice.

## 173

Goebbels's diary, February 26, 1942:

Heydrich sends me a very detailed report on the situation in the Protectorate. It hasn't really changed. But what stands out very

239

clearly is that his tactics are the right ones. He treats the Czech ministers as his subjects. Hacha puts himself completely at the service of Heydrich's new politics. As far as the Protectorate is concerned, nothing more needs to be done at the moment.

## 174

Heydrich does not neglect his cultural life. In March, he organizes the greatest cultural event of his reign: an exhibition entitled Das Sowjet Paradies, inaugurated by the vile Karl Frank, in the presence of the old president Emil Hácha and the infamous collaborator Emanuel Moravec.

I don't know what the exhibition is like exactly, but the idea is to show that the USSR is a barbaric, underdeveloped country with disgraceful living conditions, while underlining the intrinsic perversity of Bolshevism. It is also a chance to praise the German victories on the Eastern Front. Tanks and other military hardware taken from the Russians are exhibited like trophies.

The exhibition lasts four weeks and attracts half a million visitors, among them Gabčík and Kubiš. This is probably the first and only time that our heroes will see a Soviet tank.

To begin with, this seemed a simple-enough story to tell. Two men have to kill a third man. They succeed, or not, and that's the end, or nearly. I thought of all the other people as mere ghosts who would glide elegantly across the tapestry of history. Ghosts have to be looked after, and that requires great care—I knew that. On the other hand, what I didn't know (but should have guessed) is that a ghost desires only one thing: to live again. Personally, I'd like nothing better, but I am constrained by the needs of my story. I can't keep leaving space for this ever-growing army of shadows, these ghosts who—perhaps to avenge themselves for the meagre care I show them—are haunting me.

But that's not all.

Pardubice is a town in eastern Bohemia. The Elbe runs through it. The town has a population of about 90,000 and a pretty square in the centre with some handsome Renaissance-style buildings. It is also the birthplace of Dominik Hašek, the legendary goaltender and one of the greatest ice-hockey players of all time.

There is a fairly chic hotel-restaurant here called Vaselka. This evening, as every other evening, it is full of Germans. The men of the Gestapo sit around a table, making a lot of noise. They've had lots to eat and drink. They hail the waiter. He comes over, smart and obsequious. I imagine they want some brandy. The waiter takes their order. One of the Germans puts a cigarette to his lips. The waiter takes a lighter from his pocket and, with a bow, offers the German a light.

The waiter is very handsome. He was hired recently. Young, smiling, clear-eyed, and honest-looking, he has fine features on a large face. Here, in Pardubice, he answers to the name of Mirek Šolc. At first glance, there is no reason why we should be interested in this waiter. Except that the Gestapo is interested in him.

One fine morning, they summon the hotel boss. They want information on Mirek Šolc: where he comes from, who he hangs out with, where he goes when he's not at work. The boss replies that Šolc comes from Ostrava, where his father runs a hotel. The policemen pick up the phone and call Ostrava. But nobody there has ever heard of a hotelier called Šolc. So the Gestapo of Pardubice summon the hotel boss again, and Šolc with him. The boss comes on his own. He explains that he fired the waiter because he broke some dishes. The Gestapo let him go, and have him followed. But Mirek Šolc has vanished forever.

176

Between them, the parachutists operating in the Protectorate would have used an incalculable number of false identities. Mirek Šolc was one of them. Now we must turn our attention to the man who used this identity—because he plays an important role in this story. His real name is Josef Valčík. And, unlike Mirek Šolc, this is a name you need to remember. So Valčík is the handsome twenty-seven-year-old man who worked as a waiter in Pardubice. Now he's on the run, attempting to reach Moravia so he can take a break at his parents' country house. Valčík, like Kubiš, is Moravian—although that is not the most important thing they have in common. Sergeant Valčík was in the same Halifax that carried Gabčík and Kubiš over their homeland on the night of December 28. He belonged to another group (code name Silver A), whose mission was to be dropped with a transmitter (code name Libuse) in order to re-establish contact between London and A54—the German superspy with his priceless information—through the intermediary of Morávek: the last of the Three Kings, the Resistance chief with the severed finger.

Naturally, nothing went as planned. During the jump, Valčík became separated from his colleagues and had terrible difficulties retrieving the transmitter. Having tried to transport it on a sled, he ended up reaching Pardubice in a taxi. There, local agents found him work as a waiter: this provided him with excellent cover, and the fact that the restaurant was so popular with the Gestapo tickled his sense of irony.

Unfortunately, his cover is now blown. But, in a way, this misfortune forces him to go to Prague—where two other parachutists are waiting for him, along with his destiny.

If this were a novel, I would have absolutely no need for Valčík. He is more of an encumbrance than anything else—a pointless copy of the two heroes, even if he does prove himself just as cheerful, optimistic, courageous, and likable as Gabčík and Kubiš. But it's not up to me to decide what Operation Anthropoid needs. And Operation Anthropoid is definitely going to need a lookout.

The two men know each other. They've been friends since England, where they underwent the same training with the special forces of the SOE, and perhaps even since France, where they might have met in the Foreign Legion or in one of the divisions of the Czech liberation army. They also share the same Christian name. But, shaking hands with unconcealed joy, they introduce themselves as follows:

'Hello, I'm Zdenek.'

'Hello, I'm Zdenek too.'

They smile at the coincidence. Jozef Gabčík and Josef Valčík have been given the same false Christian name by London. If I were paranoid or egocentric, I would believe that London did this on purpose just to make my story even more confusing. It doesn't matter anyway, because they use a different name with practically each person they meet. I've already made fun of how lightly Gabčík and Kubiš spoke of their mission—sometimes openly—but they knew how to be rigorous when they had to be. And they must have been very professional not to get muddled, to forget who they were supposed to be each time they talked to somebody.

Between fellow parachutists it's different, and if Valčík and Gabčík introduce themselves as though they're meeting for the first time, that's simply so they know what to call each other. Or rather, as this changes so often, which Christian name is on the false ID papers they're using at that moment.

'Are you staying with the aunt?'

'Yes, but I'm moving soon. Where can I get hold of you?'

'Leave a message with the concierge. He's safe. Ask to see his collection of keys—he'll trust you then. The password is "Jan".'

'Yeah, the aunt told me that, but . . . "Jan" as in Jan?'

'No. Here, he's called Ota. It's just a coincidence.'

'Oh, right.'

This scene is not really useful, and on top of that I practically made it up. I don't think I'm going to keep it.


## 178

With Valčík's arrival in Prague, there are now nearly a dozen parachutists roaming around town. Theoretically, each one works on the mission for which his group was sent. The aim is to keep things compartmentalized, so the different groups are meant to communicate as little as possible. That way, if one falls, the others aren't dragged down with it. In practice, though, this is almost impossible. The number of addresses where the parachutists can find shelter is limited, but at the same time it is prudent to move as often as possible. As soon as one group or parachutist leaves an address, another takes his place—so all the members of the different groups cross one another's paths on a fairly regular basis.

In the Moravec family apartment especially,

there's a never-ending procession of all Prague's parachutists. The father asks no questions; the mother—whom they affectionately call 'the aunt'—bakes them cakes; the son, Ata, is overcome with admiration for these mysterious men who hide pistols in their sleeves.

The result of this game of musical chairs is that Valčík, originally part of Operation Silver A, quickly gets closer to Operation Anthropoid. Soon, he's helping Gabčík and Kubiš scout for locations.

The other result is that Karel Čurda, from the group Out Distance, meets pretty much everybody: the parachutists and their hosts. So many names to drop, so many addresses to let slip.

### 179

'I adore Kundera, but the novel of his I love the least is the one set in Paris. Because he's not truly in his element. As if he were wearing a very beautiful jacket that was just a little bit too big or a little bit too small for him [laughs]. But when Milos and Pavel are walking through Prague, I believe it totally.'

This is Marjane Satrapi, in an interview given to *Les Inrockuptibles* magazine to promote the release of her beautiful film, *Persepolis*. I feel a vague sense of anxiety as I read this. Flicking through the magazine in the apartment of a young woman, I confide my anxiety to her. 'Yes, but you've been to Prague,' she reassures me. 'You've lived there, you love that city.' But the same is true for Kundera and Paris. Anyway, Marjane Satrapi adds: 'Even if I've lived in France for twenty years, I didn't grow up here. There will always be a little Iranian core to my work. I love Rimbaud, of course, but Omar Khayyám will always speak to me more.' Strange, I've never thought about the problem in those terms. Does Desnos speak to me more than Nezval? I don't know. I don't think that Flaubert, Camus, or Aragon speak to me more than Kafka, Hašek, or Holan. Nor, for that matter, more than García Márquez, Hemingway, or Anatoly Rybakov. Will Marjane Satrapi sense that I didn't grow up in Prague? Won't she believe it when the Mercedes suddenly appears at the bend in the road? She goes on: 'Even if Lubitsch became a Hollywood filmmaker, he always reinvented and reimagined Europe—an eastern, Jewish Europe. Even when his films are set in the United States, for me they take place in Vienna or Budapest. And that's a good thing.' But does that mean she'll think my story is happening in Paris, where I was born, and not in Prague, the city my whole being yearns for? Will there be images of Paris in her mind when I drive the Mercedes to Holešovice, near the Troie Bridge?

No, my story begins in a town in northern Germany, followed by Kiel, Munich, and Berlin, then moves to eastern Slovakia. Passing briefly through France, it continues in London and Kiev before returning to Berlin, and it is going to end in Prague, Prague, Prague! Prague, city of a hundred towers, heart of the world, eye of my imagination's hurricane, Prague with fingers of rain, the emperor's Baroque dream, the soul's music flowing under bridges, Emperor Charles IV, Jan Neruda, Mozart and Wenceslaus, Jan Hus, Jan Žižka,

Josef K, *Praha s prsty deste*, the chem engraved in the Golem's forehead, the headless horseman in Liliova Street, the iron man waiting to be liberated by a young girl once every hundred years, the sword hidden in a bridge support, and today the sound of boots marching, which will echo for . . . how much longer? A year. Perhaps two. Three more, in fact. I am in Prague—not in Paris, in Prague. It's 1942. It's early spring and I'm not wearing a jacket. 'Exoticism is something I hate,' says Marjane. There is nothing exotic about Prague, because it's the heart of the world, the true centre of Europe, and because in this spring of 1942 it is going to be the site of one of the greatest scenes in the great tragedy of the universe.

Unlike Marjane Satrapi, Milan Kundera, Jan Kubiš, and Jozef Gabčík, I am not a political exile. But that is perhaps why I can talk of where I want to be without always being dragged back to my starting point. I don't owe my homeland anything, and I don't have a score to settle with it. For Paris, I feel neither the heartbreaking nostalgia nor the melancholy disenchantment of the great exiles. That is why I am free to dream of Prague.

## 180

Valčík helps his two comrades in their search for the perfect spot. One day, surveying the city, he attracts the attention of a stray dog. What strange or familiar quality does the animal detect that draws it to this man? It follows his footsteps. It doesn't take Valčík long to sense a presence behind him. He turns around. The dog stops. He sets off again. The dog follows him. Together, they cross the city. When Valčík gets back to the apartment belonging to the Moravecs' concierge, where he's staying, he adopts and names the dog. When the concierge comes home, Valčík introduces him to Moula. From now on, the two of them will scout for locations together, and when Valčík can't take him, he begs the good concierge to 'look after his dragon' (so it must have been a big dog, or a very small one if Valčík was being ironic). When his master goes away, Moula waits quietly for him—curled up under the livingroom table, immobile for hours. The dog probably won't have a decisive role to play in Operation Anthropoid, but I would rather jot down a useless detail than risk missing a crucial one.

## 181

Speer returns to Prague, but is received with less pomp than on his previous visit. The minister of armaments is here to discuss manpower with the Protector of one of the Reich's biggest industrial centres. And in the spring of 1942, much more so than in December 1941—with millions of men fighting on the Eastern Front, with Soviet tanks destroying German tanks, and British bombers striking German cities with ever greater frequency—the question of manpower is vital. More workers are needed to produce more tanks, more airplanes, more artillery, more rifles, more grenades, more submarines. Not to mention those new weapons that should help the Reich finally win the war.

This time, Speer dispenses with the tour of the city and the official procession. He's come alone, without his wife, for a work meeting with Heydrich. Neither has time to waste on small talk. Speer's efficiency in his domain is considered the equal of Heydrich's in his, and he is undoubtedly pleased about this. But he can't help noticing that Heydrich not only travels without an escort but that he calmly cruises the streets of Prague in an unarmoured, open-top car, with no bodyguard at all except his chauffeur. He expresses his concerns to Heydrich, who replies: 'Why should my Czechs shoot at me?' Heydrich probably hasn't read the 1937 newspaper article by Joseph Roth—the Jewish writer from Vienna, now exiled in Paris—mocking the vast amounts of money and men dedicated to protecting Nazi dignitaries. In this article, he has them say: 'Yes, you see, I've become so great that I'm even forced to be afraid; I am so precious that I don't have the right to die; I believe so utterly in my star that I must beware the risks that can be fatal to many a star. Who dares wins! But who has won three times over no longer needs to dare!' Joseph Roth no longer mocks anybody because he died in 1939, but perhaps Heydrich did read this article after all. It appeared in a newspaper for dissident refugees—subversive elements, no doubt closely watched by the SD. In any case, Heydrich feels duty-bound to explain part of his weltanschauung to this pampered civilian Speer: surrounding yourself with bodyguards is petit-bourgeois behaviour, in very poor taste. He leaves this kind of thing to Bormann and other Party higher-ups. In fact, he

250

refutes Joseph Roth: better to die than to let them believe you're afraid.

Nevertheless, Heydrich's initial reaction must have disturbed Speer: Why would anyone want to kill Heydrich? As if there weren't already enough reasons to kill Nazi leaders in general, and Heydrich in particular! Speer has no illusions about the popularity of the Germans in the occupied territories, and he assumes that Heydrich is the same. But this man seems so sure of himself. Speer can't tell if Heydrich's paternalistic tone, speaking of 'his' Czechs, is just an idle boast, or if Heydrich really is as powerful as he claims to be. Call him a petit-bourgeois coward if you must, but in the open-top Mercedes inching its way through the streets of Prague, Speer doesn't feel entirely at ease.


## 182

Colonel Morávek—sole survivor of the Three Kings, last remaining chief of the three-headed Czech Resistance organization—knows that he shouldn't attend the meeting. It has been arranged by his old friend René, alias Colonel Paul Thümmel, Abwehr officer; alias A54, the most important spy ever to have worked for Czechoslovakia. A54 has managed to warn him: his cover has been blown, and this meeting is a trap. But Morávek probably believes his own audacity will protect him. Wasn't it audacity that saved his life so many times before? This man who used to send postcards to the head of the Gestapo to tell him what he'd done isn't going to let himself get scared now. Arriving in the Prague park where the meeting is due to take place, he sees his contact, but also the men who are watching him. He gets ready to run off, but two men in raincoats call out from behind him. I have never witnessed a shoot-out and I have trouble imagining what it would be like in a city as peaceful as Prague is now. But there are more than fifty gunshots during the chase that follows. Morávek runs across one of the bridges that span the Vltava (unfortunately, I don't know which) and jumps onto a moving tram. But the Gestapo are everywhere—it's as if they've been teleported. They're even inside the tram carriage. Morávek jumps off the tram, but he's been shot in the legs. He collapses on the rails and, completely surrounded, he shoots himself. This is obviously the surest means of not telling the enemy anything. But his pockets will talk: on his body, the Germans find a photo of a man who (although they don't know it yet) is Josef Valčík.

This story marks the end of the last chief of the Three Kings. It proves a thorn in the side of Anthropoid, because at this date—March 20, 1942—Valčík is still closely involved in the operation. It also represents a double success for Heydrich: as Protector of Bohemia and Moravia, he manages to decapitate one of the most dangerous remaining Resistance organizations, thus fulfilling his mission. And as head of the SD, he unmasks a superspy who is also an officer of the Abwehr—the secret service run by his rival and former mentor Canaris. For the Allies this isn't the first setback and it won't be the last, but March 20, 1942, is assuredly not a redletter day in their secret war against the Germans.

252

In London they are growing impatient. It is five months now since the agents of Operation Anthropoid were parachuted into their homeland, but since then there's been hardly any news at all. London does know, however, that Gabčík and Kubiš are alive and operational. Libuse, the only secret transmitter still working, sends information of this kind whenever there is any. So London decides to give the two agents a new mission. As ever, employers are obsessed by their employees' productivity. This new mission adds to rather than replaces the previous one. But it also delays it. Gabčík and Kubiš are furious. They have to go to Pilsen to take part in a sabotage operation.

Pilsen is a large industrial town in the west of the country, quite close to the German border. Its famous beer, Pilsner Urquell, is named after it. However, London is not interested in Pilsner for its beer but for its Škoda factories. In 1942, Škoda doesn't make cars—it makes armaments. An air raid is planned for the night of April 25–26. The parachutists have to light fires around the industrial complex to help the British bombers pick out their target.

So at least four parachutists travel to Pilsen. They meet up in town, at a place agreed on in advance (the Tivoli restaurant—I wonder if it still exists?), and, that night, set fire to a stable and a stack of straw near the factory.

When the bombers arrive, all they have to do is drop their bombs between these two bright marks.

Unfortunately, all their bombs miss the target. So the mission is a total failure, even though the parachutists did exactly what they were asked.

Then again, Kubiš did get to know a young female shop assistant during his brief stay in Pilsen—a member of the Resistance, who helped the group fulfil its mission. With his handsome movie-star face—imagine a hybrid of Cary Grant and Tony Curtis—Kubiš was always a hit with the ladies. So, even if the operation was a bitter failure, at least *he* didn't waste his time. Two weeks later—two weeks before the assassination attempt—he will write a letter to this young woman, Marie Zilanova. A careless thing to do, but luckily without consequences. I would love to know the contents of that letter. I should have copied it down in Czech when I had the chance.

Returning to Prague, the parachutists are very annoyed. They've been forced to risk compromising their principal mission—their historic mission—and for what? Nothing but a few big guns. They send London a sharp message suggesting that next time they send pilots with some knowledge of the region.

To tell the truth, I can't even be sure that Gabčík was present for this mission in Pilsen. All I know is that Kubiš, Valčík, and Čurda were.

I've just realized that apart from one elliptic allusion in Chapter 178, I haven't mentioned Karel Čurda before now. And yet, historically and dramatically, he is going to play an essential role in this story.

All good stories need a traitor. The one in mine is called Karel Čurda. He's thirty years old, and I can't tell, judging from the photos I've seen, whether his betrayal can be read upon his face. He is a Czech parachutist whose background is so similar that it could be mistaken for those of Gabčík, Kubiš, or Valčík. Demobilized from the army after the German occupation, he leaves the country via Poland and travels to France, where he enlists in the Foreign Legion. He joins the Czechoslovak army-in-exile and, after the defeat of France, crosses to England. Unlike Gabčík, Kubiš, and Valčík, he is not sent to the front during the French retreat—but this is not what makes him fundamentally different to the other parachutists. In England, he volunteers for special missions and follows the same intensive training. He is parachuted over the Protectorate with two other comrades on the night of March 27–28. As for what follows . . . well, it's still too early to tell you that.

But it's in England that the seeds of the drama are sown, because it's here that it might have been avoided. Here, Karel Čurda's dubious character gradually reveals itself. He is a heavy drinker. Not a crime, obviously, but when he drinks too much he says things that alarm his regimental comrades. He says he admires Hitler. He says he regrets having left the Protectorate; that he would have a better life if he'd stayed there. His comrades consider him so unreliable that they write to General Ingr, the minister of defence in the Czech government-in-exile, warning him about Čurda. They add that he has also attempted to con two English girls who were in love with him. Heydrich, in his day, was kicked out of the navy for less than that. The minister passes on this information to Colonel Moravec, who is in charge of special operations. And this is precisely where the fate of many men is sealed. What does Moravec do? Nothing. He just notes in the files that Čurda is a good sportsman with impressive physical capacities. He does not remove him from the list of parachutists chosen for special missions. And on the night of March 27–28, Čurda is dropped over Moravia with two other comrades. Helped by the local Resistance, he manages to reach Prague.

After the war, someone will note that almost all of the dozens of parachutists chosen to be sent on special missions in the Protectorate gave patriotism as their motive for volunteering. Only two—one of them Čurda—said they volunteered because they were seeking adventure, and both turned out to be traitors.

But in terms of its impact, the betrayal committed by the other man will bear no comparison at all with that of Karel Čurda.

185

The train station in Prague is a magnificent dark stone building with two perfectly disturbing towers. Today is the Führer's birthday—April 20, 1942— and President Hácha is going to present him with a gift from the Czech people: a medical train. The ceremony is taking place in the station, naturally enough, with the highlight being a personal inspection of the train by the Protector himself. While Heydrich boards the train, a crowd of gawkers gathers outside. They stand in the vicinity of a white sign planted in the ground, declaring: 'Here stood the memorial of Wilson, removed on the orders of Reich-Protector SS-Obergruppenführer Heydrich.' I would like to be able to tell you that Gabčík and Kubiš are in that crowd, but I have no idea if it's true—and I suspect it isn't. To see Heydrich in these circumstances is of no practical use to them as it's a one-off event, unlikely to reoccur. And with the station so heavily guarded, being here would expose them to pointless risk.

On the other hand, I'm almost certain that the joke which is immediately spread around town has its origin here. I imagine someone in the crowd— probably an old man, a guardian of the Czech spirit—saying in a loud voice, so that everyone around him can hear: 'Poor Hitler! He must be really ill if he needs a whole train to make him better . . .' That's straight out of the good soldier Švejk.

## 186

Lying on his little iron bed, Jozef Gabčík listens to the sound of the tramway bell outside as the tram approaches Karlovo náměstí—Charles Square. Very close to here is Resslova Street, which leads down to the river: the street still knows nothing of the tragedy whose setting it will soon provide. A few shafts of sunlight force their way through the closed shutters of the apartment where, these days, Gabčík lives in hiding. From time to time you can hear the floorboards creak in the corridor, or on the landing, or in a neighbour's apartment. Gabčík is alert but calm, as always. His eyes stare at the ceiling while in his mind he draws maps of Europe. In one map, Czechoslovakia has its old borders back. In another, the brown plague has spread across the Channel, attaching Great Britain to one of the swastika's arms. But Gabčík, like Kubiš, tells anyone who'll listen that the war will be over in less than a year—and he probably believes it too. And not over in the way the Germans want it to be, obviously. Their first fatal error was declaring war on the USSR. Their second was declaring war on the United States in order to honour their alliance with Japan. It's quite ironic that, if France was defeated in 1940 because she didn't honour her promises to Czechoslovakia in 1938, Germany should now be about to lose the war because she *did* honour hers to Japan. But one year! In retrospect, this is touchingly optimistic.

I'm sure these political musings occupy Gabčík's mind, and the minds of his friends; I'm sure they have endless discussions at night, when they can't sleep, when they're able to relax a little by chatting. As long as they can forget the possibility of a nocturnal visit from the Gestapo. As long as they can stop themselves jumping at the slightest noise in the street, on the staircase, in the house. As long as they don't hear imaginary bells ringing in their heads, and yet are still able to listen out for the sound of real bells ringing.

This is another age—one where, each day, people eagerly look forward not to sports results

258

but to news from the Russian front.

The Russian front, however, is not uppermost in Gabčík's mind. The single most important thing in the war today is his mission. How many people believe this? Gabčík and Kubiš are convinced. Valčík too. And Colonel Moravec. And President Beneš, for the moment. And me. That's all, I think. In any case, only a handful of men know about Operation Anthropoid's objective. But even among this handful, there are some who disapprove.

This is true of certain parachutists working in Prague, and also of certain Resistance leaders—because they fear the reprisals that will be unleashed if the operation succeeds. Gabčík had a tedious argument with them the other day. They wanted to persuade him to give up his mission, or at least to change his target—to choose a prominent Czech collaborator, Emanuel Moravec, for instance, instead of Heydrich. This fear of the German! It's like a man who beats his dog: the dog may sometimes refuse to obey his master, but he will never turn on him.

Lieutenant Bartos wanted to cancel the operation. Sent by London to carry out other Resistance missions, Bartos is the highest-ranking officer among the Prague parachutists. But here, rank means nothing. The Anthropoid team, consisting only of Gabčík and Kubiš, received its instructions from London—from President Beneš himself. There are no more orders to be given now. The mission has to be accomplished, and that's that. Gabčík and Kubiš are men, and everyone who rubbed shoulders with them has emphasized their human qualities: their generosity, their good nature, their dedication. But Anthropoid is a machine.

Bartos asked London to stop Anthropoid. In reply he received a coded message, indecipherable to everyone except Gabčík and Kubiš. Lying on his little iron bed, Gabčík holds the text in his hand. Nobody has found this document. But in a few encrypted lines, their destiny is mapped out: the objective remains the same. The mission is confirmed. Heydrich must die. Outside, creaking metallically, a tram moves away.

## 187

SS-Standartenführer Paul Blobel, the leader of Sonderkommando 4a of Einsatzgruppe C—the group that so zealously performed its task at Babi Yar—is going mad. At night, in Kiev, his car passes the scene of his crimes. In the headlights' glare he contemplates the staggering spectacle of that ravine of the damned, and he is like Macbeth, haunted by his victims' ghosts. The dead of Babi Yar are not easily forgotten, because the earth in which they're buried is itself alive. Smoke rises from it. As the decomposing corpses produce gas bubbles that escape upward, clods jump out like popping champagne corks. The stench is foul. Blobel, laughing dementedly, explains to his guests: 'Here lie my thirty thousand Jews!' And he makes a sweeping gesture that takes in the whole immense gurgling belly of the ravine.

If it goes on like this, the corpses of Babi Yar will be the death of him. At the end of his tether, Blobel travels all the way to Berlin to plead with

Heydrich in person to transfer him elsewhere. He gets a suitable welcome: 'So you're feeling sick, are you? You spineless queer. You're no good for anything but selling crockery.' But Heydrich quickly calms down. The man in front of him is a drunken wreck, no longer capable of carrying out the work entrusted to him. It would be pointless and dangerous to keep him in that job against his will. 'Go and see Gruppenführer Müller. Tell him you want to go on vacation. He'll remove you from your command in Kiev.'

## 188

The working-class district of Žižkov in eastern Prague is supposed to have the highest concentration of bars in the whole city. It also has lots of churches, as you'd expect in the 'city of a hundred bells'. In one of these churches, a priest recalls that a young couple came to see him 'when the tulips were in flower'. The man was short, with thin lips and piercing eyes. The young woman, I know, was charming and full of joie de vivre. They seemed to be in love. They wanted to get married, but not straightaway. The date they wanted to book was precise but uncertain: 'two weeks after the war ends'.

## 189

I wonder how Jonathan Littell, in his novel *The Kindly Ones*, knows that Blobel had an Opel. If Blobel really drove an Opel, then I bow before his superior research. But if it's a bluff, that weakens the whole book. Of course it does! It's true that the Nazis were supplied in bulk by Opel, and so it's perfectly *plausible* that Blobel possessed, or used, a vehicle of that make. But *plausible* is not *known*. I'm drivelling, aren't I? When I tell people that, they think I'm mental. They don't see the problem.

## 190

Valčík and Ata (the Moravecs' young son) have just had a miraculous escape during a police inspection that ended in the deaths of two parachutists. They are hiding out in the concierge's apartment and telling him the story of their misadventure. I could tell this story, too, but what would it add, I wonder, to have yet another scene from a spy novel? Modern novels are all about narrative economy, that's just how it is, and mine can't keep ignoring this parsimonious logic. So, basically, all you need to know is that it was because of Valčík's cool head and his perfect grasp of the situation that he and Ata were not arrested or killed.

Seeing how strongly this adventure and he himself have impressed the teenage boy, Valčík tells him helpfully:

'You see this wooden box, Ata? The Krauts could beat it till it started to talk. But you, no matter how much they beat you, you must say nothing. Nothing, you understand?'

That line, by contrast, is not at all superfluous to my story.

## 191

You might have guessed that I was a bit disturbed by the publication of Jonathan Littell's novel, and by its success. And even if I can comfort myself by saying that our projects are not the same, I am forced to admit that the subject matter is fairly similar. I'm reading it at the moment, and each page gives me the urge to write something about it. I have to suppress this urge. All I will say is that there's a description of Heydrich at the beginning of the book, from which I will quote only one line: 'His hands seemed too long, like nervous algae attached to his arms.' I don't know why, but I really like that image.

## 192

This is what I think: inventing a character in order to understand historical facts is like fabricating evidence. Or rather, in the words of my brother-in-law, with whom I've discussed all this: *It's like planting false proof at a crime scene where the floor is already strewn with incriminating evidence.*

Prague in 1942 looks like a black-and-white photo. The passing men wear crumpled hats and dark suits, while the women wear those fitted skirts that make them all look like secretaries. I know this—I have the photos on my desk. All right, no, I admit it. I was exaggerating a bit. They don't all look like secretaries. Some look like nurses.

The Czech policemen directing the traffic look strangely like London bobbies with their funny helmets. And just when the Czechs had adopted the system of driving on the right . . .

The trams that come and go to the sound of little bells resemble old red-and-white train carriages. (But how can I know that, when the photos are in black and white? I just know, okay!) They all have round headlights that look like lanterns.

Neon signs decorate the façades of the buildings in Nové Město, advertising beer, brands of clothing, and Bata, the famous shoe manufacturer. In fact, the whole city seems to be covered in writing—and not only adverts. There are *V*s everywhere: originally they were symbols of the Czech Resistance, but the Nazis appropriated them as an exhortation to the Reich's final victory. There are *V*s on tramways, on cars, sometimes carved into the ground; *V*s everywhere, battling it out between two opposed ideologies.

Graffiti on a wall: *Židi ven*—Jews out! In shop windows, a sign to reassure the customers: *Čisté árijské obchod*—pure Aryan shop.

And in a bar: *Zada se zdvorile, by se nehovorilo*

*o politice*—Customers are kindly requested not to talk politics.

And then those sinister red posters, written in two languages like all the city's road signs. And that's without even mentioning flags and other banners. Never has any flag signalled its meaning so powerfully as this black cross in a white circle on a red background.

Prague in the 1940s didn't lack style, even if serenity was harder to come by. Looking at the photos, I keep expecting to see Humphrey Bogart among the passersby, or Lida Baarova, the beautiful and famous Czech actress who was Goebbels's mistress before the war. Strange times.

I know a restaurant called the Two Cats in the old town, under the arcades: there's a fresco above it, with two giant cats painted on either side of an arch. But as for the inn the Three Cats, I don't know where it is or even if it still exists.

Three men are drinking there, and not talking politics. Instead, they're talking timetables. Gabčík and Kubiš are sitting at a table opposite a carpenter. But this is no ordinary carpenter. He's the carpenter at Prague Castle, and in this capacity he sees Heydrich's Mercedes arrive every day. And every evening, he sees it leave.

Kubiš is talking to him because the carpenter is a Moravian, like him, and the familiar accent reassures him. 'Don't worry, you're going to help us before, not during. You'll be a long way away when we shoot him.'

Oh, really? So this is Operation Anthropoid's great secret? Even the carpenter who's being asked merely to provide the timetable is, without any further ado, told exactly what's going to happen.

I did read somewhere that the parachutists were not always rigorously discreet. Then again, is there any point in trying to conceal everything? The carpenter is hardly going to believe that they're asking him for Heydrich's schedule because they're compiling traffic statistics. But when I reread the carpenter's testimony I see that Kubiš did tell him, in his best Moravian accent: 'Don't breathe a word of this at home!' Well, as long as he told him . . .

So every day the carpenter has to write down the time of Heydrich's arrival and departure. He also has to note whether or not he's escorted by another car.

Heydrich is everywhere: in Prague, in Berlin, and—this month of May—in Paris.

In the wood-panelled rooms of the Majestic Hotel, the head of the SD gathers the principal field officers of the occupying SS troops to inform them about the operation he's leading—and which none of his men, nor the world at large, yet know by the name of 'the Final Solution'.

By this time, the mass slaughter perpetrated by the Einsatzgruppen has finally been judged too distressing for the soldiers who must carry it out. The old-style killings are gradually phased out in favour of mobile gas chambers. This new system is both simple and ingenious. The Jews have to climb into a truck with the exhaust pipe connected to a length of hose; the victims are then asphyxiated with carbon monoxide. This has two advantages:

first, you can kill more Jews at a time; and second, it is easier on the executioners' nerves. It also produces a curious side effect that the people in charge find amusing: the corpses turn pink. The only inconvenience is that the suffocating victims tend to defecate, so the floor of the truck, smeared with excrement, has to be cleaned after each gassing.

But these mobile gas chambers, Heydrich explains, are still not sophisticated enough. He says: 'Better solutions, more advanced and more productive, are on their way.' Then, his audience hanging on his every word, he adds abruptly: 'All the Jews in Europe have been sentenced to death.' Given that the Einsatzgruppen have already executed more than a million Jews, you have to wonder who among his audience hasn't yet understood this.

This is the second time I've caught Heydrich overdramatizing this kind of statement. When he informed Eichmann, just before Wannsee, that the Führer had decided upon the physical elimination of all the Jews, his colleague was struck by the dramatic silence that followed this announcement. In both cases, even if nothing was really official beforehand, you can't say it came as a great surprise. More than the pleasure of delivering a scoop, I think Heydrich enjoyed verbalizing the incredible, the unthinkable, as if to give substance to the unimaginable truth. This is what I've got to tell you—you already know it, but it's up to me to tell you, and it's up to us to do it. The orator, dizzy from speaking the unspeakable. The monster, drunk on the thought of the monstrosities he heralds.

The carpenter shows them the place where Heydrich gets out of his car each day. Gabčík and Kubiš look around. They pick a spot behind a house where they could wait for him, and from where they could shoot him. But the area is heavily guarded, of course. The carpenter makes it clear they wouldn't have time to flee, that they would never get out of the castle alive. Gabčík and Kubiš are ready to die—they have been since the beginning, no question about it. But all the same they do want to *try* to stay alive. They need a plan that gives them a chance of getting away—a small chance but a chance nonetheless—because they both have hopes and dreams for after the war. In the Resistance, among all the Czechs who are risking their lives to help them, there are some brave and pretty young women. I know very few details of my heroes' love lives, but I do know that after these few months operating secretly in Prague, Gabčík wants to marry Libena, the Fafek family's daughter, and Kubiš the beautiful Anna Malinova, with her raspberry lips. After the war . . . They're not deluding themselves. They know they have only one chance in a thousand of surviving the war. But they want to take that chance. They must, above all, accomplish their mission—absolutely. But that doesn't mean they want to commit suicide. What a terrible thought.

The two men walk back down Nerudova, the long street with its alchemists' shop signs, connecting the castle to Malá Strana. Farther down, the Mercedes will have to go around a nice curve.

Could be a spot worth looking at . . .

196

Heydrich is wrong about the Czech Resistance—it's not dead yet. In order to collect the carpenter's daily bulletin on Heydrich's movements, they find a ground-floor apartment just below the castle. Whenever necessary (every day, I suppose), the carpenter comes and knocks at the window. A young girl opens it. Two of them take turns; the carpenter thinks they are not only sisters but also the two parachutists' girlfriends—which they might well be. The carpenter and the girls never exchange a word. The carpenter hands over his piece of paper and leaves. Today, he has written: '9–5 (without)'. In other words: 9:00 a.m. to 5:00 p.m. Without an escort.

Gabčík and Kubiš are confronted by an insoluble problem. They have no way of knowing in advance whether Heydrich will be escorted by a second car, filled with bodyguards. The statistics based on the carpenter's reports do not show any fixed pattern. Sometimes without, sometimes with. Without: they'll have a small chance of getting out alive. With: no chance at all.

So, to carry out their mission, the two parachutists must surrender themselves to this horrifying lottery. They must choose a date with no idea whether Heydrich will be escorted. Whether their mission is extremely risky, or whether it's actually a suicide mission.

Riding bicycles, the two men keep making the same journey—from Heydrich's home to the castle, from curve to curve. Heydrich lives in Panenské Břežany, a little spot in the suburbs a quarter of an hour by car from the city centre. One part of the journey is particularly isolated: a long straight line with no houses nearby. If they managed to immobilize the car they could shoot Heydrich here without anyone seeing. They consider stopping the car with a steel cable strung tightly across the road. But afterward, how would they get away? They'd need their own car or motorbike. And the Czech Resistance has neither. No, it has to be done in the middle of town, in the middle of the day, in the middle of a crowd. They need a curve in the road. Gabčík's and Kubiš's thoughts are curved and twisting. They dream of the ideal curve.

And they end up finding it.

Well, 'ideal' is perhaps not the right word.

The curve in Holešovice Street (ulice v Holešovičkách in Czech), in the Libeň district, has several advantages. First of all, it is almost a hairpin, so the Mercedes will be forced to slow right down. Next, it's at the foot of a hill where they can post a lookout to warn them of the Mercedes's arrival. Finally, it's in the suburbs, midway between

Panenské Břežany and Hradčany: neither in the city centre nor in the countryside. So it offers the possibility of escape. The Holešovice curve also has some disadvantages. It's at a crossroads intersected by tram tracks. If a tram goes by at the same time as the Mercedes, there's a danger the operation will be compromised—because the car might be hidden or civilians put at risk.

I have never assassinated anyone, but I suppose there is no such thing as ideal conditions: a moment comes when you have to decide. And anyway, there isn't time to find anything better. So Holešovice it is: this curve that no longer exists, swallowed up by a highway ramp and by modernity, which couldn't care less about my memories.

Because I do remember now. Each day, each hour, the memory grows clearer. On this bend of Holešovice Street, I feel I've been waiting forever.


## 199

I'm spending a few days on vacation in a beautiful house in Toulon, and I'm doing a bit of writing. This is no ordinary house: it's the former residence of an Alsatian printer who, in the course of his job, rubbed shoulders with Paul Eluard and Elsa Triolet. [Paul Eluard (1895–1952) was a French surrealist poet. Elsa Triolet (1896–1970) was a French writer of Russian origin who fought in the French Resistance alongside her husband, Louis Aragon.] During the war he was in Lyon, where he printed false papers for Jews and stocked books by the underground publisher Éditions de Minuit.

At the same time, the land surrounding his house in Toulon was occupied by German army camps, but apparently no one lived in the house, which remained in good condition. The furniture and the books were not touched, and they're still here.

This man's great-niece, knowing of my interest in the period, shows me a slim volume taken from the family library. It's the original edition of *The Silence of the Sea* by Vercors, published on July 25, 1943, 'the day the Roman tyrant fell', as it says in the back of the book. It is signed by the author and dedicated to the great-uncle:

> *To Madame and Pierre Braun, with feelings that link all those engulfed in dark days by*
> The Silence of the Sea
> *Sincerely yours, Vercors*

I am on vacation and I hold a bit of history in my hands. It is a very sweet and pleasant feeling.

## 200

There are alarming rumours about Heydrich. He will leave Prague. For good. Tomorrow, he must take the plane to Berlin. No one knows if he will return. This would obviously be a relief to the Czech people, but it would be a disaster for Operation Anthropoid. Alarming news for the parachutists, and also—although they know nothing about it—for the French. It is whispered among historians that perhaps Heydrich, having accomplished his mission in the Protectorate, now has his eye on

272

what today we would call 'a new challenge'. Having dealt so ruthlessly and brutally with Bohemia and Moravia, Heydrich would now sort out France.

He has to go to Berlin to discuss this with Hitler. France is in turmoil; Pétain and Laval are worms; if Heydrich could deal with the French Resistance the way he dealt with the Czech Resistance, that would be perfect.

This is only a theory, although it is backed up by Heydrich's trip to Paris two weeks earlier.

## 201

That's right—in May 1942, Heydrich spent a week in Paris. I have found the film of his visit in the archives of the National Audiovisual Institute. A clip from the day's French news: fifty-nine seconds of filmed reportage. Speaking in that nasal voice so typical of the 1940s, the newsreader announces:

'Paris. Arrival of Mr Heydrich, the SS general, chief of police, Reich representative in Prague, asked by the head of the SS and the German police, Mr Himmler, to officially appoint Mr Oberg, major general of the SS and of the police in the occupied territories. Mr Heydrich is the head of the International Commission of the Criminal Police, and France has always been represented at this commission. The general took advantage of his stay in Paris to receive Mr Bousquet, secretary-general of the police, and Mr Hilaire, secretary-general of the administration. Mr Heydrich also made contact with Mr Darquier de Pellepoix, who, along with Mr de Brinon, has just been named commissioner

273

for Jewish affairs.'

I have always been intrigued by this meeting between Heydrich and Bousquet. I would really like to have the minutes of their conversation. After the war, Bousquet let it be known for a long time that he stood up to Heydrich. And it's true that he categorically refused to give in on one point: that the powers of the French police should not be reduced; these powers consisting essentially of the right to arrest people. Jews in particular. Heydrich is happy to let the local police deal with this: it's less work for the Germans, after all. As he tells Oberg, his experience in the Protectorate has shown him that an autonomous police and administration will produce better results. Provided, of course, that Bousquet leads his police 'in the same spirit as the German police.' But Heydrich has no doubt that Bousquet is the right man for the job. At the end of his stay, he says: 'The only person who has youth, intelligence, and authority is Bousquet. With men like him, we will be able to build the Europe of tomorrow—a Europe very different from that of today.'

When Heydrich tells René Bousquet about the next deportation of stateless (that is, non-French) Jews interned at Drancy, Bousquet spontaneously suggests that stateless Jews interned in the free zone should be deported as well. How very obliging of him.

René Bousquet was a lifelong friend of François Mitterand. But that is far from his worst offence.

Bousquet is not a cop like Barbie, or a militiaman like Touvier; nor is he a prefect like Papon [Klaus Barbie (1913–91) was a Gestapo member and war criminal known as the Butcher of Lyon. Paul Touvier (1915–96) was head of the Lyon militia. Maurice Papon (1910–2007) was a French politician later condemned for complicity in crimes against humanity during the Second World War.] in Bordeaux. He is a high-level politician destined for a brilliant career, but who chooses the path of collaboration and gets mixed up in the deportation of Jews. He is the one who ensures that the raid on Vél' d'Hiv [The raid on the Vélodrome d'Hiver took place on July 16–17, 1942, and involved the arrests of 13,152 Jews, including 5,802 women and 4,051 children. They were sent to concentration camps. Only 25 people survived.] (code name: Spring Wind) is carried out by the French police rather than the Germans. He is thus responsible for what is probably the most infamous deed in the history of the French nation. That it was committed in the name of the French state obviously changes nothing. How many World Cups will we have to win in order to erase such a stain?

After the war, Bousquet survives the purge of Nazi collaborators that took place in France, but his participation in the Vichy government nevertheless deprives him of the political career that had appeared his destiny. He doesn't live on the streets, though, and gets positions on various boards of directors, including that of the newspaper *La Dépêche du Midi*; he is the main force behind its hard-line anti-Gaullist stance between 1959 and 1971. So, basically, he benefits from the usual tolerance of the ruling class for its most compromised members. He also enjoys the company—not without malice, I imagine—of Simone Weil, an Auschwitz survivor who knows nothing of Bousquet's collaborationist activities.

His past finally catches up with him in the 1980s, however, and in 1991 he is charged with crimes against humanity.

The investigation ends two years later when he is shot in his own house by a madman. I vividly remember seeing that guy give a press conference just after killing Bousquet and just before the cops arrested him. I remember how pleased with himself he looked as he calmly explained that he'd done it to make people talk about him. I found that utterly idiotic.

This ridiculous moron deprived us of a trial that would have been ten times more interesting than those of Papon and Barbie put together, more interesting than those of Pétain and Laval . . . the trial of the century. As punishment for this outrageous attack on history, this unimaginably cretinous man was given ten years; he served seven, and is now free. I feel a great repulsion and mistrust for someone like Bousquet, but when I think of his assassin, of the immense historical loss that his act represents, of the revelations the trial would have produced and which he has forever denied us, I feel overwhelmed by hate. He didn't kill any innocents, that's true, but he is a destroyer of truth. And all so he could appear on TV for three minutes! What a monstrous, stupid, Warholian piece of shit! The only ones who ought to have a moral right to judge whether this man should live or die are his victims—the living and the dead who fell into the Nazis' claws because of men like him—but I am sure they wanted him *alive*. How disappointed they must have been when they heard about this absurd murder! I can feel only disgust for a society that produces such behaviour, such lunatics. Pasternak wrote: 'I don't like people who are indifferent to truth.' And worse still are those bastards who are not only indifferent to it but work actively against it. All the secrets that Bousquet took with him to his grave . . . I have to stop thinking about this because it's making me ill.

Bousquet's trial: that would have been the French equivalent of Eichmann in Jerusalem.

## 203

Anyway, let's talk about something else. I have just discovered the testimony of Helmut Knochen, appointed chief of the German police in France by Heydrich. He claims to reveal something that Heydrich told him in confidence and which he never repeated to anyone until now. His testimony dates from June 2000. Fifty-eight years later!

Heydrich supposedly told him: 'The war can no longer be won. We must reach a negotiated peace and I am afraid that Hitler can't accept that. We must think about this.' We are meant to believe that Heydrich reached this conclusion in May

1942—before Stalingrad, at a time when the Reich had never looked stronger.

Knochen sees in that an extraordinary clairvoyancy on Heydrich's part. He considers the Blond Beast much more intelligent than all the other Nazi dignitaries. He also believes that Heydrich was thinking of overthrowing Hitler. And based on this he proposes the following theory: that the assassination of Heydrich would have been a high priority for Churchill, who absolutely refused to be deprived of total victory over Hitler. In other words, the British would have supported the Czechs because they were afraid that a wise Nazi like Heydrich might remove Hitler and save the regime through a negotiated peace.

I suspect it's in Knochen's interests to associate himself with the theory of a plot against Hitler, in order to minimize his own (very real) role in the police machine of the Third Reich. It is even perfectly conceivable that, sixty years later, he actually believes what he's saying. Personally, I think it's bullshit. But I report it anyway.

## 204

A poster on an Internet forum expresses the opinion that Max Aue, Jonathan Littell's protagonist in *The Kindly Ones*, 'rings true because he is the mirror of his age.' What? No! He rings true (for certain, easily duped readers) because he is the mirror of *our* age: a postmodern nihilist, essentially. At no moment in the novel is it suggested that this character believes in Nazism. On the contrary, he displays an often critical detachment towards National Socialist doctrine—and in that sense, he can hardly be said to reflect the delirious fanaticism prevalent in *his* time. On the other hand, this detachment, this blasé attitude towards everything, this permanent malaise, this taste for philosophizing, this unspoken amorality, this morose sadism, and this terrible sexual frustration that constantly twists his guts . . . but of course! How did I not see it before? Suddenly, everything is clear. *The Kindly Ones* is simply 'Houellebecq does Nazism.'

## 205

I think I'm beginning to understand. What I'm writing is an *infranovel*.

## 206

The moment is getting closer, I can feel it. The Mercedes is on its way. It's coming. Something floating in the Prague air pierces me to my bones. The twists of the road are spelling out the destiny of a man, and of another, and another, and another. I see pigeons take off from the bronze head of Jan Hus and, in the background, the most beautiful view in the world: Týn Church with its sharp black turrets, whose grey and evil-looking façade is so majestic that it makes me want to fall to my knees every time I see it. The heart of Prague beats in my chest. I hear the bells of the tramway. I see men in grey-green uniforms, hear their boots clicking on the cobbles. I'm nearly there. I have to go. Yes, I must travel to Prague. I have to be there when this happens.

I have to write it there.

I hear the engine of the Mercedes as it glides along the road. I hear Gabčík breathing, wrapped up in his raincoat, waiting on the pavement. I see Kubiš standing opposite, and Valčík posted at the top of the hill. I feel the smooth cold mirror at the bottom of his coat pocket. Not yet, not yet, *uz nie, noch nicht*.

Not yet.

I feel the wind that whips the faces of the two Germans in the car. Yes, the chauffeur is driving that fast—I know this: a thousand witnesses have attested to it, I have no doubts at all on that score. The Mercedes speeds past, and the most precious part of my imagining follows silently in its slipstream. The air rushes past, the engine drones, the passenger keeps telling his giant chauffeur, *'Schneller! Schneller!'* Faster, faster, he shouts, but he doesn't know that time has already started to slow down. Soon, the course of the world will freeze at a bend in the road. The earth will stop moving at exactly the same time as the Mercedes.

But not yet. It is still too early. Not everything is in place yet. Not everything has been said. I would like to be able to delay this moment forever, I think, even as my whole being stretches out longingly towards it.

The Slovak, the Moravian, and the Bohemian Czech are also waiting, and I would pay dearly to feel what they felt then. But I am too corrupted by literature. 'Yet have I something in me dangerous,'

280

says Hamlet, at a similar moment. I hope I can be forgiven. I hope they can forgive me. I am doing all of this for them. I had to start up the black Mercedes—that wasn't easy. I had to put everything in place, take care of the preparations. I had to spin the web of this adventure, erect the gallows of the Resistance, cover death's hideous iron fist in the sumptuous velvet glove of the struggle. Scorning modesty, I had to join forces with men so great that I am a mere insect in comparison.

I had to cheat sometimes, to betray my literary principles—because what I believe is insignificant next to what is being played out now. What will be played out in a few minutes. Here. Now. On this curve in Holešovice Street in Prague, where—later, much later—they will build some kind of access road. Because cities change faster, alas, than men's memories.

But that doesn't really matter. A black Mercedes is sliding along the road like a snake—from now on, that's the only thing that matters. I have never felt so close to my story.

Prague.

I feel metal rubbing against leather. And that anxiety rising inside the three men, and the calmness they display. This is not the manly self-confidence of those who know they are going to die. Even though our heroes are prepared for death, the possibility of escaping alive has never been dismissed. And this makes their psychological tension even more unbearable. I don't know what incredible power over their nerves they must possess in order to remain in control. I make a quick inventory of all the times in my life when I've had to show sangfroid. What a joke! On each

281

occasion, the stakes were tiny: a broken leg, a night at work, a rejection. There you go, that's pretty much all I've ever risked in the course of my pathetic existence. How could I convey even the tiniest idea of what those three men lived through?

But it's too late for this kind of mood. After all, I, too, have responsibilities and I must face up to them. I have to stay in the slipstream of the Mercedes. Listen to the sounds of life on this May morning. Feel the wind of history as it begins, gently, to blow. Watch as all the actors in this drama—from the dawn of time in the twelfth century, up until the present and Natacha—file past in my mind. And then retain only five names: Heydrich, Klein, Valčík, Kubiš, and Gabčík.

In the narrowing flow of this story, those five are about to reach the waterfall.

207

It's the afternoon of May 26, 1942. Heydrich is about to attend the opening concert of Prague's weeklong music festival, featuring music composed by his father. A few hours before the first notes are played, he holds a press conference for the Protectorate's journalists:

'I am obliged to observe that incivilities, or what one might call indelicacies, if not examples of outright rudeness, particularly towards Germans, are once again on the rise. You are well aware, gentlemen, that I am generous and that I encourage all plans for reform. But you also know that, however patient I may be, I will not hesitate to strike with the most extreme harshness if I get the feeling that people consider the Reich to be weak, and if they mistake the goodness of my heart for weakness.'

I am a child. This speech is interesting on more than one level. It shows Heydrich at the height of his powers, utterly self-assured, expressing himself like the enlightened despot he imagines himself to be—the viceroy proud of his governance, the master firm but fair, as if the title of Protector were printed upon his conscience; as if Heydrich really considered himself a 'protector'. Proud of his sharp political sense, Heydrich wields the carrot and the stick in all his speeches. It is typical of totalitarian rhetoric that Heydrich the Hangman, Heydrich the Butcher, should ingenuously tell us how generous and progressive he is, wielding his irony as knowingly and insolently as the wiliest of tyrants. But it is none of this that stands out for me in this speech. What stands out is his use of the term 'incivilities'.


## 208


On the evening of May 26, Libena goes to see Gabčík, her fiancé. But he has gone out to calm his nerves because he can no longer stand the prevarications of those Resistance members who fear the consequences of the assassination attempt. So it's Kubiš who lets her in. She's brought cigarettes. After a brief hesitation, she gives them to Kubiš. 'But, Jeniček [this is the affectionate diminutive of Jan, which means that she knows his real name], you mustn't smoke them all!' And the young girl leaves, not knowing whether she will ever see her fiancé again.

## 209

I think all men for whom life is not an endless series of misfortunes are bound to experience, at least once, a moment they consider, rightly or wrongly, to be the apotheosis of their existence. For Heydrich, this moment has arrived. And by one of those delicious ironies that forge our destinies, it occurs the day before his assassination.

When Heydrich enters the chapel of Wallenstein Palace, all the guests rise. Ceremonious but smiling, his eyes lifted, he walks on the red carpet that leads him to his place in the front row. His wife, Lina, accompanies him. She is pregnant and radiant, wearing a dark dress. Everyone's eyes turn their way and all the men in uniform make the Nazi salute as they pass. Heydrich is overcome by the majesty of the place—I can read it in his eyes. He proudly contemplates the altar, surmounted by sumptuous bas-reliefs, and the space below it where the musicians will soon take their seats.

This evening he remembers (if he'd ever forgotten) that music is his life. Music has been with him since his birth. It has never left him. Within Heydrich, the artist has always fought against the man of action. His career has been decided by the course of the world. But music always lives inside him—it will be there until his death.

Each guest holds the evening's programme.

Here, he can read the bad prose that the interim Protector has seen fit to compose as an introduction:

Music is the creative language of those who are artists and music lovers, the means of expressing their interior life. In difficult times, it brings relief to he who listens, and in times of greatness and fighting, it encourages him. But music is, above all, the great expression of the German race's cultural productivity. In this sense, the festival of music in Prague is a contribution to the excellence of the present, conceived as the foundation of a vigorous musical life in this region at the heart of the Reich for years to come.

Heydrich does not write as well as he plays the violin, but he doesn't care about that—because music is the true language of artistic souls.

The programme is exceptional. He has brought over the greatest musicians to play the greatest Germanic music. Beethoven, Handel, even Mozart . . . and probably, for once, no Wagner. (I can't be certain, because I haven't been able to get hold of the complete programme.) But it is when he hears the first notes of Bruno Heydrich's Concerto for Piano in C Minor—played by former pupils of the Halle Conservatory, accompanied by a famous virtuoso pianist flown in expressly—that Heydrich, letting the music flow through him like a stream of well-being, experiences his feeling of apotheosis. I would be curious to hear this work. When Heydrich applauds at the end, I can read on his face the arrogant daydream of all great, self-centred megalomaniacs. Heydrich tastes his personal triumph through the posthumous triumph of his father. But triumph and apotheosis are not exactly the same thing.


## 210

Gabčík is back. Neither he nor Kubiš smokes in the apartment, because they don't want to put out the family they're staying with—and also because they don't want to arouse the neighbours' suspicions.

Through the window, the silhouette of the castle stands out against the night. Kubiš, lost in contemplation of its imposing mass, thinks aloud: 'I wonder what it will be like there, this time tomorrow . . .' His hostess, Mrs Ogounova, asks: 'What is supposed to happen?' Gabčík is the one who replies: 'Nothing, Mrs Ogounova.'


## 211

The morning of May 27, Gabčík and Kubiš get ready to leave earlier than usual. The Ogoun family's young son is doing lastminute revision because today is the day of his final exam and he's nervous. Kubiš tells him: 'Be calm, Luboš. You'll pass it. You have to pass it. And tonight, we'll all celebrate your success together . . .'

# 212

As usual, Heydrich eats his breakfast while reading the day's newspapers, delivered to him from Prague every morning at dawn. At nine o'clock his black (or dark green) Mercedes arrives, driven by his chauffeur—a giant SS guard, about six feet five inches tall, called Klein. But this morning, Heydrich makes him wait. He plays with his children (I have trouble imagining Heydrich playing with his children) and goes for a walk with his wife in the immense gardens that surround their house. Lina probably has to keep him up-to-date on the work that's being done. The plan is to cut down the ash trees and replace them with fruit trees. At least, that's what Ivanov says in his historical account of the assassination. I wonder if he made it up? According to him, the Heydrichs' youngest child, Silke, told her father that someone called Herbert had taught her how to load a revolver. Silke is three years old. But I suppose nothing, in such troubled times, should surprise me.

# 213

It is May 27: the anniversary of Joseph Roth's death. He died three years before in Paris, of alcoholism and sorrow. Roth was a fierce and prophetic observer of the Nazi regime during its early years. In 1934, he wrote: 'What swarmings of people in this world, an hour before its end!'

Two men board a tram. Thinking it might be their last journey, they watch avidly as the streets of Prague rush past the window. Then again, they might have chosen to see nothing, to think about nothing, gathering their concentration by blocking out the outside world . . . but I doubt it. They've been on the alert for so long it's become second nature. Boarding the tram, they automatically check out the appearances of all the other male passengers: who gets on and off, who stands in front of each door. They can tell instantly who's speaking German, even at the other end of the carriage. They note the vehicle in front of the tram, and the one behind it, and how far away they are. They spot the Wehrmacht motorbike and sidecar as they overtake on the right; they glance at the patrol going back up the pavement; they note the two men in leather raincoats standing guard outside the building opposite . . . okay, I'll stop there. Gabčík is also wearing a raincoat, but although the sun is shining it's still cool enough for him not to attract unwanted attention. Or perhaps he's carrying it on his arm? He and Kubiš have dressed smartly for the big day, and each grips a heavy briefcase.

They get off somewhere in Žižkov, the district named after the legendary Jan Žižkov, the greatest and most ferocious Hussite general—the one-eyed man who for fourteen years resisted the armies of the Germanic Holy Roman Empire; the Taborite leader who brought down the wrath of heaven on all Bohemia's enemies. They go to the house of a contact to pick up two bicycles. One of the bikes belongs to Aunt Moravec. On Holešovice Street, they stop to greet another lady of the Resistance— another surrogate mother who sheltered them and made them cakes: a Mrs Khodlova, whom they wish to thank. You haven't come to say goodbye, have you? No, not at all, we'll come to see you soon—perhaps even today. Will you be at home? Yes, of course, please come . . .

When they finally get there, Valčík is already waiting for them. There is perhaps a fourth parachutist—Lieutenant Opalka from Out Distance, come to give them a hand—but his role has never been clarified, nor has his presence even been verified. So I'll stick to what I know.

It is not yet nine o'clock. After a brief discussion, the three men go to their posts.


## 214

It is nearly ten o'clock and Heydrich still hasn't left for work. That evening, he must fly to Berlin for a meeting with Hitler. Perhaps he is taking particular care to prepare for it? Ever the meticulous bureaucrat, he is probably checking the documents in his briefcase one last time. In any case, it's already ten o'clock when Heydrich takes his place in the front seat of the Mercedes. Klein starts the engine, the gates open, and the guards, right arms outstretched, salute the Protector as he passes. Then the Mercedes convertible accelerates up the road.

While Heydrich's Mercedes snakes along the thread of its knotted destiny, while the three parachutists keep an anxious lookout, all their senses alert, on that deadly bend of the road, I reread the story of Jan Žižka, told by George Sand in a little-known book called *Jean Zizka*. And once more I become distracted. I see the fierce general sitting enthroned on his mountain: blind, his skull shaved, his braided Asterix-style moustaches drooping onto his chest like creepers. At the foot of his improvised fortress, ready to attack, is Sigismond's imperial army. Battles, massacres, sieges, and spoils of war pass before my eyes. Žižka was the king's chamberlain in Prague. It's said that he entered the war against the Catholic Church out of hatred for priests—because a priest had raped his sister. This is the era of the first famous defenestrations in Prague. No one knows yet that this small fire in Bohemia will blaze up into more than a century of terrible religious wars, and that from the ashes of Jan Hus will rise Protestantism. I learn that the word 'pistol' comes from the Czech *pištala*. I learn that it was Žižka, with his battalions of heavily armed chariots, who practically invented tank warfare. Apparently, Žižka found the man who raped his sister and punished him terribly. Apparently, too, Žižka was one of the greatest war leaders in history, because he never suffered defeat. I am spreading myself too thinly. Everything I read takes me farther and farther away from the curve in Holešovice Street. And then I stumble on this phrase of George Sand's: 'Poor workers or sick people, you must always struggle against those who tell you: "Work hard to live badly." ' That isn't an invitation to digress—it's a demand! But I am concentrated on my objective now. I will no longer let myself be distracted. A black Mercedes glides along the road—I can see it.

## 216

Heydrich is late. It is already ten o'clock. Rush hour is over, and Gabčík and Kubiš's presence on the pavement is becoming more conspicuous. In 1942, anywhere in Europe, two men standing alone for a long time in the same place quickly attract suspicion.

I am sure they are sure that the game is up. Each passing minute increases the risk that they will be spotted by a patrol and arrested. But still they wait. The Mercedes should have been here more than an hour ago. According to the carpenter's records, Heydrich has never arrived at the castle after ten o'clock. Everything says he is not coming. He could have changed his route, or gone straight to the airport. Perhaps he's already taken off, never to return.

Kubiš is leaning against a lamppost, on the inside of the curve. Gabčík, on the other side of the crossroads, pretends to wait for a tram. He must have seen a good dozen pass already and he's no longer counting. The flood of Czech workers gradually abates. The two men are more and more exposed. Little by little the hum of the city fades and the calm that descends on the curve in the road is like an ironic echo of their disastrous mission. Heydrich is never late. He's not coming.

But obviously I wouldn't have written this whole book if Heydrich wasn't coming.

At half past ten, the two men are struck by lightning—or rather by the light of the sun reflected, from the hill above them, by the little mirror that Valčík has taken from his pocket. It's the signal. He is coming. At last! In a few seconds he'll be there. Gabčík runs across the road and positions himself at the exit of the curve, hidden by it until the last moment. Unlike Kubiš, who is farther forward (unless he's behind Gabčík, as some reconstructions claim, but that seems less likely to me), he can't see that the Mercedes outlined against the horizon is not followed by a second car. I bet he hasn't even given it a thought. At this moment, one single idea takes all the space in his fevered brain: shoot the target. But then, from behind, he hears the unmistakable noise of a tram approaching.

Suddenly the Mercedes appears. As expected, it brakes. But as they had feared, a tram filled with civilians is going to pass it at the worst possible moment: at the exact instant when the car reaches the part of the street where Gabčík waits. Oh well . . . tough shit. They have evaluated the risk of killing innocent civilians, and they have decided to take it. Gabčík and Kubiš are less scrupulous than Camus' Just Assassins, [Les Justes was a 1949 play by Camus about five revolutionaries in Russia who attempt to assassinate a grand duke.] but that's because they are real people, both greater and more flawed than any fictional character.

292

You are strong, you are powerful, you are pleased with yourself. You have killed people and you are going to kill many, many more. Everything you do succeeds. Nothing can resist you. In the space of barely ten years you have become 'the most dangerous man in the Third Reich.' Nobody makes fun of you anymore. They don't call you the Goat now—they call you the Blond Beast. You have undeniably moved up the hierarchy of animal species. Everyone is afraid of you, even your boss—a bespectacled little hamster, albeit a dangerous one.

You are sitting comfortably in your Mercedes convertible and the wind is whipping your face. You are going to work; you work in a castle. All the inhabitants of the country where you live are your subjects: you have the power of life and death over them. If you decide to, you could kill them all— every last one. In fact, that might be exactly what ends up happening.

But you won't be there to see it, because you are headed for other adventures. You have new challenges to face. Later today, you will fly away and abandon your kingdom. You came to restore order in this country and you have succeeded brilliantly. You have made an entire people submit to you; you have led the Protectorate with an iron fist; you have governed, you have ruled, you have reigned. You leave to your successor the tough task of perpetuating your legacy. They must: prevent any resurgence of the Resistance movement that you crushed; keep the entire machinery of Czech industry at the service of the German war effort; continue the process of Germanization, which you began and whose forms you defined.

Thinking of your past and your future, you are overwhelmed by an immense feeling of self-satisfaction. You tighten your grip on the leather bag that rests on your knees. You think of Halle, of the navy, of France, which awaits you, of the Jews you will kill, of this immortal Reich whose most solid foundations you have laid. But you forget the present. Is your policeman's instinct blunted by the daydreams that fill your mind as the Mercedes speeds along? You do not see, in this man carrying a raincoat over his arm on a hot spring day and crossing the road in front of you, you do not see in him the present that is catching up with you.

What's he doing, this imbecile?

He stops in the middle of the road.

Turns to face the car.

Looks into your eyes.

Pushes aside his raincoat.

Uncovers a machine gun.

Points the gun at you.

Aims.

And fires.

### 218

He fires, and nothing happens. I can't resist cheap literary effects. Nothing happens. The trigger sticks—or perhaps it gives way too easily and clicks on nothing. Months of preparation only for the

Sten—that English piece of shit—to jam. Heydrich is there, at point-blank range, at his mercy, and Gabčík's weapon fails. He squeezes the trigger and the Sten, instead of spraying bullets, remains silent. Gabčík's fingers tighten on the useless hunk of metal.

The car has stopped, and time has stopped too. The world no longer spins, nobody breathes. The two men in the car are paralyzed. Only the tram keeps rolling as if nothing were wrong, except for the faces of a few passengers, frozen in the same expression—because they've seen what's happening: nothing. The screech of wheels on steel rails rips through the petrified moment. Nothing happens, except in Gabčík's head. In his head, everything whirls, unimaginably fast. If only I could have been inside his head at this precise instant, I am absolutely convinced I would have enough material to fill hundreds of pages. But I wasn't, and I don't have the faintest idea what he felt. Examining my own safe little life, I can't think of a single situation that would allow me to imagine even a watered-down version of what filled Gabčík's mind. A feeling of surprise, of fear, with a torrent of adrenalin surging through his veins, as if all the floodgates of his body had opened at the same time.

'We who perhaps one day shall die, proclaim man as immortal at the flaming heart of the instant.' I spit on Saint-John Perse, but I don't necessarily spit on his poetry. It is this verse that I choose now to pay homage to these men, even if they are, in truth, above all praise.

There's a theory that the Sten was concealed in a bag that Gabčík had filled with dry grass. It seems a

295

strange idea. If the police checked him, how would he explain the fact that he was walking around town with a bag full of hay? Well, actually, that's easy: all he'd have to say is that it's for the rabbit. In those days, many Czechs bred rabbits at home in order to improve their daily diet, and fed them on grass taken from the city's parks. Anyway, the theory is that it was this grass that got stuck in the mechanism.

So the Sten doesn't fire. And everybody remains rigid with shock for several long tenths of seconds. Gabčík, Heydrich, Klein, Kubiš. It's so kitsch! It's like a Western! These four men turned into stone statues, all eyes trained on the Sten, everyone's brains working at incredible speed, a speed no ordinary man can even comprehend. At the end of this story, there are these four men at a curve in the road. And then, on top of that, there's a second tram coming up behind the Mercedes.

### 219

In other words, we don't have all day. It's now Kubiš's turn to enter the action—Kubiš, moving unseen behind the two Germans, who are still transfixed by Gabčík's appearance. Calm and gentle Kubiš, taking a bomb out of his briefcase.

### 220

I, too, am transfixed—because I'm reading *Europe Central* by William T. Vollmann, which has just appeared in French. Finally, feverishly, I read this book that I would love to have written, and I wonder, reading the endless first chapter, how long he'll keep it up, this style, this incredible tone. In fact, it lasts only eight pages, but those eight pages are magical, with phrases streaming past as in a dream, and I understand nothing, and understand everything. This is perhaps the first time that the voice of history has resounded so perfectly, and I am struck by this revelation: history is a prophet who says 'We'. The first chapter is entitled 'Steel in Motion', and I read: 'In a moment steel will begin to move, slowly at first, like troop trains pulling out of their stations, then more quickly and ubiquitously, the square crowds of steel-helmed men moving forward, flanked by rows of shiny planes; then tanks, planes and other projectiles will accelerate beyond recall.' And, further on: 'Serving the sleepwalker's rapture, Göring promises that five hundred more rocket-powered planes will be ready within a lightning-flash. Then he runs out for a tryst with the film star Lida Baarova.' The Czech. When I quote an author, I must be careful to cut my quotations every seven lines. No longer than seven lines. Like spies on the telephone: no more than thirty seconds, so they can't track you down. 'In Moscow, Marshal Tukhachevsky announces that *operations in a future war will unfold as broad maneuver undertakings on a massive scale.* He'll be shot right away. And Europe Central's ministers, who will also be shot, appear on balconies supported by nude marble girls, where they utter dreamy speeches, all the while listening for the ring of the telephone.' In the newspaper, somebody explains to me that this is an account of 'slow-burning intensity'. a novel that is 'more fantastical than historical', the reading of which 'requires a psychoanalytic listening'. I understand. I will remember.

So . . . where was I?

## 221

Here I am, exactly where I wanted to be. A volcano of adrenalin sets ablaze the curve in Holešovice Street. It is the precise instant when the sum of individual microdecisions, transformed solely by the forces of instinct and fear, will allow history to perform one of its most resounding convulsions, or hiccups.

Each man's body has its own responsibilities. Klein, the chauffeur, does not restart the engine, and that's a mistake.

Heydrich stands up and draws his gun. A second mistake. Had Klein shown Heydrich's presence of mind, or had Heydrich remained paralyzed in his seat like Klein, then probably everything would have been different, and I might not even be here to tell you about it.

Kubiš's arm describes an arc and the bomb flies through the air. But nobody ever does exactly what they're supposed to do. Kubiš has aimed for the front seat but the bomb lands next to the right rear wheel. Nevertheless, it does explode.

# Part Two

An alarming rumour comes from Prague.
GOEBBELS'S DIARY, May 28, 1942

The bomb explodes and instantly the windows in the tram opposite are blown out. The Mercedes jumps a few feet in the air. Fragments from the explosion hit Kubiš in the face and hurl him backwards. A cloud of smoke fills the air. Screams burst from the smashed tram. An SS jacket, laid out on the backseat, flies upward. For several seconds, this is all the suffocating witnesses see: a black uniform floating above a cloud of dust. It is, in any case, all I can see: the jacket, twisting and spiralling gracefully like a dead leaf, while the aftershock of the explosion travels calmly outward to echo as far away as Berlin and London. Apart from the spreading sound and the fluttering jacket, nothing moves. There is no sign of life at the curve in Holešovice Street. From now on, I am talking in seconds. A second later, everything will have changed. But here, now—on this clear morning of Wednesday, May 27, 1942—time has stopped. For the second time in two minutes, albeit rather differently.

The Mercedes lands heavily on the asphalt. In Berlin, Hitler has not the faintest suspicion that Heydrich won't report for their meeting that evening. In London, Beneš still believes Anthropoid will succeed. What arrogance, in both cases. When the blown tyre of the right rear wheel—the last of those four suspended in the air—touches the ground, time starts up again for good. Instinctively, Heydrich brings his hand around to his back—his right hand, the one that holds his pistol. Kubiš gets to his feet. The passengers on the second tram press their faces to the windows to see what's happening, while those in the first tram cough, scream, and push each other to get off. Hitler is still sleeping. Beneš leafs nervously through Moravec's reports. Churchill is already on his second whisky. Valčík, from the top of the hill, watches the confusion unfolding at the crossroads below, cluttered with all these vehicles: one Mercedes, two trams, two bicycles. Opálka is somewhere nearby, but I can't put my finger on him. Roosevelt is sending American pilots to Britain to help the RAF. Lindbergh does not want to give back the medal that Göring awarded him in 1938. De Gaulle is fighting to convince the Allies to recognize the Free French. Von Manstein's army is besieging Sebastopol. The day before, the Afrika Korps began its attack on Bir Hakeim. Bousquet is planning the raid on Vél' d'Hiv. In Belgium, from today, all Jews must wear a yellow star. The first Resistance fighters are appearing in Greece. Two hundred and sixty Luftwaffe planes are en route to intercept a navy convoy headed towards the USSR, attempting to bypass Norway via the Arctic Ocean. After six months of daily bombings, the German invasion of Malta is indefinitely postponed. The SS jacket comes to rest gently on the tram's electric cables, like an item of washing hung out to dry. Here we are again. But Gabčík still hasn't moved. More than the explosion, the tragic click of his Sten has been like a slap in his face. As if in a dream, he sees the two Germans get out of the car, covering each other just like in a training exercise. Klein turns towards Kubiš, while Heydrich, reeling, stands in front of him—alone, gun in hand. Heydrich: the most dangerous man in the Third

Reich, the Hangman of Prague, the Butcher, the Blond Beast, the Goat, Süss the Jew, the Man with the Iron Heart, the worst creature ever forged in the burning fires of hell, the fiercest man ever to come from a woman's womb, his target, standing right there in front of him, reeling and armed. Released from a trance, Gabčík suddenly recovers his wits. He grasps the situation immediately. Putting aside all considerations of mythology and grandiloquence, he comes to a quick and correct decision, one that allows him to do exactly what he ought to do: he drops his Sten and runs. The first shots ring out. Heydrich is shooting at him. But despite being a champion in all categories in practically every human discipline, the Reichsprotektor is clearly not at his best. All his shots miss. For now. Gabčík manages to throw himself behind a telegraph pole—and it must have been a seriously thick telegraph pole, because he decides to stay there. He doesn't know when Heydrich might start shooting straight. Meanwhile, there's a rumble of thunder. On the other side, Kubiš, wiping away the blood that's streaming over his face and blurring his vision, discerns the gigantic silhouette of Klein moving towards him. What madness, or what supreme effort of lucidity, reminds him of the existence of his bicycle? He grabs the machine's frame and jumps on the seat. Now, anyone who's ever ridden a bike will know that a cyclist racing against a man on foot is going to be vulnerable for the first ten, fifteen, let's say the first twenty yards after starting up, beyond which he will outdistance his opponent easily. Given the decision he's just made, Kubiš must have this in mind. Because instead of fleeing in precisely the opposite direction to the one Klein is approaching from—which would seem the natural thing to do for 99 per cent of people in a similar situation: that is, a situation where you must very quickly escape from an armed Nazi with at least one very good reason to want you dead—he decides to pedal towards the tram (where the suffocating passengers are starting to stagger out onto the street), meaning that the angle of his escape, with reference to Klein, is less than 90 degrees. I don't like putting myself inside people's heads, but I think I can explain Kubiš's calculation. In fact, he has two reasons for doing what he does. Reason one: in order to counteract the relative slowness of those first few yards, and to gather speed as quickly as possible, *he goes downhill.* In all likelihood, he has calculated that pedalling uphill pursued by an enraged SS stormtrooper is not a viable option. Reason two: in order to have a chance, even an infinitesimally small chance, of getting out of this alive, he must meet two contradictory demands: Don't expose yourself, and put yourself out of range of enemy fire. But to put himself out of range, he must first cover a certain distance, though he cannot know the exact length until he has already covered it. The gamble that Kubiš makes is the opposite of Gabčík's: he tries his luck now. But he is not merely giving himself up to chance. Instead, he considers the unfortunate presence of this tram—a presence the parachutists had always feared—and decides to use it to his advantage. The passengers who have escaped from the tram are not numerous enough to constitute a crowd, but all the same he is going to try to use them as a shield. I don't suppose he's counting too heavily on an SS stormtrooper's scruples about shooting through a group of innocent civilians, but at least the shooter's vision of his target will be reduced. This seems to me a brilliantly conceived escape plan, particularly if you bear in mind that the man behind it has just been blown up by a bomb, that he has blood in his eyes, and that he's had about three seconds to come up with it. However, there is a moment when Kubiš will have to abandon himself to pure chance—the moment before he reaches his shield of suffocating passengers. Now, as is often the case, fortune decides to distribute her favours equally. So when Klein, still shocked by the explosion, squeezes the trigger of his gun, something jams. (The firing pin? The breech? The trigger itself? I don't know.) Does this mean Kubiš's plan is going to work? No, because the passengers in front of him are standing too close together. Some of them have already regained their senses and—whether because they're German, or Nazi sympathizers, or because they're eager for praise or a reward, or because they're terrified of being accused of complicity, or simply because they're so shocked that they can't budge an inch— they don't seem inclined to get out of his way. I doubt whether any of them showed any intent to actually apprehend Kubiš, but perhaps they looked vaguely menacing. Whatever, we now have a burlesque scene (there seems to be one in every episode) in which Kubiš, on a bicycle, fires into the air to create a passage for himself through the stunned tram passengers. And he makes it. Realizing that his prey has escaped him, the bemused Klein remembers that he has a boss to protect and runs back towards Heydrich, who is still shooting. But suddenly the Reichsprotektor's body betrays him by collapsing. Klein rushes up. The silence that follows this cease-fire is not lost on Gabčík, who decides that if he wants to try his luck it's now or never. He leaves the precarious shelter of his telegraph pole and starts running. He is thinking clearly now: in order to maximize Kubiš's chances of escaping, he needs to choose a different direction. So he runs up the hill. His analysis, however, is not entirely flawless because in doing so he is heading towards Valčík's observation post. But Valčík has not as yet been identified as a participant in the operation. Heydrich manages to lift himself up on an elbow. As Klein reaches him, he barks: 'Catch the *Schweinehund*!' Klein finally manages to cock his damn pistol, then runs off in pursuit. He fires and Gabčík, equipped with a Colt 9mm (that he had, thankfully, kept in reserve), shoots back. I don't know how many yards ahead he is. At this point, I don't think Gabčík is shooting to hit his opponent, just to warn him off getting too close. Running, the two men leave the chaotic crossroads behind them. But up ahead a silhouette stands out ever more clearly: it's Valčík, who is coming towards them. Gabčík sees him raise his gun, stop to aim, then collapse before he's had time to fire.

*'Do pici!'* When he falls to the ground, a violent pain in his thigh, all Valčík can say is: 'Shit, what an idiot!' Hit by one of the German's bullets—tough luck. The SS giant is now only a few yards away. Valčík thinks the game is up. There's no time to pick up his gun, which he dropped. But then a miracle happens: Klein doesn't slow down. Either the German regards Gabčík as the more important

306

target, or—in concentrating on him—he hasn't noticed that Valčík was armed and about to shoot at him. Or perhaps he hasn't seen him *period*. He runs past without stopping, without even glancing at him. Valčík can think himself lucky, but he's cursing all the same. If that's what really happened, he's been hit by a *stray bullet*. When he turns around, the two men have vanished.

Farther down the hill, things are hardly any less confused. A young blonde woman, however, has grasped the situation. She is German and has recognized Heydrich, who is lying across the road, clutching his back. With the authority born of believing oneself part of a race of natural leaders, she stops a car and orders the two occupants to take the Reichsprotektor to the nearest hospital. The driver protests: his car is loaded with boxes of candy, which cover the whole backseat. 'Get them out! *Sofort!* ' barks the blonde. So now we have another surreal scene, described by the driver himself: the two Czechs, clearly less than thrilled, start unloading the boxes of candy as if in slow motion, while the pretty and elegantly dressed young blonde woman babbles away in German to Heydrich, who seems not to hear. But this is the blonde's lucky day. Another vehicle arrives, which she judges at a glance to be more suitable. It's a little Tatra van, delivering shoe polish and floor wax. The blonde runs towards it, yelling at its driver to stop.

'What's going on?'

'An attack!'

'So?'

'You must drive Herr Obergruppenführer to the hospital.'

'But . . . why me?'

'Your car is empty.'

'But it's not going to be very comfortable. There are boxes of polish, it smells bad. You can't transport the Protector in conditions like that . . .'

'*Schnell!*'

Tough luck for the worker in the Tatra—he's stuck with the job now. Meanwhile, a policeman has arrived, and he helps Heydrich towards the van. The Reichsprotektor tries to walk on his own, but he can't. Blood seeps from his torn uniform. He manoeuvres his too-tall body with difficulty into the front passenger seat, holding his revolver tightly in one hand and his briefcase in the other. The van starts up and takes off down the hill. But the driver realizes that the hospital is in the other direction, so he makes a U-turn. Heydrich notices this and shouts: '*Wohin fahren wir?*' Even I, with my poor German, understand that this means 'Where are we going?' The driver understands, too, but he can't remember the German word for 'hospital' (*Krankenhaus*), so he doesn't say anything. Heydrich threatens him with the gun. Luckily, the van is now back at its starting point. The young blonde woman sees them arrive and rushes towards them. The driver begins to explain, but Heydrich murmurs something to the blonde. He can't stay in front—it's too cramped. So they help him out, then put him in the back of the van, lying facedown, surrounded by boxes of polish and wax. Heydrich orders them to give him his briefcase. They throw it in next to him. The Tatra starts up again. With one hand Heydrich holds his back, and with the other he hides his face.

While this is going on, Gabčík keeps running.

Tie flapping in the wind, hair messed up, he looks like Cary Grant in *North by Northwest* or Jean-Paul Belmondo in *That Man from Rio*. But obviously Gabčík, though very fit, does not have the supernatural endurance that the French actor would later display in his spoof role as a hero. Unlike Belmondo, Gabčík cannot keep running forever. By zigzagging through the neighbouring residential streets he has managed to put a bit of distance between himself and his pursuer, but he still hasn't shaken him off completely. Each time he turns into a new street, though, there is a period of a few seconds when he disappears from the other man's field of vision. He has to use this to his advantage. Breathless, he spots an open shop doorway and throws himself inside, precisely during this brief window of opportunity. Unfortunately, Gabčík didn't have time to read the name of the establishment: Brauner the butcher. So when, panting, he asks the shopkeeper to help him hide, the butcher rushes outside, sees Klein belting towards him, and—without a word—points at his shop. Not only is Brauner a German Czech, but on top of that his brother is in the Gestapo. This is bad news for Gabčík, who now finds himself cornered in a Nazi butcher's back room. But Klein has had time during the pursuit to notice that the fugitive is armed, so instead of entering the shop he takes shelter behind a little garden post and starts shooting like crazy through the doorway. Thus Gabčík's position has not really improved much since he was hiding behind the telegraph pole being shot at by Heydrich. But whether because he remembers his abilities as a marksman, or because an ordinary SS stormtrooper standing six feet away impresses him less than the Hangman of Prague in person, he reacts very differently. Moving into the open for a second and seeing part of a silhouette sticking out from behind the post, Gabčík aims and fires—and Klein collapses, hit in the leg. Without any hesitation Gabčík springs out, runs past the felled German and back up the street. But he's lost in this maze of residential alleys. At the next crossroads, he freezes. At the end of the street he's about to enter, he can see the beginning of the curve in Holešovice Street. In his frantic flight, he has gone around in a circle, and now he's back to where he started. It's like a Kafkaesque nightmare stuck on fast-forward. Hurrying to the other side of the crossroads, he runs down towards the river. And I, limping through the streets of Prague, dragging my leg as I climb back up Na Poříčí, watch him run into the distance.

The Tatra reaches the hospital. Heydrich is yellow; he can barely stand up. He is taken immediately to the operating room, where they remove his jacket. Bare-chested, he scornfully eyes the female nurse, who runs out without asking him to take off the rest of his clothes. He sits alone on the operating table. I'd love to know how long this solitary wait lasts. Eventually a man in a black raincoat arrives. He sees Heydrich and his eyes widen. After looking quickly around the room, he leaves to make an urgent telephone call: 'No, it's not a false alarm! Send an SS squadron over here immediately. Yes, Heydrich! I repeat: the Reichsprotektor is here, and he's injured. No, I don't know. *Schnell!* ' Then the first doctor arrives—a Czech. He is as white as a sheet but immediately begins to examine the wound, using swabs and a pair of tweezers. The wound is three inches long and contains many fragments and bits of dirt. Heydrich doesn't flinch while it's cleaned. A second doctor, a German, bursts in. He asks what's happening, then he sees Heydrich. Instantly he clicks his heels and shouts: *'Heil!'* They return to examining the wound. There is no damage to the kidney, nor to the spinal column, and the preliminary diagnosis is encouraging. They put Heydrich in a wheelchair and take him to the X-ray department. The corridors are full of SS guards. Security measures are being taken: all exterior windows are painted white to protect them from snipers, and machine gunners are posted on the roof. And, of course, they get rid of any patients who are in the way. Making a visible effort to retain his dignity, Heydrich gets out of the wheelchair and stands in front of the X-ray machine. The X-rays reveal further injuries: one rib is broken, the diaphragm is perforated, and the thoracic cage is damaged. They discover something lodged in the spleen—a fragment of shrapnel or a piece of the car's bodywork. The German doctor leans close to his patient:

'Herr Protektor, we're going to have to operate . . .'

Heydrich, white-faced, shakes his head.

'I want a surgeon sent from Berlin!'

'But your condition requires . . . would require immediate intervention.'

Heydrich thinks about it. He realizes his life is at risk, and that time is not on his side, so he agrees instead to summon the best specialist working at the German clinic in Prague. He is taken back to the operating room. Karl Hermann Frank and

311

the first members of the Czech government are beginning to arrive. The little local hospital is busier than it's ever been, or ever will be again.

Kubiš keeps looking over his shoulder but he is not being followed. He's done it. But what exactly? He hasn't killed Heydrich, who seemed perfectly fine when he left him, spraying bullets at Gabčík. Nor has he helped Gabčík, who looked in serious difficulty, with his jammed Sten. As for putting himself out of danger, he is well aware that this is only a provisional escape. The manhunt will begin any minute, and they won't have much trouble describing who they're looking for: a man on a bike with an injured face. He could hardly be any more conspicuous. Once again he is faced with a dilemma: the bicycle allows him to escape more quickly but it also makes him easier to find. Kubiš decides to dump it. He thinks while he's riding. Bypass the curve in Holešovice Street, and leave the bike outside the Bata shoe shop in the old Libeň district. It would have been better to move to a different district, but each passing second outside increases the likelihood of him being arrested. That's why he decides to seek refuge with his nearest contact—the Novak family. Inside the workers' apartment building, he climbs the stairs four at a time. A female neighbour calls out: 'Are you looking for someone?' He clumsily hides his face.

'Mrs Novak.'

'She's not here just now, but she should be back soon.'

'I'll wait.'

Kubiš knows that good Mrs Novak never locks her door, precisely in case he or one of his friends

312

turns up. He enters the apartment and throws himself on the sofa. It's the first respite he's had on this very long and very testing morning.

The hospital on Bulovka now looks like a cross between the Reich Chancellery, Hitler's bunker, and the Gestapo headquarters. Shock SS troops are posted around, inside, above, and beneath the building; enough of them to take on a Soviet tank division. Everyone waits for the surgeon. Karl Frank chain-smokes cigarettes as if he's about to become a father. In fact, he's brooding: he ought to inform Hitler.

The town is in pandemonium: uniformed men run in all directions. There is a great deal of agitation to very little purpose. Had Gabčík and Kubiš wanted to leave the city by taking the train from Wilson Station (although it's no longer called that) during the first two hours after the attack, they could have done so without any difficulties.

Having got off to a bad start, Gabčík now has fewer problems. He has to get hold of a raincoat—because the description of him broadcast by the Germans will doubtless mention that he doesn't have one, having dropped his next to the Mercedes—but on the other hand he has no injuries at all, visible or otherwise. He runs until he reaches the Žižkov district, where he stops to catch his breath and calm down. He buys a bouquet of violets and calls at the apartment of Professor Zelenka, a member of the Jindra Resistance group. He hands the bouquet of violets to Mrs Zelenka, borrows a raincoat, then leaves. Either that or he borrows the coat from the Svatoš family, who have already lent him their briefcase—which he also dropped at the scene of the crime. But the Svatošes

313

live farther away, near Wenceslaus Square. At this point in the narrative the witness accounts are unclear, and I'm a bit lost. Somehow he ends up at the Fafeks' place, where a nice hot bath is waiting for him, along with his young fiancée, Libena. What they do, what they say, I have no idea. But Libena knew all about the assassination attempt. She must have been very happy to see him alive again.

Kubiš washes his face, and Mrs Novak applies tincture of iodine to his wounds. The neighbour, a good sort, lends Kubiš one of her husband's shirts so he can change—a white shirt with blue stripes. His disguise is completed with a railway worker's uniform, borrowed from Mr Novak. Dressed like this, his swollen face will attract less attention: everyone knows that workers are far more likely to have accidents than gentlemen in suits. But one problem remains: someone has to pick up the bicycle he left outside the Bata shoe shop. It's too close to the curve in Holešovice Street—the police will soon find it. Happily, young Jindriska bursts in at that very moment: the Novaks' youngest daughter is hungry after a day at school—people eat lunch early in Czechoslovakia—so, while preparing her meal, her mother gives her an errand: 'A man I know has left his bicycle in front of the Bata shop. Go and get it, will you, and bring it back to the yard? And if someone asks you who it belongs to, don't say anything. He had an accident, and it might make things difficult for him . . .' As the young girl dashes off, her mother shouts: 'And don't try to use it—you don't know how! And watch out for cars!'

Fifteen minutes later, she returns with the bike. A lady questioned her, but she did what she was told and didn't reply at all. Mission accomplished. Kubiš can leave now, his mind at ease. Well, when I say 'at ease' . . . obviously I mean as at ease as anyone could be when they know they're fated to become one of the two most wanted men in the Reich within hours or even minutes.

As for Valčík, his predicament is not quite so delicate, as his participation in the attack has not yet been clearly established. But still, limping around Prague during a state of emergency with a bullet wound in his leg is probably not the best way to secure an untroubled future. So he finds refuge with a friend and colleague of Alois Moravec— another railway worker; another Resistance fighter who has helped the parachutists; another husband of a woman utterly devoted to fighting the German occupation. It's this man's wife who lets Valčík in. He's very pale. She knows him well, having often looked after him and hidden him, but she calls him Mirek because she doesn't know his real name. With the whole city buzzing with rumours, the first thing she asks him is: 'Mirek, have you heard? There's been an attack on Heydrich.' Valčík lifts his head: 'Is he dead?' Not yet, she says, and Valčík lowers his head again. But she can't stop herself asking the burning question: 'Were you in on it?' Valčík manages to smile: 'You're kidding! I'm much too softhearted for that kind of thing.' Knowing from experience that this man is made of sterner stuff, she realizes he is lying. And in fact Valčík does so only as a reflex; he doesn't really expect her to believe him. She has no idea he's limping, but asks him if he needs anything. 'A very strong coffee, please.' Valčík also asks if she might go into town to find out what people are saying.

Then he's going to take a bath, because his legs hurt. The woman and her husband assume he must have walked too far. It's not until the next morning, when they discover bloodstains on his sheets, that they understand he's been injured.

Around noon, the surgeon arrives at the hospital. The operation begins straightaway.

At a quarter past twelve, Frank bites the bullet and rings Hitler. As expected, the Führer is not happy. The worst bit is when Frank has to admit that Heydrich drove around town in an unarmoured Mercedes convertible without bodyguards. At the other end of the line, Hitler screams, just for a change. The contents of the Führer's ravings can be divided into two parts: first, that pack of dogs that they call the Czech people are going to pay dearly for this. Second: How could Heydrich, the best of them all, a man of such importance for the good of the Reich—the whole Reich, you understand—how could he be cretinous enough to be guilty of such self-neglect? Yes, guilty! It's very simple. They must immediately:

1. Shoot ten thousand Czechs.
2. Offer one million Reichsmarks as a reward for any information leading to the criminals' arrests.

Hitler has always been fond of figures. And, where possible, nice round figures.

In the afternoon, Gabčík—accompanied by Libena, because a couple always looks less suspicious than a man on his own—goes out to buy a Tyrolean hat. It's a little green hat with a pheasant feather. He does this to look more German. And

316

this hasty disguise works better than he could have hoped: a uniformed SS guard calls him over and asks for a light. Ceremoniously, Gabčík takes out his lighter and touches it to the German's cigarette.

I'm going to light one too. I feel a bit like a graphomanic depressive, roaming around Prague. I think I'll take a pause here.

But only a short pause. We have to get through this Wednesday. The man in charge of the inquest is Commissioner Pannwitz: the black-coated man glimpsed earlier in the hospital, sent by the Gestapo to find out the news. Judging by the clues left at the crime scene—a Sten, a bag containing an English-made antitank bomb—there is nothing very mysterious about the origin of the attack: London. Pannwitz makes his report to Frank, who calls Hitler back. The internal Resistance is not responsible. Frank advises against mass reprisals because they would suggest that the local population was largely opposed to the Germans. Executing individuals suspected of the crime, or of complicity—and their families, for good measure—would seem the best way of putting the event back in its true perspective: an individual action, organized abroad. Above all, they must not let the public form the unpleasant impression that the attack is an expression of national revolt. Surprisingly, Hitler seems more or less convinced by this argument in favour of moderation. The mass reprisals are put on hold for the time being. However, as soon as he puts the phone down, Hitler starts ranting at Himmler. So that's how it is, eh? The Czechs don't like Heydrich? Well, we'll find them someone worse! At this point, obviously, he needs some time to reflect, because finding someone worse than Heydrich is no easy task. Hitler and Himmler rack their brains. There are a few high-ranking Waffen—SS leaders who might be suitable for organizing a good slaughter, but they're on the Eastern Front—and in the spring of 1942 they've got their hands full. In the end, they fall back on Kurt Dalüge because he happens to be in Prague already, for medical reasons. Ironically, Dalüge—the chief of the Reich's regular police, and just promoted to Oberstgruppenführer—is one of Heydrich's direct rivals, although he has nothing like the same stature. Heydrich refers to him only as 'the moron'. If the Blond Beast regains consciousness, he is not going to be pleased. As soon as he's back on his feet, they must think about promoting him.

He regains consciousness. The operation has gone well. The German surgeon is quietly optimistic. It's true that they had to remove the spleen, but there are no apparent complications. The only slightly surprising discovery was some tufts of hair, which were inside the wound and all over his body. It took the doctors a while to figure out where they came from: the Mercedes's leather seats, ripped open by the explosion, were stuffed with horsehair. In the X-ray department, they were worried that there might be small fragments of metal lodged in some vital organs. But there's nothing, and the German elite in Prague can begin to breathe again. Lina, who wasn't told about the attack until 3:00 p.m., is at his bedside. Still groggy, he speaks to her in a weak voice: 'Take care of our children.' Right now, he doesn't seem very sure about his future.

Aunt Moravec is ecstatic. She bursts into the

318

concierge's apartment and asks: 'Have you heard about Heydrich?' Yes, they've heard: it's all they're talking about on the radio. But they have also broadcast the serial number of the second bicycle, abandoned at the scene of the crime. *Her* bicycle. They forgot to scratch it out. Her happy mood is instantly extinguished and replaced by bitter reproach. Ashen-faced, she curses the men for their negligence. But she still firmly intends to help them. Aunt Moravec is a woman of action and now is not the time for self-pity. She doesn't know where they are; she must find them. Indefatigable, she leaves.

All over town, they are plastering the bilingual red posters to the walls—the posters they use whenever they need to proclaim something to the local population. There are many such posters, but this one will undoubtedly remain the highlight of the collection. It says:

1. IN PRAGUE ON MAY 27, 1942, THERE WAS AN ATTACK ON THE INTERIM REICHSPROTEKTOR, SS OBERGRUPPENFÜHRER HEYDRICH.

For information leading to the arrest of the perpetrators, there will be a reward of ten million crowns. Whoever shelters these criminals, or helps them, or who, having any knowledge of them, does not denounce them, will be shot, along with his entire family.

2. A state of emergency has been declared in the Oberlandrat region of Prague. The state of emergency will be proclaimed by the reading of this declaration on the radio. The following measures have been decided:

1. All civilians, without exception, are forbidden to go out on the streets between 9:00 p.m. on May 27 and 6:00 a.m. on May 28;
2. All bars and restaurants, all cinemas, theatres, and other places of entertainment are to be closed, and all traffic on public highways stopped during these hours;
3. Whoever, in contradiction of this order, is found on the street between these hours will be shot if they do not stop at the first command;
4. Further measures are anticipated and, if necessary, will be announced on the radio.

At 4:30 p.m. this declaration is read out on German radio. From 5:00, Czech radio begins to broadcast it every thirty minutes; from 7:40, every ten minutes; and from 8:20 until 9:00, every five minutes. I suppose anyone who lived through this day in Prague—if they are still alive—would be able to recite the entire text by heart. At 9:30 the state of emergency is extended throughout the Protectorate. Meanwhile, Himmler has called Frank to confirm Hitler's new orders: the hundred most important people imprisoned as hostages since Heydrich's arrival the previous October are to be executed.

In the hospital, they are emptying the cupboards of all the morphine they can find for the relief of their most important patient.

That evening, an insane raid is organized. The city is invaded by 4,500 men from the SS, the SD, the NSKK, the Gestapo, the Kripo, and other Schupos, plus three Wehrmacht battalions. Add

320

to this the Czech police, who must help them, and there are more than 20,000 men taking part in the operation. All access routes are cut off, all main roads blocked, streets closed, buildings searched, people checked. Everywhere I look, I see armed men jumping from uncovered trucks, running in columns from one building to the next, filling stairwells with the pounding of boots and the clanking of steel, hammering on doors, shouting orders in German, dragging people from their beds, turning their apartments upside down, pushing them about and barking at them. The SS in particular seem to have completely lost control: they pace up and down the streets like angry madmen, shooting at lighted windows or open windows, expecting at any moment to be the victims of snipers waiting in ambush. This is not a state of emergency—it's a state of war. The police operation plunges the entire city into indescribable chaos. That night 36,000 apartments are visited— for a meagre yield, compared with the means deployed. They arrest 541 people—of whom three or four are tramps, one a prostitute, one a juvenile delinquent, and one a Resistance leader with no link whatsoever to Anthropoid—and immediately release 430 of them. And they do not find a single trace of the parachutists. What's worse, this is only the beginning. Gabčík, Kubiš, Valčík, and their friends must have had a strange night. I wonder if any of them managed to sleep? I would be very surprised. As for me . . . I'm sleeping very badly these days.

## 223

On the hospital's second floor, emptied of all but one of its patients, Heydrich is lying in bed. He is weak, his senses are numbed, his body aching, but he's conscious. The door opens, and the guard lets his wife, Lina, into the room. He tries to smile at her—he's happy she's here. She, too, is relieved to see her husband alive, albeit very pale and bedridden. Yesterday, when she saw him just after his operation, all white and unconscious, she thought he was dead. Even after waking up, he looked barely any better. She didn't believe the doctors' reassuring words. And if the parachutists had trouble sleeping, Lina's night wasn't very pleasant either.

This morning she brings him hot soup in a thermos flask. Yesterday: victim of an assassination attempt. Today: already convalescent. The Blond Beast has thick skin. He'll be fine, as always.

## 224

Mrs Moravec goes to fetch Valčík. Her husband, the kindhearted railway worker, does not want to let Valčík leave in his current state. He gives him a book to read on the tram, so he can hide his face: *Thirty Years of Journalism* by H. W. Steed. Valčík thanks him. After he's gone, the railwayman's wife tidies his room and, stripping his bed, finds blood on the sheets. I don't know how serious his injury was, but I do know that all doctors in the Protectorate were legally obliged to tell the police about any bullet wounds, under pain of death.

## 225

A crisis meeting is taking place behind the black walls of Peček Palace, Commissioner Pannwitz summing up: after studying the clues gathered at the crime scene, his initial conclusion is that the attack was planned in London and executed by two parachutists. Frank agrees. But Dalüge, named as interim Protector the day before, believes the attack points to an organized national uprising. As a preventive measure, he orders that lots of people be shot and every policeman in the region rounded up to reinforce the city's police presence. Frank looks like he's going to throw up. All the evidence suggests that this attack was organized by Beneš, and even if that were not true . . . politically, he couldn't care less if the internal Resistance is implicated or not. 'We must not let people believe that there is a national revolt! We have to say that this was an individual action.' On top of that, if they pursue a campaign of mass arrests and executions, they risk disturbing the country's industrial production. 'Need I remind you of the vital importance of Czech industry for the German war effort, Herr Oberstgruppenführer?' (Why have I made up this phrase? Probably because he actually said it.) Frank, the second-in-command, thought his hour had come. Instead of which, they promoted this Dalüge, who has no experience as a statesman, knows nothing of the Protectorate's business, and can barely even locate Prague on a map. Frank doesn't object to a show of force: it costs nothing to unleash terror in the streets, and he knows it. But he remembers the political lessons learned from his master: no stick without a carrot. The previous night's hysterical raid exemplified the uselessness of such actions. What they need is a well-organized and well-funded campaign of denouncements. That would produce better results.

Frank leaves the meeting. He's wasted enough time with Dalüge. A plane is waiting to take him to Berlin, where he has a meeting with Hitler. He hopes that the Führer's political genius will not be overpowered by one of his famous rages. In the plane, Frank carefully plans his presentation of the measures he will recommend. Given yesterday's phone conversation, it's in his interests to be convincing. In order not to look like a wimp, he suggests invading the city with tanks and regiments, and cutting off a few heads. But, once again, there must be no mass reprisals. Rather, he would advise that Hácha and his government be leaned on: threatened with the loss of the Protectorate's autonomy, and with German control of all Czech organizations. Plus all the usual methods of intimidation: blackmail, harassment, et cetera. But all of this, for now, in the form of an ultimatum. The ideal solution would be for the Czechs themselves to deliver the parachutists into their hands.

Pannwitz's concerns are different. His area of expertise is not politics but investigation. He is collaborating with two brilliant detectives sent by Berlin, both of whom are still stunned by the chaos of 'catastrophic proportions' that they found here on arrival. They say nothing about this to Dalüge, but to Pannwitz they complain that they needed an escort just to reach their hotel safely. As for the behaviour of those rabid SS dogs, their judgement is damning: 'They're completely mad. They won't even be able to find their way out of the insane maze they're creating, never mind find the assassins.' They must proceed more methodically. In less than twenty-four hours, the three detectives have already obtained some important results. Thanks to the witness accounts they've collected, they are now in a position to reconstruct exactly how the attack unfolded, and they have a description—albeit rather vague (those bloody witnesses can never agree on what they saw!)—of the two terrorists. But there are no leads on the men's whereabouts. So they're searching. Not in the streets, though, like the SS imbeciles: they are going through the Gestapo files with a fine-tooth comb.

And they find that old photo taken from the corpse of brave Captain Morávek—the last of the Three Kings, killed in a tramway shoot-out two months earlier. In this photo, the handsome Valčík looks inexplicably bloated. But it's him, all the same. The policemen have no clues at all linking this man to the attack. They could easily pass on to the next file, but they decide to investigate this photograph *just on the off chance*. If this were a detective novel, we'd call it a hunch.

## 226

A young female Czech liaison officer called Hanka rings the Moravecs' doorbell. They show her through to the kitchen. And there, sitting in an armchair, she finds Valčík, whom she knows from his days as a waiter in Pardubice, her hometown. As affable as ever, he smiles at her and apologizes for not being able to stand up: he's twisted his ankle.

It's Hanka's job to send Valčík's report to the Bartos group in Pardubice, so that they can inform London via the Libuse transmitter. Valčík asks the young woman not to mention his injury. As the leader of Silver A, Captain Bartos is still officially his head of mission. But Bartos has never approved of the assassination attempt. Somehow Valčík managed to transfer himself from Silver A to Anthropoid. Given what's happened, he doesn't believe he owes an explanation to anyone apart from his two friends, Gabčík and Kubiš (he hopes they're safe); to Beneš himself (if need be); and, perhaps, to God (Valčík is a believer).

The young woman rushes to the station. But before boarding her train, she stops dead before a new red poster. Immediately she phones the Moravecs: 'You should come here and see—there's something interesting.' There is the photo of Valčík, and beneath: *100,000 crowns reward*. There follows a fairly inaccurate description of the parachutist—and that's another piece of luck to add to the fact that the picture doesn't look much like him. His surname is mentioned, but his first name and date of birth are both wrong (they've

326

made him five years younger). A little note at the end reminds you of the true nature of wanted posters: 'The reward will be given with the greatest discretion.'

## 227

But that poster isn't the best bit.

Bata built his empire before the war. Starting as a small shoemaker in the town of Zlín, he developed an immense business with shops all over the world, and above all in Czechoslovakia. Fleeing the German occupation, he emigrated to the United States. But even during the boss's exile, the shops remained open. At the bottom of Wenceslaus Avenue, number 6, is a gigantic Bata boutique. In the shop window this morning the usual display of shoes has been replaced by an assortment of other objects. A bicycle, two leather bags, and—displayed on a mannequin—a raincoat and a beret. All these exhibits were found at the crime scene. They are accompanied by an appeal for witnesses. Passersby who stop before the shop window can read:

> With regard to the reward of ten million crowns for information leading to the arrest of the perpetrators, which is to be paid in full, the following questions must be asked:
> 1. Who can provide information on the criminals?
> 2. Who saw them at the scene of the crime?
> 3. To whom do these objects belong? Above all, whose is the ladies' bicycle,

the coat, the beret, and the bag?
Whoever is able to provide this information and who fails to do so voluntarily will be shot with his family in accordance with the notice of May 27 declaring the state of emergency.
Be assured that all information received will be dealt with in the strictest confidence.
Furthermore, from May 28, 1942, all owners of houses, apartments, hotels, etc., in the Protectorate must declare to the police all persons staying with them who have not already been reported. Failure to do so will be punishable by death.

SS-Obergruppenführer
Chief of Police
Office of the Reichsprotektor of Bohemia
    and Moravia
K. H. Frank

## 228

The Czech government-in-exile declares the assassination attempt on the monster Heydrich an act of vengeance, a rejection of the Nazi yoke, and a symbol of hope for all the oppressed peoples of Europe. The shots fired by the Czech patriots are a show of solidarity sent to the Allies and of faith in the final victory which will ring out all over the world. Already, new Czech victims are being killed by German firing squads. But this latest fit of Nazi fury will once again be broken by the unbending resistance of the Czech people, and will succeed only in reinforcing their will and determination.

The Czech government-in-exile encourages the population to hide these unknown heroes and threatens punishment for anyone who betrays them.


## 229


In his Zurich postbox, Colonel Moravec receives a telegram sent by agent A54: 'Wunderbar—Karl'. Paul Thümmel (alias A54, alias René, alias Karl) has never met Gabčík and Kubiš, and took no direct part in the attack's preparations. But with this single word he echoes the joy felt on hearing the news by everyone, all over the world, fighting against Nazism.


## 230


The concierge's doorbell rings. It's Ata, the young Moravec son, come to fetch Valčík. The concierge doesn't want Valčík to leave. He could live in the attic, he says, on the fifth floor: nobody would look for him up there. Here, Valčík plays cards and listens to the BBC and eats the delicious cakes made by the concierge's wife, which he says are as good as his mother's. The first evening, he had to hide in the cellar because there was a Gestapo agent in the building. But he feels very safe, staying with these people. So why not stay? the concierge insists. Valčík explains that he's been given orders, that he's a soldier, that he is bound to obey, and that he must rejoin his comrades. The concierge shouldn't worry: a safe haven has been found for them. Only, it's very cold. They'll need blankets and warm clothes. Valčík picks up his coat, puts on a pair of green glasses, and follows Ata, who is taking him to the new hiding place. But by accident he leaves behind the book lent to him by his previous host. The owner's name is written inside. The fact that he forgets this book will save the owner's life.

## 231

Capitulation and servility are the lifeblood of Pétainism, and old President Hácha—every bit as senile as his French counterpart—is a master in the art. To show his goodwill, he decides, in the name of the puppet government he leads, to double the reward. So Gabčík's and Kubiš's heads are now valued at ten million crowns *each*.

## 232

The two men at the church door are not here to attend Mass. The Orthodox church of St Charles Borromeo (today renamed the Saints Cyril and Methodius Cathedral) is an immense building, and one side of it faces Resslova Street—that sloping street which runs from Charles Square down to the river, right in the heart of Prague. One of the men is Professor Zelenka, alias 'Uncle Hajsky' of the Jindra organization. He is met at the door by Father

Petrek, an Orthodox priest. Zelenka has brought a friend with him. This is the seventh friend he's brought to the church. It's Gabčík. They take him through a trapdoor to the church crypt. There, amid stone recesses that used to hold dead bodies, he is reunited with his friends: Kubiš and Valčík, but also Lieutenant Opalka and three other parachutists, Bublik, Svarc, and Hruby. One by one, Zelenka has brought them all here. Because, while the Gestapo is still tirelessly searching all the city's apartments, no one has yet thought to look in the churches. Only one parachutist is missing: they've had no news of Karel Čurda at all. Nobody knows where he is, whether he's hiding or he's been arrested, or even if he's still alive.

Gabčík's arrival causes a sensation in the crypt. His comrades rush to hug him. He recognizes Valčík, his hair dyed brown, sporting a thin brown moustache, and Kubiš, whose eye is swollen and whose face still bears the scars of the explosion. These two are clearly the most demonstrative in their joy at seeing him again. Gabčík's feelings are torn: he doesn't know whether to laugh or cry. Naturally he is very happy to see his friends, all of them pretty much safe and sound. But he's so sorry for the way things turned out. He's barely been reunited with them before he begins his bitter litany of excuses and self-reproach. They will soon become accustomed to this. He curses the bloody Sten, which jammed just when he had Heydrich at his mercy. It's all my fault, he says. I had him there in front of me, he was a dead man. And then this piece-of-shit Sten . . . ah, it's too stupid. But he's injured—you got him, Jan? Seriously injured? You think? Lads, I am so sorry. It's all my fault. I

331

should have finished him off with the Colt. But there were bullets flying everywhere, and I ran, with that giant hot on my heels . . . Gabčík hates himself, and nothing his friends say can console him. It doesn't matter, Jozef. What you did is huge, don't you realize? The Hangman himself! You injured him! Heydrich is injured, that's true, he saw him fall, but apparently he's recovering in hospital. A month from now, he'll be back at work—perhaps even earlier. It's true what they say: those bastards are bulletproof. Anyway, the Nazis have always had the luck of the devil when it comes to surviving assassination attempts. (I think of Hitler in 1939, who had to give his annual speech at the famous Munich beer hall between 8:00 and 10:00 p.m., but who left the building at 9:07 to catch his train—and the bomb went off at 9:30, killing eight people.) But Anthropoid is a pitiful failure—there you go, that's what he thinks—and it's all his fault. Jan did nothing wrong. He threw the grenade. Sure, it missed the car, but he was the one who injured Heydrich. Thank God Jan was there! They didn't fulfil their mission, but thanks to him at least they hit the target. Now the Germans know that Prague isn't Berlin, and that they can't treat this place like home. But frightening the Germans was not the objective of Anthropoid. Perhaps they were too ambitious after all: no Nazi as high-ranking as Heydrich has ever been shot. But no, what am I saying? If it wasn't for the stupid, stinking Sten, he'd be dead, that pig . . . The Sten, the Sten! . . . It's a piece of shit, I'm telling you.

Heydrich's condition has suddenly and inexplicably deteriorated. He's in the grip of a powerful fever. Himmler has rushed to his bedside. Heydrich's tall body lies weakly under a thin white sheet drenched with sweat. The two men philosophize about life and death. Heydrich quotes a line from his father's opera: 'The world is just a barrel organ, which the Lord God turns Himself. We all have to dance to the tune that is already on the drum.'

Himmler asks the doctors for explanations. The patient seemed to be recovering well until he was laid low by a sudden infection. Perhaps the bomb contained poison or the horsehairs from the Mercedes's seats got into his spleen. There are various theories, but nobody knows which one is correct. But if, as they believe, this is the beginning of septicaemia, the infection is going to spread very quickly and he will be dead within forty-eight hours. To save Heydrich, they would need something that is not to be found anywhere in the vast territory of the Reich: penicillin. And the British aren't about to give them any.

On June 3, the Libuse radio receives the following message, for the attention of Anthropoid:

From the president. I am very happy that you

have been able to keep in contact. I thank you most sincerely, and take note of your absolute determination, and that of your friends. This shows me that the whole nation is united. I can assure you that this will bear fruit. The events in Prague had a huge impact here and have done a great deal for international recognition of the Czech Resistance.

But Beneš doesn't know that the best is yet to come. And the worst.

## 235

Anna Maruscakova, a young and pretty factory worker, called in sick today. So when the afternoon post arrived and the factory boss found a letter addressed to her, he opened and read it without a second thought. The letter was from a young man, and this is what it said:

Dear Ania,
Sorry for taking so long to write to you, but I hope you will understand, because you know I have many worries.
What I wanted to do—I've done it. On the fatal day, I slept in Cabarna. I'm fine. I'll come to see you this week, and afterward we will never see each other again.
Milan

The factory boss is a Nazi sympathizer—or perhaps not even that: just an ordinary person conditioned by that ignoble mentality that exists almost everywhere but which finds its true voice in occupied countries. Deciding that there is perhaps something fishy going on, he forwards the letter to the relevant authority. The Gestapo's inquiry has stalled so badly that they are desperate for a new bone to chew. They treat the dossier with a diligence all the greater because after making more than three thousand arrests they still haven't found anything useful. Very quickly, they determine that the letter concerns a love affair: the author is a married man. He probably wishes to put an end to an adulterous relationship. The details of the story are not very clear, but it's true that certain phrases could be construed as ambiguous. Perhaps this young man even wanted, between the lines, to suggest an imaginary involvement in the Resistance—either to impress his mistress, or to create an atmosphere of mystery so he could break up with her without having to justify himself. Whatever the truth of this, he had nothing to do in any shape or form with Gabčík, Kubiš, and their friends. They've never heard of him and he's never heard of them. But the Gestapo is so desperate for leads that they decide to dig deeper on this one. And this leads them to Lidice.

Lidice is a peaceful and picturesque little village. It is also the birthplace of two Czechs who enrolled in the RAF. This is all the Germans have discovered in the course of their inquiry. Even to them, it is obviously a false trail. But Nazi logic is complex and mysterious. Either that or it's very simple: they're out for blood and their patience is running thin.

I spend a long time looking at Anna's photo. The

poor girl is posed as if for a Hollywood glamour shot, even though it's just an identity photo for her work permit. The more I examine this portrait, the more beautiful I find her. She looks a bit like Natacha: high forehead, well-drawn mouth, with that same look in her eyes of gentleness and love, slightly darkened, perhaps, by a premonition of disappointment.

236

'Gentlemen, if you'll follow me . . .' Frank and Dalüge give a start. The corridor is perfectly silent as they walk its mazelike turns for I don't know how long. Holding their breath, they enter the hospital room. The silence here is even more overpowering. Lina is there, hieratic and pale. They approach the bed stealthily, as if fearful of waking a wildcat or a snake. But Heydrich's face remains impassive. In the hospital they write down the time of his death—4:30 a.m.—and the cause: infection caused by a wound.

237

Opportunity makes not only the thief but the assassin too. Therefore, supposedly heroic behaviour such as driving around in an open-topped, unarmoured car or walking the streets without a bodyguard are nothing but damned stupidity, and are against the national interest. That a man as

336

irreplaceable as Heydrich should expose himself to danger in that way . . . it's idiotic and stupid! Men as important as Heydrich should always know that they are like targets at a fairground, and that a certain number of people are constantly watching for any opportunity to shoot them.

Goebbels is listening to something he will hear more and more often until May 2, 1945: Hitler, adopting a sententious tone and lecturing the world, in a vain attempt to keep his temper. Next to him, Himmler listens in approving silence. He is not in the habit of contradicting the Führer anyway, but he, too, is angry—with the Czechs and with Heydrich. Naturally, Himmler was wary of the ambitions of his right-hand man. But without him—deprived of the abilities of this machine of terror and death—Himmler feels more vulnerable. To lose Heydrich is to lose a potential rival, but above all a trump card. Heydrich was his jack of clubs. And everyone knows the story: once Lancelot left the kingdom of Logres, that was the beginning of the end.

## 238

For the third time, Heydrich makes a solemn journey to the castle of Hradčany. But this time he is in a coffin. A Wagnerian setting has been organized for the occasion. The coffin, wrapped in a huge SS standard, is carried on a gun carriage. A torchlit procession leaves from the hospital, an endless line of military vehicles moving slowly through the night. Armed Waffen-SS guards march alongside, brandishing torches, which illuminate the route. Throughout its journey the convoy is saluted by soldiers standing to attention at the sides of the road. No civilians have been authorized to attend, but in truth nobody would want to risk going outside tonight anyway. Among the guard of honour, accompanying the coffin on foot, are Frank, Dalüge, Böhme, and Nebe, all wearing helmets and combat uniform. And so, after a journey that began at 10:00 a.m. on May 27, Heydrich finally reaches his destination. For the last time, he passes through the open gates and enters the walls of the castle of the kings of Bohemia.

## 239

I'd like to spend my days with the parachutists in the crypt, reporting their discussions, describing how they live from hour to hour in the cold and the damp, what they eat, what they read, what rumours they hear from the town, what they do with their girlfriends when they visit. I would like to tell you about their plans, their doubts, their hopes, their fears, their dreams and thoughts. But that isn't possible, because I know almost nothing about any of it. I don't even know how they reacted when they heard about Heydrich's death, although that ought to make one of the best bits of my book. I know the parachutists were so cold in the crypt that, when night fell, some of them took their mattresses to the gallery that overhung the nave because it was slightly warmer. That's not much, is it? I also know that Valčík had a fever (probably as a result of his injury), and that Kubiš was one of those who tried sleeping in the church rather than the crypt. Or that he tried it at least once.

On the other hand, I have a colossal amount of information about Heydrich's funeral, from his body being taken from the castle in Prague until its burial in Berlin, including the rail journey in between. Dozens of photos, dozens of pages of speeches made in praise of the great man. But that's too bad, because I don't really care. I am not going to copy out Dalüge's funeral eulogy (although it is quite amusing, given that the two men hated each other), nor Himmler's interminable encomium for his subordinate. I think I'll quote Hitler instead, because at least he kept it short:

I will say only a few words to pay homage to the deceased. He was one of the best National Socialists, one of the most ardent defenders of the idea of the German Reich, one of the greatest opponents of all the Reich's enemies. He is a martyr for the preservation and protection of the Reich. So, my dear comrade Heydrich, as head of the Party and as Führer of the German Reich, I award you the highest decoration that it is in my power to bestow: the medal of the German Order.

My story has as many holes in it as a novel. But in an ordinary novel, it is the novelist who decides where these holes should occur. Because I am a slave to my scruples, I'm incapable of making that decision. I flick through the photos of the funeral cortège crossing the Charles Bridge, going back up to Wenceslaus Square, passing in front of the museum. I see the beautiful stone statues on the balustrade of the bridge with swastikas beneath them, and I feel slightly sick. I think I'd rather take my mattress to the gallery in the church, if they've got a bit of room for me there.

## 240

Evening, and all is calm. The men are home from work, and in the little houses the lights are going out one after another. The houses still exhale the pleasant smell of dinner, mixed with the slightly acrid stench of cabbage. Night falls on Lidice. The inhabitants go to bed early because, as always, they'll have to get up early tomorrow to go to the mine or the factory. Miners and steelworkers are already sleeping when a distant sound of engines is heard. The sound gets slowly closer. Covered trucks move in single file through the silence of the countryside. Then the motors are silenced, and a continuous clicking sound is heard. The clicking extends through the streets like liquid rushing through tubes. Black shadows spread all over the village. And then, when the silhouettes have congregated in compact groups, and when everyone is in position, the clicking stops. A human voice rips open the night. It's an order shouted in German. And so it begins.

Torn from sleep, the inhabitants of Lidice understand nothing of what's happening to them— or they understand all too well. They are dragged from their beds, they are driven from their houses with rifle butts, and herded into the village square, in front of the church. Nearly five hundred men, women, and children, dressed hastily, stand there dumbstruck and terrified, surrounded by the uniformed men of the Schutzpolizei. They cannot know that this unit has been brought here specially from Halle-an-der-Saale, Heydrich's hometown. But they do know that nobody will be going to work tomorrow. Then the Germans begin to do what will soon become their favourite occupation: they divide the group in two. Women and children are locked up in the school, while the men are led to a farmhouse and crammed into the cellar. Now they must wait, interminably, the anguish etched into their faces. Inside the school, the children weep. Outside, the Germans are let off the leash. Frenetically but conscientiously, they pillage and ransack each of the ninety-six houses in the village, plus all the public buildings, including the church. All books and paintings, considered to be useless objects, are thrown from the windows, piled up in the square, and burned. Anything considered useful—radios, bicycles, sewing machines—is taken away. This work takes several hours, and by the time it's finished, Lidice is in ruins.

At five in the morning, the soldiers come back to get them. The inhabitants find their village turned upside down and filled with running, shouting policemen who continue to plunder everything they can find. The women and children are taken in trucks toward the neighbouring town of Kladno. For the women, this is the first stage on their journey to Ravensbrück. The children will be separated from their mothers and gassed in Chełmno—with the exception of a few judged suitable for Germanization, who will be adopted by

341

German families. The men are assembled before a wall where the mattresses have been dumped. The youngest is fifteen, the eldest eighty-four. Five are lined up and shot. Then five more, and so on. The mattresses are there to prevent the bullets ricocheting. But the men of the Schupo are not as experienced in such matters as the Einsatzgruppen, and—with all the pauses for carrying away the corpses and forming new firing squads—it takes forever. Hours pass while the men await their turn. To speed the process up, they decide to double the rate and shoot them ten by ten. The village mayor, whose job it is to identify the men before their execution, is among the last to be killed. Thanks to him, the Germans spare nine men who are not from the village but simply visiting friends and trapped there by the curfew or invited to stay the night. They will, however, be executed in Prague. When nineteen night workers return from their shifts, they find their village devastated, their families vanished, the bodies of their friends still warm. And, as the Germans are still there, they, too, are shot. Even the dogs are killed.

But that isn't all. Hitler has decided to vent all his frustrations on Lidice, so the village will serve as a means of catharsis and as a symbol of his avenging rage. The Reich's inability to find and punish Heydrich's assassins provokes a systematic hysteria beyond all human bounds. The order is that Lidice must be wiped off the map—literally. The cemetery is desecrated, the orchards destroyed, all the buildings burned, and salt thrown over the earth to make sure that nothing can ever grow here. The village is now nothing more than a hellish furnace. Bulldozers have even been sent to raze the ruins. Not a single trace of the village must remain, not even a hint of its former location.

Hitler wants to show people the price to be paid for defying the Reich, and Lidice is his expiatory victim. But he has committed a serious error. It is so long since Hitler and his colleagues lost touch with reality that they do not anticipate the worldwide repercussions that will be provoked by news of the village's destruction. Up to now, the Nazis, if somewhat half-hearted in the concealment of their crimes, have nevertheless kept up a superficial discretion that has enabled some people to avert their gaze from the regime's true nature. With Lidice, the scales have fallen from the whole world's eyes. In the days that follow, Hitler will understand. For once, it is not his SS who will be let loose but an entity whose power he does not fully grasp: world opinion. Soviet newspapers declare that, from today, people will fight with the name of Lidice on their lips—and they're right. In England, miners from Stoke-on-Trent launch an appeal to raise money for the future reconstruction of the village and come up with a slogan that will be echoed all around the world: 'Lidice shall live!' In the United States, in Mexico, in Cuba, in Venezuela and Uruguay and Brazil, town squares and districts, even villages, are renamed Lidice. Egypt and India broadcast official messages of solidarity. Writers, composers, filmmakers, and dramatists pay homage to Lidice in their works. The news is relayed by newspapers, radio, and television. In Washington, D.C., the naval secretary declares: 'If future generations ask us what we were fighting for, we shall tell them the story of Lidice.' The name of the martyred village is scrawled on the bombs dropped by the Allies on German cities, while in the East, Soviet soldiers do the same on the gun turrets of their T34s. By reacting like the crude psychopath that he is (rather than the head of state that he also is), Hitler will suffer his most devastating defeat in a domain he once mastered: by the end of the month the international propaganda war will be irredeemably lost.

But on June 10, 1942, neither he nor anyone else is aware of all this—least of all Gabčík and Kubiš. The news of the village's destruction plunges the two parachutists into horror and despair. More than ever, they are wracked by guilt. No matter that they have fulfilled their mission, that the Beast is dead—no matter that they have rid Czechoslovakia and the world of one of its most evil creatures— they feel as if they themselves have killed the inhabitants of Lidice. They also fear that, as long as Hitler does not know them to be dead, the reprisals will continue indefinitely. Enclosed in the crypt, all of this churns over and over in their heads, until— exhausted by the nervous tension—they reach the only possible conclusion: they must turn themselves in. In their fevered brains they imagine asking to see Emanuel Moravec, the Czech Quisling. When they see him, they will hand over a letter explaining that they are responsible for Heydrich's assassination; then they will shoot him, and kill themselves in his office. Lieutenant Opalka, Valčík, and the other comrades in the crypt need all their patience, friendship, diplomacy, and persuasiveness to convince the guilt-ridden parachutists not to go through with this insane plan. First of all, it's technically unfeasible. Second, the Germans will never take them at their word. Finally, even if they managed to carry out their plan, the terror and the massacres had begun long before Heydrich's death, and would continue long after their own. Nothing would change. Their sacrifice would be completely in vain. Gabčík and Kubiš weep from rage and powerlessness, but they end up being convinced. All the same, no one ever manages to persuade them that Heydrich's death was good for anything.

Perhaps I am writing this book to make them understand that they are wrong.

## 241

## CONTROVERSY ON THE CZECH NET

An Internet site designed to get young Czechs interested in the history of the village of Lidice, which was utterly destroyed by the Nazis in June 1942, is offering an interactive game, the goal of which is to 'burn Lidice in the shortest possible time.'

(LIBÉRATION, SEPTEMBER 6, 2006)

## 242

The Gestapo is so short of leads you might think they'd given up looking for Heydrich's assassins. They need a scapegoat to explain this incompetence and they think they might have found one. He is a civil servant for the Ministry of Work, and on the evening of May 27 he authorized the departure of a train full of Czech workers going to Berlin. Given that the three parachutists still haven't been found, this lead seems as good as any other—so the Gestapo 'establishes' that the three assassins (yes, the inquiry has made some progress—they now know that there were three of them) were on board the train. The men from Peček Palace are even in a position to give some surprising details: the fugitives hid beneath their seats during the journey and got off the train while it made a brief stop in Dresden, where they disappeared into the countryside. It's true that the idea of the terrorists leaving their own country to take refuge in Germany seems rather daring, but you have to be more daring than that to escape the Gestapo. Unfortunately, the civil servant is not prepared to be the scapegoat, and his defence takes them by surprise: yes, he authorized the train's departure, but only because he was told to do so by the Air Ministry in Berlin. Göring, in other words. Not only that, but the meticulous bureaucrat has kept a copy of the authorization, stamped by the Prague police services. So if there's been a mistake, the Gestapo would have to accept its own share of the responsibility. The men from Peček Palace decide not to pursue this particular lead.


243

The idea that finally solves the problem comes from that old soldier Commissioner Pannwitz, clearly a fine connoisseur of the human soul. Pannwitz begins with this observation: the climate of terror deliberately created since May 27 is counterproductive. He has nothing against terror, but in this case it's inconvenient because it scares off those who might otherwise be tempted to inform. More than two weeks after the attack, nobody is going to risk trying to explain to the Gestapo that they know something but that, up to now, they haven't admitted it. The Gestapo must promise—and deliver—an amnesty for anyone who comes forward of their own free will and provides information on the assassination, even if they themselves are implicated.

Frank is persuaded by these arguments and decrees an amnesty for whoever provides—*within five days*—information leading to the capture of the assassins. After that he won't be able to contain Hitler and Himmler's lust for blood any longer.

As soon as she hears this news, Mrs Moravec understands what it means: the Germans are staking everything. If, after five days, nobody has denounced her lads, they will be free from any further fear of informers and their chances of survival will increase considerably. Because, once the amnesty has expired, nobody will dare to go and see the Gestapo. Today, June 13, 1942, a stranger turns up at Mrs Moravec's apartment, but there's nobody there. The man asks the concierge if Mrs Moravec has by any chance left a briefcase for him. He is Czech but he doesn't give the password, 'Jan'. The concierge says he knows nothing about it. The stranger leaves. Karel Čurda has almost resurfaced.

Aunt Moravec has sent her family to the countryside for a few days, but she herself has too much to do in Prague. She washes and irons clothes, and she runs errands all over the place. In order not to attract too much attention, she is helped by the concierge's wife. They mustn't be seen too often carrying packages, and naturally the parachutists' hiding place must remain secret, so the two women arrange to meet in Charles Square, surrounded by flower beds and crowds of people. After that, the aunt walks down Resslova Street, enters the church, and disappears. Another time, they get on the same tram but the concierge's wife gets off two or three stations earlier, leaving her bags, and the aunt picks them up. She brings the men cakes still warm from the oven, and methylated spirits for their old stove. She also brings them news from the outside world. The lads are all a bit under the weather, but their morale has improved. Heydrich's death cannot erase the memory of Lidice, but gradually they come to realize the significance of what they've done. Aunt Moravec is welcomed by Valčík in his dressing gown. He looks a bit peaky, but he sports a thin moustache these days—and, my word, how very distinguished it makes him look. He asks for news of Moula, his dog. Moula is fine: he has been adopted by a family with a large garden. The swellings on Kubiš's face have gone down, and even Gabčík has recovered a bit of his old joie de vivre. They are beginning to get organized, this little community of seven: they've improvised a sieve from an undershirt and they'd like to try to make coffee. The aunt promises to find some. Meanwhile, Professor Zelenka is working with the Resistance on some very hypothetical plans to get the parachutists out of the Reich. The problem is that Anthropoid was really designed as a suicide mission, so nobody gave much thought to the question of their return. First of all, they must be smuggled into the countryside, but the Gestapo is still under great pressure to arrest them and the city is in a state of maximum alert—so this will have to wait. It will soon be St Adolf's day, and as they wish to celebrate this (because, to be clear, Lieutenant Opalka's first name is Adolf), Aunt Moravec is going to try to get hold of some veal scallops. She'd also like to make them a broth with chunks of liver. The lads no longer call her 'Aunt', but simply 'Mom'. These seven highly trained men are now reduced to a state of total inaction, as vulnerable as children, cloistered in this damp cellar and wholly in the hands of this little lady who cares for them like a mother. She keeps repeating to them: 'We just have to get through to the eighteenth.' Today is the sixteenth.


## 245


Karel Čurda stands on the pavement at the top of Bredovska Street—today renamed the Street of Political Prisoners—which comes out at the central train station. On the opposite corner is Peček Palace, a dour and menacing presence in grey stone. This huge pile was built after the

First World War by a Czech banker who owned almost all the coal mines in northern Bohemia. Perhaps the anthracite-grey façade was designed as a reminder of the origin of his fortune. But the banker gave up the mines and the palace to the government, prudently deciding to leave the country for England just before the German invasion. Even today Peček Palace is an official building—home of the Ministry of Commerce and Industry. But in 1942 it is the headquarters of the Gestapo for Bohemia and Moravia. Nearly a thousand employees work here at the blackest tasks, in rooms so gloomy it looks like night even in the middle of the day. Located in the heart of the capital and equipped with the latest technology—a printing works, a laboratory, a pneumatic postal service, and a telephone exchange—the building is, from a functional point of view, absolutely perfect for the Nazi police. Its many underground chambers and cellars have been cleverly converted for the Gestapo's particular needs. The head of the police here is a young Standartenführer called Dr Geschke. I've seen only one photo of this man, but—with his scar, his womanly skin, his mad eyes and cruel lips, his side-parted hair and half-shaved skull—it was enough to freeze my blood. Anyway, Peček Palace is the very incarnation of the Nazi terror in Prague, and you need a certain courage just to stand in front of it. Karel Čurda does not lack courage, but he is motivated by the thought of twenty million crowns. Though, to be honest, it does take courage to denounce your comrades. You have to weigh up the pros and the cons, and there is no guarantee that the Nazis will keep their word. Čurda is playing double or quits with his own life: either wealth or death awaits him. But he's an adventurer. That's why he joined the Free Czechoslovak army; that's why he volunteered for special missions in the Protectorate: because he has a taste for adventure. He hasn't enjoyed this return to his homeland because, ultimately, the clandestine lifestyle isn't very appealing. Since the assassination he's been living in the provinces with his mother, in the little town of Kolín, forty miles east of Prague. Before this, though, he did have time to meet many people involved in the Resistance, among them Kubiš and Valčík—they worked together in the Škoda operation at Pilsen—and also Gabčík and Opalka, whose paths he crossed several times when they were switching hideouts in Prague. He knows the apartment of the Svatoš family, who supplied a bicycle and a briefcase for the assassination. And above all he knows where the Moravec family lives. I don't know why he went there three days earlier. Was he already thinking of betraying them? Or was he attempting to get back in contact with the network because he'd had no news of them recently? But why come back to Prague, if not for the reward? Wasn't he safer with his mother in picturesque little Kolín? Actually, he probably wasn't: in 1942, Kolín is a German administrative centre, where the Jews of central Bohemia are rounded up, and its train station is a rail junction for deportations to Terezín. So it's possible that Čurda no longer wished to endanger his family—he had a sister in Kolín as well as his mother—and that he came back to Prague to seek support and refuge with his comrades. How important, then, was the closed door he found when he went to call on the Moravecs? And yet, Aunt Moravec was expecting

351

him, because when the concierge told her about the mysterious visitor, she asked if he had come from Kolín. But she'd gone out . . . We can never know why things turn out the way they do—malicious and mischievous fate, or the powerful forces of some higher will. Still, by Tuesday, June 16, 1942, Karel Čurda has made his decision. He doesn't know where his comrades are hiding. But he knows enough.

Karel Čurda crosses the road, presents himself to the guard standing in front of the heavy wooden gate, and tells him that he has important information to provide. Then he climbs the wide steps covered in red carpet that lead up to the vast entrance hall, and he is swallowed by the stone belly of the black palace.

I don't know when or why the father and son of the Moravec family returned to Prague. I guess they went away for just a few days. Perhaps it was the son's impatience to help the parachutists that brought them back, or his unwillingness to leave his mother in Prague alone. Or perhaps it was the father's work. It's said that the father knew nothing of what was going on, but I can't believe that. When he saw the men his wife welcomed into their house, he knew perfectly well they weren't Boy Scouts. And besides, he asked his friends on several occasions for clothes or a bicycle or a doctor or a new hiding place. So the whole family took part in the struggle—including the eldest son, who lived in

England and was an RAF pilot. He will die when his fighter plane crashes on June 7, 1944, the day after D-day. Nearly two years from now, in other words. In times like these, that's an eternity away.


## 247

Čurda has crossed the Rubicon, but he is not exactly being welcomed like a conquering hero. After being interrogated all night long—the Gestapo give him a good beating in recognition of the importance of his testimony—Čurda now waits quietly on a wooden bench in one of those dark corridors while they decide his fate. Left alone with him briefly, the requisitioned interpreter asks him a question:

'Why have you done this?'

'I couldn't bear any more innocent people being murdered.'

And also for twenty million crowns. Which he will get.


## 248

The Moravec family have lived in fear of one thing throughout these years of iron and horror, and this morning it finally comes to pass. The bell rings, and it's the Gestapo at the door. The Germans stick them up against the wall—mother, father, and son—then frantically ransack the apartment. 'Where are the parachutists?' barks the German commissioner, and the translator translates. The father replies quietly that he doesn't know any. The commissioner goes off to inspect the other rooms. Mrs Moravec asks if she can go to the toilet. One of the Gestapo agents slaps her face. But then he is called away by his boss and she asks the translator, who agrees. Mrs Moravec knows she has only a few seconds. So she locks herself quickly in the bathroom, takes out her cyanide pill, pops it in her mouth, and—without hesitating—bites down on it. She dies instantly.

Coming back to the living room, the commissioner asks where the woman is. The translator explains. The German understands immediately. Enraged, he rushes to the bathroom and breaks down the door with his shoulder. Mrs Moravec is still standing, a smile upon her face. Then she sinks to the ground. *'Wasser!'* yells the commissioner. His men bring water and try hopelessly to revive her, but she's dead.

But her husband is still alive, and so is her son. Ata watches the Gestapo guards carry off his mother's body. The commissioner approaches, smiling. Ata and his father are arrested and taken away in their pyjamas.

249

It goes without saying that he was tortured horribly. Apparently, they showed him his mother's head floating in a jar. 'You see this box, Ata . . .' He must have remembered Valčík's words. But a box has no mother.

And now I am Gabčík. What do they say? I am inhabiting my character. I see myself arm in arm with Libena, walking through liberated Prague, people laughing and speaking Czech and offering me cigarettes. We are married now, she's expecting a baby. I've been promoted to captain. President Beneš is leading a reunified Czechoslovakia. Jan comes to see us with Anna, behind the wheel of the latest-model Škoda. He wears his cap backwards. We go to drink a beer in a *kaviaren* by the riverside. Smoking English cigarettes, we laugh as we think back to the time of the struggle. Remember the crypt? God, it was cold! It's a Sunday. The river flows by. I hug my wife. Josef comes to join us, and Opalka with his Moravian fiancée—the one he used to talk about all the time. The Moravecs are there, too, and the colonel, who offers me a cigar. Beneš brings us sausages, and flowers for the girls. He wants to make a speech in our honour. Jan and I plead with him: no, no, not another speech! Libena laughs and teases me gently. She calls me her hero. Beneš begins his speech in the church at Vyšehrad—it's cool in there, and I'm dressed in my wedding suit. I hear people come into the church behind me. I hear Nezval recite a poem. It's a Jewish story, of the Golem, of Faust on Charles Square, with golden keys and the shop signs in Nerudova Street, and numbers on a wall that form my date of birth until the wind scatters them . . .

I have no idea what time it is.

I am not Gabčík and I never will be. At the

last second, I resist the temptation of the interior monologue and in doing so perhaps save myself from ridicule at this crucial point. The gravity of the situation is no excuse. I know perfectly well what time it is, and I am wide-awake.

It is 4:00 a.m. I am not asleep in the stone recesses reserved for dead monks in the church of Saints Cyril and Methodius.

In the street, black shapes begin their furtive ballet once again. Except we are no longer in Lidice, but in the heart of Prague. It is now much too late for regrets. Covered trucks arrive from all directions, forming the shape of a star, with the church at its centre. On a control panel, we see the luminous streaks of vehicles slowly converging on the target, but stopping before they meet. The two main stopping points are the bank of the Vltava and Charles Square, at either end of Resslova Street. Headlights and engines are switched off. Shock troops clatter out from beneath the covers on the trucks. An SS guard stands at his post before each doorway, each sewer opening. Heavy machine guns are placed on the roofs. Prudently, night flees the scene. The first glimmers of dawn have already begun to lighten the sky because summer time has not yet been invented and Prague— though slightly farther west than, say, Vienna—is sufficiently eastern for these cold, clear mornings to come while the city is still sleeping. The block of houses is already surrounded when Commissioner Pannwitz arrives, escorted by a small group of his agents. The interpreter accompanying him breathes in the fragrant smell of the flower beds in Charles Square (and to still be in a job after allowing Mrs Moravec to commit suicide, he must be one hell of an interpreter). Pannwitz is in charge of the whole operation; this is both an honour and a heavy responsibility. Above all, there must be no repeat of the fiasco of May 28, that unbelievable fuckup, which—thank God—had nothing to do with him. If all goes well, this will be the crowning glory of his career; if, on the other hand, the operation ends with anything other than the arrests or the deaths of the terrorists, he will be in deep trouble. Everyone is playing for high stakes today, even on the German side, where a lack of results can easily look like sabotage to the leaders—all the more so when they have to conceal their own errors or quench their thirst for blood (and here both factors are in play). Scapegoats at all costs—that could be the Reich's motto. So Pannwitz spares no effort to keep himself in his bosses' good books, and who can blame him? He is a professional cop and he will proceed methodically. He has given his men strict instructions. Absolute silence. Several security cordons. A very tight dragnet of the area. Nobody to fire without his authorization. We need them alive. Not that anyone will hold it against him if he happens to kill them, but an enemy captured alive brings the promise of ten new arrests. The dead don't talk. Although, in a way, the Moravec woman's corpse told them a few things. Does Pannwitz snigger quietly when he thinks this? Now that the time has finally come to arrest the assassins, who have been making fools of the Reich police for three weeks, he must be feeling a little nervous. After all, he has no idea what's waiting for him inside. He sends a man to get the church door open. At this instant, nobody knows that the silence that reigns over Prague will be broken in only a

357

few minutes. The agent rings the doorbell. Time passes. At last, the hinges turn. A sleepy sacristan appears in the doorway. He is hit and handcuffed before he even has time to open his mouth. But they do still have to explain to him the objective of this morning's visit. They wish to see the church. The interpreter translates. The group crosses a vestibule, a second door is opened, and they enter the nave. The men in black spread out like spiders. Except that they don't climb the walls—only the echo of their footsteps does that, ringing out and ricocheting off the high stone surfaces. They search everywhere but find nobody. The only place they haven't yet searched is the gallery over the nave. Pannwitz spots a spiral staircase behind a locked gate. He demands the key from the sacristan, who swears he doesn't have it. Pannwitz orders the lock smashed with a rifle butt. Just as the gate is opened, a round (perhaps slightly oblong) object rolls down the stairs. Hearing the metal chiming on the steps, Pannwitz understands. I'm sure he does. He understands that he's found the parachutists' lair, that they are hiding in the gallery above, that they are armed, and that they are not going to give themselves up. The grenade explodes. A curtain of smoke falls inside the church and then the Stens enter the action. One of the Nazi agents—the most zealous of the lot, according to the interpreter— begins to yell. Pannwitz immediately orders the retreat, but his men, blinded and disoriented, just run around shooting in all directions, caught in the cross fire from high and low. The battle of the church has begun. Clearly, the visitors were not prepared for this. Perhaps they thought it would be easy? After all, the smell of their leather raincoats is usually enough to petrify their prey. So the element of surprise is on the defenders' side. Somehow the Gestapo gather up their wounded and manage to evacuate. The shooting from both sides stops suddenly. Pannwitz sends in an SS squadron, who receive the same welcome. Up above, the invisible marksmen know exactly what they're doing. Perfectly positioned to cover every angle in the nave, they take their time, aim carefully, shoot sparingly, and hit their targets more often than not. Each burst of gunfire is answered with an enemy scream. The narrow, twisting staircase is as good as the most solid barricade for barring access to the gallery. The second attack ends in a second withdrawal. Pannwitz realizes there is no chance of taking them alive. To add to the atmosphere of chaos, someone orders the machine gunners posted on the roof opposite to open fire. The MG42s smash the windows to pieces.

In the gallery, three men are showered in a rain of stained glass. Yes, only three men—Kubiš of Anthropoid, Opalka of Out Distance, and Bublik of Bioscope—but they know exactly what they have to do: bar access to the staircase (Opalka is stuck with that job), spend as little ammunition as possible, and kill as many Nazis as they can. Outside, their assailants are growing wild with impatience. When the machine guns go silent, the next wave surges into the nave. Pannwitz yells: *'Attacke! Attacke!'* Short, judicious bursts of fire are enough to push them back. The Germans rush into the church and immediately rush out again, squealing like puppies. Between the two attacks, the German machine guns spit out long, heavy bursts of fire, eating into the stone and shredding everything else. Kubiš and

359

his two comrades—unable to return fire, or to do anything but wait for the storm to pass—protect themselves as best they can, hiding behind thick columns. Luckily for them, the SS squadrons can't expose themselves to this covering fire either, so the MG42s neutralize the attackers just as much as they do the defenders. The situation is extremely precarious for the three parachutists, but as minutes turn into hours, they continue to hold out.

Karl Hermann Frank arrives at the scene. He'd been thinking, perhaps a little naively, that everything would be over by now. Instead, he is stunned to discover the most unbelievable bedlam on the streets, with Pannwitz sweating in his civilian suit, loosening his tie, and yelling, *'Attacke! Attacke!'* The assaults crash against the church like waves, one after another. You can see the relief on the faces of the injured when they're dragged from this hell and taken to the medical centre. Frank's face, by contrast, looks anything but relieved. The sky is blue, it's a beautiful day, but the thunder of weaponry must have woken the entire population. Who knows what they'll be saying about this in town? Things are not looking good. As is traditional in a crisis, the boss gives his subordinate a good dressing-down. The terrorists must be neutralized immediately. One hour later, bullets are still whistling from all directions. Pannwitz screams ever louder: *'Attacke! Attacke!'* But the SS have now realized that they are never going to take the staircase, so they change their tactics. The nest has to be cleaned out from below. Covering fire, assault, fusillade, grenades tossed upward until the most skilful (or the luckiest) grenadier hits the bull's-eye. After three hours of battle, a series of explosions finally brings silence to the gallery. For a long time, nobody dares move. Finally, it's decided to send someone up to see. The soldier ordered to climb the staircase waits, resigned yet anxious, for the burst of gunfire that will kill him. But it doesn't come. He enters the gallery. When the smoke clears, he discovers three motionless bodies: one a corpse, the other two wounded and unconscious. Opalka is dead, but Bublik and Kubiš are still breathing. Pannwitz calls an ambulance. He never expected to get this chance; now he must take advantage of it. The men must be saved so they can be interrogated. One has broken legs and the other's in equally bad shape. The ambulance tears through the streets of Prague, its siren screaming, but by the time it reaches the hospital Bublik is dead. Twenty minutes later, Kubiš, too, succumbs to his wounds.

Kubiš is dead. I wish I didn't have to write that. I would have liked to get to know him better. If only I could have saved him. According to witnesses, there was a boarded-up door at the end of the gallery that led to the neighbouring buildings, and which might have allowed the three men to escape. If only they'd gone through that door! History is the only true casualty: you can reread it as much as you like, but you can never rewrite it. Whatever I do, whatever I say, I will never bring Jan Kubiš back to life—brave, heroic Jan Kubiš, the man who killed Heydrich. It has given me no pleasure at all to write this scene. Long, laborious weeks I've spent on it, and for what? Three pages of comings and goings in a church, and three deaths. Kubiš, Opalka, Bublik—they died as heroes, but they died all the same. I don't even have time to mourn them, because history waits for no man.

The Germans search through the rubble and find nothing. They dump the body of the third man on the pavement and bring Čurda along to identify him. The traitor lowers his head and mumbles: 'Opalka.' Pannwitz is delighted. He's struck lucky. He presumes that the two men in the ambulance are the two assassins, whose names Čurda gave up during the interrogation: Jozef Gabčík and Jan Kubiš. He has no idea that Gabčík is just beneath his feet.

When the shooting stopped, Gabčík realized his friend was dead. None of them would ever let the Gestapo take them alive. Now he waits alongside Valčík and his two other comrades—Jan Hruby of Operation Bioscope and Jaroslav Svarc of Operation Tin, the latter having just been sent by London to assassinate Emanuel Moravec, the collaborationist minister—for the Germans either to burst into the crypt or to leave without having flushed them out.

Above them the search goes on, but still they haven't found anything. The church looks like it's been hit by an earthquake, and the trapdoor to the crypt is concealed beneath a carpet that nobody thinks to lift. When you don't know what you're looking for, you are far less likely to find it. And of course the Germans' nerves have been sorely tested. Everybody thinks that there is probably nothing more to do here: the mission is over and Pannwitz is about to suggest to Frank that they pack up and go home when one of his men finds something and brings it to him. It's a piece of clothing—I don't even know if it's a jacket, a sweater, a shirt, or a pair of socks—

362

that he discovered in a corner of the church. The policeman's instinct is immediately on alert. I don't know how he decides that this item of clothing does not belong to one of the three men they've just killed in the gallery, but in any case he orders the search to be continued.

It is after seven o'clock when they find the trapdoor.

Gabčík, Valčík, and their two comrades are trapped like rats. Their hiding place is now their prison, and everything points towards it becoming their tomb. But until then they're going to make it a bunker. The trapdoor opens. As soon as the legs of an SS stormtrooper appear, they each release a short burst of gunfire. This is like their signature—a demonstration of the cool blood that flows through their veins. There's screaming and the legs disappear. Their situation is hopeless, but at the same time quite safe, in a way, at least in the short term—safer than the situation in the gallery had been. Kubiš and his two comrades had the benefit of a position overlooking the nave, which allowed them to dominate their attackers. Here, it's the opposite, because the enemy is coming from above, but the entrance is so narrow that the SS have to come down one by one—and that gives the defenders plenty of time to shoot them one after another. It's the same principle as at Thermopylae, if you like, except that Leonidas's task has already been accomplished by Kubiš. So, protected by thick stone walls, Gabčík, Valčík, Hruby, and Svarc do at least have time—to think, if nothing else. How can they get out of there? Above them, they hear: 'Give yourselves up. Nothing bad will happen to you.' The only way out of the crypt is this trapdoor.

There is also a kind of horizontal vent in the wall, about ten feet above the floor: they've got a ladder, so they could reach it, but it's too narrow for a man to pass through, and besides, it would only take them out to Resslova Street, which is crawling with hundreds of SS stormtroopers. 'You will be treated as prisoners of war.' There are also a few steps leading to an old, boarded-up door, but even if they did manage to break it down, it only leads to the nave—and that, too, is swarming with Germans. 'They told me to tell you that you have to give up. So I've told you. They said that nothing bad will happen to you, that you'll be treated as prisoners of war.' The parachutists recognize the voice of Father Petrek, the priest who welcomed them and hid them in his church. One of them replies: 'We are Czechs! We will never give ourselves up, you hear? Never! Never!' This is almost certainly not Gabčík, who would have specified: 'Czechs and Slovaks.' In my opinion it's Valčík. But another voice repeats 'Never!' and follows it with a burst of gunfire. That seems to me more Gabčík's style. (Although the truth is that I don't have a clue.)

Anyway, the endgame has reached a stalemate. Nobody can enter the crypt, and nobody can leave it. Outside, loudspeakers repeat the same words in a loop: 'Give yourselves up and come out with your hands in the air. If you do not give yourselves up, we will blow up the whole church and you will be buried in the rubble.' Each announcement is met by a salvo of bullets from the crypt. Even if the Resistance is often deprived of its ability to speak, it can still express itself with a marvellous eloquence. Outside, the ranks of SS are asked to volunteer to go into the crypt. Nobody blinks. The commander repeats his request, more threateningly. A few soldiers step forward, pale-faced. Those who didn't move are automatically volunteered. Another man is selected to descend through the trapdoor. He gets the same treatment: bullets in the legs—a bloodcurdling scream; another crippled superman. If the parachutists have plenty of ammunition, this could go on for a long time.

The truth is that I don't want to finish this story. I would like to suspend this moment for eternity, when the four men decide not to surrender to their fate but to dig a tunnel. Beneath the sort of fanlight/vent thing, with God knows what tools, they notice that the wall—which is below ground level—is made of bricks that crumble and come loose easily. Perhaps there is a way after all . . . perhaps, if we can dig through the stone . . . Behind the fragile brick wall, they find soft earth, and this makes them redouble their efforts. How far until they reach a pipe, or a sewer, or some kind of path leading to the river? Sixty feet? Thirty feet? Less? There are seven hundred SS outside, fingers on triggers, paralyzed or overexcited by nerves, by their fear of these four men, by the prospect of having to dislodge these enemies who are entrenched, resolute, and not at all intimidated, these enemies who know how to fight. They don't even know how many of them there are! (As if there might be a whole battalion down there! The crypt is less than fifty feet long.) Outside, Pannwitz barks orders and men run in all directions. Inside, they dig with the energy of the damned. Perhaps they are just struggling for the sake of struggling, and nothing more. Perhaps nobody actually believes in this insane, delirious, Hollywood-style escape plan. But

365

I believe in it. The four men dig away. Do they take turns while they listen to the fire engines' sirens in the street? Or perhaps there weren't any sirens. I'll have another look at the testimony of the fireman who took part in that terrible day. Gabčík puts everything into digging the tunnel. He's sweating now, having been so cold for days. I'm sure the tunnel was his idea: he's a natural optimist. And I'm also sure that he's digging now: he can't stand being inactive. He wouldn't just sit there and wait for death, not without doing something, not without trying something. Kubiš will not die in vain— let nobody say that Kubiš died in vain. Had they already begun digging the tunnel during the assault on the nave, taking advantage of the noise to cover the sound of their pickaxe? I don't know that either. How is it possible to know so much and yet so little about people, a story, historical events that you've lived with for years? But, deep down, I know they're going to make it. I can feel it. They're going to get out of this trap. They are going to escape from Pannwitz's clutches. Frank will be mad as hell and there'll be films made about them.

Where is that bloody fireman's testimony?

Today is May 27, 2008. When the firemen arrive, about 8:00 a.m., they see the SS everywhere and a corpse on the pavement. No one has thought to move Opalka's body. The firemen listen as they are told what they have to do. It was Pannwitz's brilliant idea: to smoke them out, and—if that doesn't work—to drown them. None of the firemen want this job. Among their ranks, one hisses: 'If you want that done, don't look at us.' The head fireman chokes with anger: 'Who said that?' But who would have become a fireman to end up lumbered with

366

such a job? So a volunteer is chosen to smash off the iron bars that protect the vent. They fall after a few blows and Frank applauds. And thus a new battle begins around this horizontal orifice, barely three feet long and ten inches high; this black hole that, for the Germans, seems to open onto the unknown and the prospect of death; this shaft of light for the men in the crypt, which also signifies death. This small opening is now the one square on the chessboard coveted by all the pieces remaining in the game. Occupy this square, and you have a crucial positional advantage in an endgame where white—because, in this particular game, it's black who moved first and who holds the initiative—will stage a heroic, against-all-odds defence.

May 28, 2008. The firemen manage to slide their firehose through the vent. The hose is connected to a fire hydrant, and the pumps are activated. Water pours through the opening.

May 29, 2008. The water begins to rise. Gabčík, Valčík, and their two comrades have wet feet. As soon as a shadow approaches the vent, they shoot. But the water keeps rising.

May 30, 2008. The water is rising, but very slowly. Frank is getting impatient. The Germans toss tear-gas grenades into the crypt to smoke out its occupants, but it doesn't work, because the grenades fall in the water. Why didn't they try this before? It's a mystery. I don't think you should rule out the possibility that they are acting, as is often the case, in a rushed and disorderly way. Pannwitz seems to me the kind of man who thinks things through carefully, but I suppose he may not be in charge of all the military operations. And perhaps he, too, gives in to panic? Gabčík and his friends

367

have wet feet, but at this rate they will die of old age before they're drowned.

June 1, 2008. Frank is extremely nervous. The more time passes, the more he fears that the parachutists will find a way of escaping. The water could even help them if they manage to find a leak, because, obviously, the crypt is not exactly watertight. Inside, they're getting organized. One is in charge of gathering up the grenades and throwing them back outside. Another keeps digging unrelentingly in the tunnel. A third uses a ladder to push the firehose away from the vent. And the other one lets off bursts of gunfire whenever someone approaches. On the other side of the stone wall, soldiers and firemen, bent double, have to keep putting the firehose back in place while avoiding the spray of bullets.

June 2, 2008. The Germans bring a gigantic searchlight to dazzle the men in the crypt, so they can't aim properly. But before they've even had time to switch it on, a burst of gunfire, like an ironic punctuation mark, puts it out of service.

June 3, 2008. The Germans keep sliding the hose into the crypt, to drown them or smoke them out, but each time the parachutists use the ladder like a telescopic arm to push it back. I don't understand why the Germans couldn't put the firehose through the trapdoor in the nave, which is still—as far as I'm aware—wide open. Perhaps the hose is too short, or they can't get into the nave with the kind of equipment required? Or perhaps it's an unlikely providence that is depriving them of all tactical lucidity?

June 4, 2008. The water is up to their knees. Outside, Čurda and Ata Moravec are brought to

368

the vent. Ata refuses to speak, but Čurda shouts through the opening: 'Give yourselves up, lads! They've treated me well. You'll be prisoners of war—it'll be all right.' Gabčík and Valčík recognize his voice; now they know who betrayed them. They reply in the usual way: with a burst of gunfire. Ata stands with his head lowered. His face is swollen and he has the absent look of a young man with one foot in the land of the dead.

June 5, 2008. After about ten feet, the earth in the tunnel becomes hard. Do the parachutists stop digging so they can concentrate on shooting? I can't believe that. They go at it even harder. They'll dig with their fingernails if they have to.

June 9, 2008. Frank can bear it no longer. Pannwitz tries to think. There must be some other way in. They used to put dead monks in the crypt. How did they get the bodies down there? Inside the church, his men continue their search. They clear away the rubble. They pull up the carpets. They demolish the altar. They tap on the stone walls. They search high and low.

June 10, 2008. And they find something else. Beneath the altar, there's a heavy slab that sounds hollow when you tap it. Pannwitz sends for the firemen and orders them to break the slab. A sectional drawing at this moment would show the firemen hammering away with a pickaxe at ground level while the parachutists do the same underground. The picture would be captioned: 'Race against death—and against all odds.'

June 13, 2008. Twenty minutes have passed and the firemen have worn themselves out on the stone slab, to no effect. In bad German, they stammer to the watching soldiers that it's impossible to break this stone with the tools at hand. The weary SS guards dismiss them and bring in some dynamite. The explosives experts fuss around the slab for a while, and when everything's ready they evacuate the church. Outside, everyone is told to move back. Below, the parachutists have surely stopped digging. The sudden silence must have alerted them, coming after such a racket. Something is about to happen—they can't help but be aware of it. The explosion confirms it. A cloud of dust falls over them.

June 16, 2008. Pannwitz orders the rubble cleared away. The slab has been smashed in two. A Gestapo agent puts his head through the gaping hole. Straightaway, bullets whistle around his face. Pannwitz gives a satisfied smile. They've found the way in. They send two stormtroopers down, but it's the same old problem: a cramped wooden staircase allows only one man at a time to pass. The first unlucky SS guards are shot down like skittles. But from now on, the parachutists have to watch over three different openings. Taking advantage of this distraction, one of the firemen grabs the ladder as it's being used to push the firehose away from the vent for the umpteenth time, and manages to hoist it up to the street outside. Frank applauds. The fireman will be rewarded for his zeal (but punished after the liberation).

June 17, 2008. The situation is getting more and more difficult. The defenders have been deprived of their makeshift telescopic arm, and now their bunker is shipping water everywhere—both figuratively and literally. As soon as the SS have two entry points, added to the danger posed by the vent, the parachutists realize it's all over. They're screwed and they know it. They stop digging, if they haven't already, and concentrate entirely on shooting their enemies. Pannwitz orders a new attack through the main entrance while grenades are thrown into the crypt and another man tries to get down through the trapdoor. Inside the crypt, the Stens spray bullets at the assailants. It's total chaos. It's the Alamo. And it goes on and on, and it doesn't end, it comes from all sides, through the trapdoor, down the stairs, through the vent; and while the grenades fall in the water and don't explode, the four men empty their guns at everything that moves.

June 18, 2008. They come to their last clip, and it's the kind of thing that you grasp very quickly, I suppose, even (perhaps especially) in the heat of battle. The four men don't need to speak. Gabčík and his friend Valčík smile at each other—I'm sure of that, I can see them. They know they've fought well. It's noon when four dull explosions pierce the tumult of gunfire, which stops immediately. Silence falls once again on Prague, like a shroud of dust. The SS are like statues: nobody dares fire, or even move. They wait. Pannwitz stands rigid. He signals to an SS officer, who hesitates—where is the manly confidence that he ought, by law, to show in all circumstances?—then orders two of his men to go and see. Carefully, they descend the first few steps. Then, like two little boys, they stop and look back up at their commander, who signals that they should continue—weiter, weiter! Everybody in the church watches, breath held. They disappear into the crypt. Time passes slowly then a call is heard, in German, from beyond the grave. Revolver in hand, the officer jumps to his feet and rushes down the staircase. He comes back up, his trousers soaked up to his thighs, and yells: *'Fertig!'* It's all over. Four bodies float in the water. Gabčík, Valčík, Svarc, and Hruby killed themselves in order not to fall into the Gestapo's hands. On the surface of the water float ripped-up banknotes and identity papers. Among the objects scattered around the crypt are a stove, some clothes, mattresses, and a book. There are bloodstains on the wall and a pool of blood on the stairs—though that, at least, is German blood. And cartridge cases but not a single cartridge: they kept the last ones for themselves.

It is noon. It has taken eight hundred SS stormtroopers nearly eight hours to get the better of seven men.

## 251

I am coming to the end and I feel completely empty. Not just drained but empty. I could stop now, but that's not how it works here. The people who took part in this story are not characters. And if they became characters because of me, I don't wish to treat them like that. With a heavy heart—and without turning it into literature, or at least, without meaning to—I will tell you what became of those who were still alive on June 18, 1942.

When I watch the news, when I read the paper, when I meet people, when I hang out with friends and acquaintances, when I see how each of us struggles, as best we can, through life's absurd meanderings, I think that the world is ridiculous, moving, and cruel. The same is true for this book:

the story is cruel, the protagonists are moving, and I am ridiculous. But I am in Prague.

I fear that I am in Prague for the last time. The stone ghosts that people the town surround me, as always, with their threatening, welcoming, or indifferent presences. I see a young woman's body, like an evanescent sculpture, with brown hair and white skin, pass under the Charles Bridge: a summer dress clings to her stomach and her thighs, the water streams over her bared chest, and on her breasts magical incantations are vanishing. The river water washes the hearts of men taken by the current. From Liliova Street I hear the echo of horses' hooves striking the cobbles. In the tales and legends of old Prague, the city of alchemists, it's said that the Golem will return when the city is in danger. But the Golem did not come back to protect the Jews or the Czechs. Nor, frozen in his centuries-old curse, did the iron man move when they opened Terezín, or when they killed people, when they despoiled, bullied, tortured, deported, shot, gassed, executed them in every conceivable way. By the time Gabčík and Kubiš landed, it was already too late. The disaster had occurred; there was nothing left to do but wreak vengeance. And it was stunning. But they, and their friends, and the Czech people, paid dearly for it.

Leopold Trepper, head of the French arm of the legendary Resistance organization Red Orchestra, made an observation: when a Resistance fighter fell into enemy hands and was offered the chance to cooperate, he had a choice: to accept or not. If he accepted, the damage could still be limited by saying as little as possible, hemming and hawing, releasing information drop by drop, and playing for time. This was the strategy Trepper adopted when he was arrested, and it was also the strategy used by A54. But they were both extremely high-level professional spies. Most of the time, the spy who accepted the offer to swap sides—even if he had until then resisted the worst kinds of torture—cracked very suddenly. From the moment he made his decision, he (to use Trepper's memorable expression) 'wallowed in betrayal as if in mud.' Karel Čurda is not content to lead the Gestapo to Heydrich's assassins but also provides the names of all his contacts, and of all those who helped him after his return to his homeland. He *sold* Gabčík and Kubiš to the Nazis, but he *gave* them all the others. Nothing forced him to mention the existence of Libuse, the radio transmitter, for example. Yet he puts the Gestapo on the trail of the final two escapees from Valčík's group, Silver A— Captain Bartos and the radiotelegrapher Potůček. The trail leads to Pardubice, where Bartos— surrounded, after being chased on foot through the town—follows his comrades' example and kills himself. Unfortunately, when they search his body they find a little book containing lots of addresses. Thus Pannwitz is able to keep following the thread. It passes through a tiny village called Ležáky, which becomes the Nagasaki to Lidice's Hiroshima. On June 26, Potůček the radiotelegrapher—the last parachutist still alive—sends the final message from Libuse: 'The village of Lezaky, where I ended up with my transmitter, has been razed to the ground. The people who helped us were arrested [only two little blonde girls suitable for Germanization would survive]. Thanks to their support, I was able to save myself and the transmitter. That day, Freda

[Bartos] was not in Lezaky. I don't know where he is and he doesn't know where I am now. But I hope that we will manage to find one another. For now, I am alone. Next transmission: June 28 at 23 hours.' He roams through forests, is picked up at another village, and manages to escape once more. But, hunted, starving, exhausted, he is finally captured and shot on July 2 near Pardubice. I said he was the last of the parachutists, but that's not true: there is still Čurda. The traitor gets his money, changes his name, marries a woman of good German stock, and becomes a full-time double agent on behalf of his new masters. During this time, A54, the German superagent, is sent to Mauthausen, where he manages to endlessly defer his own execution by playing the same game as Scheherezade. But not everyone has that many stories to tell.

Ata Moravec and his father; Kubiš's fiancée, Anna Malinova; Gabčík's fiancée, Libena Fafek (nineteen years old, probably pregnant), along with all her family; the Novaks, the Svatošes, the Zelenkas, Piskaceks, Khodls . . . I'm forgetting so many. The Orthodox priest of the church and all his colleagues; the people of Pardubice; all those who helped the parachutists in any way at all are arrested, deported, shot, or gassed. Professor Zelenka, however, has time to bite his cyanide pill when he's arrested. It's said that Mrs Novak, the mother of the little girl with the bicycle, went mad before being sent to the gas chamber with her children. Very few slipped through the net, like the Moravecs' concierge. Even Moula the dog, entrusted to the concierge by Valčík, died of grief at having lost his master—or so the story goes. Well, the animal did accompany Valčík on

375

his scouting missions. But we must also add to this list everyone who had nothing to do with the assassination—hostages, Jews, political prisoners executed as part of the reprisals; whole villages; Anna Maruscakova and her lover, whose innocent letter led to the massacre at Lidice. There were also the parachutists' families, whose only crime was to be related to them: handfuls of Kubišes and Valčíks were sent to Mauthausen and gassed. Only Gabčík's family—his father and his sisters—would escape the massacre, thanks to their Slovak nationality. Because Slovakia was a satellite state rather than an occupied state, it kept up a semblance of independence by deciding not to execute its own countrymen, not even to please its threatening ally. In sum, thousands perished as a consequence of the assassination. But it's said that all those who were tried for having helped the parachutists bravely declared to their Nazi judges that they regretted nothing and that they were proud to die for their country. The Moravecs did not betray their concierge. The Fafeks did not betray the Ogoun family, who also survived. I wish to pay my respects to these men and women: that's what I'm trying to say, however clumsily. That's what I didn't want to forget to say, despite the inherent clumsiness of tributes and condolences.

Today, Gabčík, Kubiš, and Valčík are heroes in their country, and their memory is regularly celebrated. Each has a street named after him, close to the scene of the assassination, and in Slovakia there is a small village called Gabčíkovo. They even continue to rise posthumously through the ranks; I think they're captains at the moment. The men and women and children who helped

376

them, directly or indirectly, are not so well-known. Worn-out by my muddled efforts to salute these people, I tremble with guilt at the thought of all those hundreds, those thousands, whom I have allowed to die in anonymity. But I want to believe that people exist even if we don't speak of them.


## 252

The most appropriate tribute paid by the Nazis to Heydrich's memory was not Hitler's speech at his zealous servant's funeral, but probably this: in July 1942 the programme to exterminate all Poland's Jews began, with the opening of Belzec, Sobibor, and Treblinka. Between July 1942 and October 1943, more than two million Jews and almost fifty thousand Romany will die as part of this programme. Its code name is Aktion Reinhard.


## 253

What is he thinking of, this Czech worker behind the wheel of a van one morning in October 1943? He drives through Prague's winding streets, a cigarette in his mouth, and his head, I imagine, full of worries. Behind him, he can hear wooden crates or boxes sliding around and banging against the walls in rhythm with the curves through which he passes. Whether because he's late or just because he's impatient to get his chore over with so he can go and have a drink with his friends, he is driving fast over the snow-damaged tarmac. He doesn't see the little blond figure running along the pavement. When this figure rushes into the road with that suddenness typical of children, he brakes—but it's too late. The van hits the child, who rolls into the gutter. The driver does not know that he has killed little Klaus, eldest son of Reinhard and Lina Heydrich. Nor does he know that this moment of inattention will see him sent to a concentration camp.

## 254

Paul Thümmel (alias René, alias Karl, alias A54) has survived in Terezín until April '45. But now that the Allies are at the gates of Prague, the Nazis are evacuating the country and they don't want to leave any embarrassing witnesses behind. When they come to fetch him so he can be shot, Paul Thümmel asks his cell mate to send his regards to Colonel Moravec, if he ever gets the chance. He adds this message: 'It was a real pleasure to work with the Czechoslovak information services. I am sorry it has to end like this, but I am comforted to think that all we accomplished was not in vain.' The message will get through.

'How could you have betrayed your comrades?'

'I think you'd have done the same thing for a million marks, Your Honour!'

Arrested by the Resistance near Pilsen during the last days of the war, Karel Čurda is tried and sentenced to death. He is hanged in 1947. As he climbs onto the scaffold, he tells the hangman an obscene joke.

My story is finished and my book should be, too, but I'm discovering that it's impossible to be finished with a story like this. My father calls me to read out something he copied down at the Museum of Man in Paris, where he visited an exhibition on the recently deceased Germaine Tillion, an anthropologist and Resistance fighter who was sent to Ravensbrück. This is what the text said:

The vivisection experiments on 74 young female prisoners constitute one of Ravensbrück's most sinister episodes. The experiments, conducted between August '42 and August '43, consisted of mutilating operations aimed at reproducing the injuries that caused the death of Reinhard Heydrich, the gauleiter of Czechoslovakia. Professor Gerhardt, having been unable to save

Heydrich from a gaseous gangrene, wished to prove that the use of sulphonamides would have made no difference. So he deliberately infected the young women with viruses, and many of them died.

Passing over the inaccuracies ('gauleiter', 'Czechoslovakia', 'gaseous gangrene'), I now know that this story will never truly end for me, that I will always be learning new details relating to the extraordinary story of the assassination attempt on Heydrich on May 27, 1942, by Czechoslovak parachutists sent from London.

'Above all, do not attempt to be exhaustive,' said Roland Barthes. There you go—some good advice I never took.

257

A rusty steamboat glides across the Baltic, like a Nezval poem. Jozef Gabčík is leaving behind the dark coastline of Poland and a few months spent inhabiting Kraków's alleyways. He and the other ghosts of the Czechoslovak army have finally managed to set sail for France. They walk around the boat, tired, worried, uncertain, but at the same time joyful at the prospect of finally fighting the invader, although they don't as yet know anything about the Foreign Legion, Algeria, the French campaign, or London fog. They bump into one another clumsily in the narrow gangways, searching for a cabin, a cigarette, or a familiar face. Gabčík leans on his elbows and watches the sea:

such a strange sight for someone, like him, from a landlocked country. That's probably why his gaze is not fixed on the horizon—too obvious a symbol of his future—but on the boat's waterline, where the waves swell and crash against the hull, then retreat and crash again in a hypnotic, deceptive movement. 'Got a light, comrade?' Gabčík recognizes the Moravian accent. The lighter's flame illuminates his countryman's face. A dimpled chin, lips made for smoking, and in the eyes—it's quite striking—a little bit of the world's goodness.

'My name's Jan,' he says. Smoke curls into the air and vanishes. Gabčík smiles silently. They'll have plenty of time to get to know each other during the journey. Mixed with the shadows of the soldiers in civilian clothes who pace around the boat are other shadows: disoriented old men, misty-eyed lone women, wellbehaved children holding a younger brother's hand. A young woman who looks like Natacha stands on deck, her hands on the railing, one leg bent up at the knee, playing with the hem of her skirt. And me? I am also there, perhaps.

# A NOTE ABOUT THE TRANSLATOR

Sam Taylor was born in Nottinghamshire. He is the author of three books of fiction, *The Republic of Trees*, *The Amnesiac*, and *The Island at the End of the World*. *HHhH* is his first translation.

# CHIVERS
# LARGE PRINT
## —direct—

If you have enjoyed this Large Print book and would like to build up your own collection of Large Print books, please contact

## Chivers Large Print Direct

Chivers Large Print Direct offers you a full service:

• Prompt mail order service

• Easy-to-read type

• The very best authors

• Special low prices

For further details either call
Customer Services on (01225) 336552
or write to us at Chivers Large Print Direct,
**FREEPOST**, Bath BA1 3ZZ

Telephone Orders:
**FREEPHONE** 08081 72 74 75